THE MANAGER

Inside the Minds
of Football's Leaders

MIKE CARSON

B L O O M S B U R Y
LONDON · NEW DELHI · NEW YORK · SYDNEY

For my father, who lifted me up to see the winning goal

First published in Great Britain 2013
This paperback edition published 2014

Copyright © by The League Managers Association (LMA)
and Mike Carson 2013

The moral right of the author has been asserted

Bloomsbury Publishing Plc
50 Bedford Square
London WC1B 3DP

www.bloomsbury.com

Bloomsbury is a trademark of Bloomsbury Publishing Plc

Bloomsbury Publishing, London, New York, Berlin and Sydney

A CIP catalogue record for this book is available from the British Library

ISBN 978 1 4088 4350 5

10 9 8 7 6 5 4 3 2 1

Typeset by Saxon Graphics Ltd, Derby
Printed in Great Britain by CPI Group (UK) Ltd, Croydon CR0 4YY

FSC
www.fsc.org
MIX
Paper from
responsible sources
FSC® C020471

CONTENTS

CONTENTS

FOREWORDS

An intensely contested environment, where the competition constantly strive to outwit, outperform and beat your best endeavours. Where the will to succeed is just the beginning and the positive combination of a hundred small differences can be the deciding factor between winning and losing. Where the investment in culture, training and implementation of the game plan are crucial. Where results are judged in the harsh light of a few numbers and the best talent available is rare, highly mobile and in increasing demand.

Elite football management… or familiar aspects of managing in the corporate world today?

This is a rare book. It looks through the eyes of the people who manage some of the most high-profile football clubs in the world and asks: how do they navigate these challenges, how do they motivate their teams to achieve tremendous success and overcome underperformance? It's an unprecedented glimpse behind the curtain at the true role of the manager.

Louis Jordan
Vice Chairman and Partner, Deloitte

What does it take to be a good leader? Whether it is business, or football, leadership is an important quality if you want to succeed. There have been a myriad of management books talking about leadership in abstract terms. But what better way to learn about real leadership skills than by reading what people like Sir Alex Ferguson, Arsène Wenger and José Mourinho say on this complex subject.

Barclays operates in over 50 countries and employs nearly 150,000 people, so effective leadership in a global business such as ours is essential to sustained success.

We have been global title sponsor of the Barclays Premier League and lead sponsor of the League Managers Association since 2001 so we are delighted to also support this book.

Mike Carson has been able to draw on some of the most successful and best known managers in football, yet they all have very individual views about what leadership means to them, and how they get the best out of their teams. What is clear from this book is that there are traits that all great managers share: passion for the game and the drive to continuously improve.

I hope you enjoy the book.

Antony Jenkins
Barclays Group Chief Executive

1992 witnessed the birth of two great football institutions, the Barclays Premier League and the League Managers Association. In the 22 years that have followed, we have worked extremely hard to look after our members – the current and former managers from the 92 professional football clubs in England – to protect their welfare and represent their collective voice. As a group, these managers have a vast wealth of accumulated knowledge and experience, acquired by managing many thousands of games at the very highest level. During this time, through the LMA's work in supporting its members, we have slowly and painstakingly earned their trust, their respect and their confidence. A priceless by-product of this process has been unprecedented access into their extremely private and personal world.

Since our beginning, the education and development of our members, and prospective members, has been a responsibility we have taken very seriously. In this respect, one of our major objectives has been to meticulously research and identify those characteristics and traits common to the best of the best. Our findings leave us in absolutely no doubt; the quality which sets apart the very best from the rest is 'leadership'. The best managers are passionate about football, obsessed and driven by the need to manage and succeed. Without exception, they also share a crystal-clear sense of where they are going; they know and understand how they will get there; and they have that precious ability to get inside the hearts and minds of those they work with and convince them to follow. They all possess an unquenchable thirst for knowledge, a passion for learning, and a willingness to successfully adapt to changing times and circumstances. In addition, they all have a huge generosity in their willingness to share information for the benefit of those taking their first treacherous steps up the slippery slope of football management. It is this willingness to share that has enabled the LMA to methodically develop our own Leadership Education Programme, 'Survive, Win, Succeed', as we have sought to ensure that all our members receive the best possible start to their careers.

We are therefore extremely proud and delighted that this, our first book, has set the bar so high. The managers and former managers who have contributed to this book have amassed in excess of a staggering 15,000 competitive matches between them and along the way have accumulated every major domestic trophy available in their respective European competitions. Their success is due – in part at least – to their awareness that a football manager has to be more than what we traditionally understand the term 'manager' to mean, and to their ability to encompass aspects of leader, father figure, coach, and psychologist roles into their daily work. It is a complex job, all the more impressive for being carried out under the unique, relentless public scrutiny that accompanies their every move. Season after season, their unique skills enable them to transform vision into reality. Season after season, they are tasked to make the aspirations and dreams of millions come true, and they do.

I thank all those who have contributed so generously to this very special book – including Mike Carson, whose energy and enthusiasm have been boundless – and I hope that you enjoy its content and the unique insights it offers into the hitherto very private workings of the football manager's mind and into that hallowed place that is the professional football dressing room.

Howard Wilkinson
Chairman, League Managers Association
www.leaguemanagers.com
June 2013

PREFACE

Football as a sport and more broadly as an industry is unique – in the breadth of its appeal, the scale of its support and its ability to generate emotion. For generations, the game has created extraordinary memories, offering us visions of sublime skill and moments of great passion. It has also generated pain and anguish, and tragically has known its own human disasters. Across the world, it both divides and unites people of different races, nationalities and every conceivable status. It is the sport of rulers and workers, of children and the elderly.

In Britain, the people with the task and privilege of leading football at the front line are the managers. In fact, their role has only a little to do with management, and much more to do with leadership. The men who lead in the upper reaches of professional British football – especially in the world-famous Barclays Premier League – are truly extraordinary. The work they do is intensive, personal, technical and critical – critical to the success of their teams, the growth of their clubs and the happiness of many. It is also subject to intense public scrutiny: their every move – whether witnessed, surmised or merely imagined – is subject to widespread analysis in almost every forum imaginable, from bar rooms through offices to internet blogs and live television and radio broadcasts.

My intention is this book will appeal to many people from different camps. At one level, it is simply a book for all football managers – both serving and aspiring. It brings together insights from the collective wisdom of almost 30 people at the very top of their game. At another level, it is written for leaders in all fields of endeavour: business, education, government, non-profit, the arts – any context where individuals lead other individuals and teams in their pursuit of meaning and success. My own work is with business leaders, enabling them to lead from their deep strengths, and I know that there is real value for them in this book. This is not to say that any one manager has all the answers – or even that the full cohort has cracked it between them. But there is a set of circumstances from which emerges a compelling language of leadership that will be useful to leaders in any and every setting and culture. And at a further level, the book is written unashamedly for the football fan: the men and women who love the game, and who – like me – are simply fascinated by the challenge and want to know how and why these people do what they do.

These managers are fascinating. For the most part, they are true natural leaders. One of them commented to me: 'You have the harder task. I just have to do this stuff – you have to explain it! I just do it all by intuition.' This may be simple modesty, but there is a considerable element of truth in it – and this perhaps explains the appeal of the book. It is written as a first-hand insight into what these leaders think, feel and do to lead in this most dramatic and demanding of settings.

In writing, I have made extensive use of the voices of the managers themselves who I was lucky enough to interview in depth. As the work progressed, powerful themes emerged: in every case I have sought to surface, illustrate and simplify these themes so that we can all come away with practical and helpful ways of thinking. My intention is for the leaders among you to identify within these pages some of your own struggles, challenges and successes, and to create a language from this that will enhance your own practices. For the fans among you, I hope you will join me in appreciating the enormous complexity of the task that our often-criticised managers undertake. And for the football managers and coaches among you, I intend it to be an interesting and memorable take on how some of the great leaders achieve success.

I would also like to acknowledge the excellent work of the League Managers' Association. In providing a professional home for its members, it is taking the art of leadership in football on to excellence. The LMA's own leadership model, emerging at the time of this publication, is perceptive and valuable. As it evolves, it will become a very valuable tool for the profession for generations to come.

Hope Powell, who managed the England women's team for 15 years, has made an important contribution to this book and a huge contribution to leadership in the sport overall. As an important point of style, in all cases except for Powell, I have used the masculine pronouns of he, him and his. This is because the book is focused almost exclusively on experiences of Premier League leaders past and present, and the Premier League at the level of players and managers is an exclusively masculine environment. This issue of style in no way passes comment on the abilities of the rapidly growing body of women leaders in football or elsewhere.

Finally, it has been a personal joy to work with the LMA and the managers themselves on this project. You have been generous with your time and your insights; and I have been struck by your humility. Thank you.

Mike Carson
June 2013

PART ONE

The Scale of the Task

CHAPTER ONE

A PIECE OF THE ACTION

THE BIG IDEA

Professional football is a crucible. Working inside that crucible, the managers of the 20 Barclays Premier League clubs in England have their leadership publicly examined, challenged, lauded and ridiculed on a daily basis. Some of us feel we could do a better job if asked. Others stand back in admiration of the great achievers, and cast a sympathetic backward glance at the ones who look like they've failed. But we actually have very little appreciation of the full scope of their work.

The role of a leader in Premier League football is fascinating, complex and tough. Fantasy football leagues may convince us that it's about buying players and selecting a team. In reality it is about creating winning environments, delivering on enormous expectations, overcoming significant challenges, handling pressure and staying centred throughout – a set of challenges familiar to leaders in all sectors.

There are plenty of people with influence around the managers – all of them having or wanting a piece of the action: owners, fans and the general public, media, the players of course, and now the agents. This massive, global interest in top-level professional football is what sustains the game. But although the influence of these various parties may be welcome – and even necessary – they pose an ever-present challenge to the managers. So how do the managers cope?

3

THE MANAGER

Roy Hodgson is a football manager of considerable international standing. Since his early 20s he has been passionate about coaching and about the global nature of football. Since beginning his work in earnest in Sweden at the age of 29, he has accumulated and deployed a wide range of experience, leading 16 teams in eight countries over 37 years – including four national teams (Switzerland, the UAE, Finland and most recently his native England).

In Sweden, he is widely acclaimed as one of the architects of the national game, introducing new thinking and styles with great success in his 12 years at Halmstads BK, Örebro SK and Malmö FF. At Malmö he led the club to domestic dominance and unprecedented European achievement – even defeating the Italian champions Inter Milan in the European Cup. In Switzerland, he transformed the national side into genuine performers on the world stage. Under Hodgson they achieved World Cup qualification for the first time in 28 years, Euro qualification in 1996 and, at their peak, third place in the world rankings.

Roy Hodgson's leadership has since been pressure tested in the toughest of club settings: the Italian Serie A with Inter Milan and the Barclays Premier League with Blackburn Rovers, Fulham, Liverpool and West Bromwich Albion. Among these, his greatest impact came at Fulham: he joined them in a mid-season relegation battle in late 2007, led them to safety that season, took them to a club record seventh in the following year and led them to a Europa League final the year after, defeating Juventus and the German champions Wolfsburg along the way. They lost the final in the last moments to Atlético Madrid. His achievements with Fulham that season saw Hodgson recognised by his managerial peers when he was voted the League Managers Association Manager of the Year. Previously holding a greater reputation outside his own country than inside, his coaching skills and leadership talent were fully recognised in 2012 when he was appointed manager of the England national team to succeed Fabio Capello.

His Philosophy

Hodgson is a thoughtful and focused leader who operates along simple and clear lines: 'The manager is employed to coach a football team. That has to be his primary focus. So I concentrate for the most part on the team: making sure they are prepared for the challenge ahead. After that it's about compartmentalising. The owner has employed me; and the fans are the people whose interest in the game has generated my job and my players' jobs. We must never lose sight of that, but you can't work for the fans or even just for the chairman. The only way you can satisfy both parties is to do your job well and win.' Simple focus: team first, then each other party in turn, giving them real attention.

But this elegant approach conceals a raft of challenges. What are the realities of life in this high-octane environment? How do the successful managers – Hodgson and others – practically navigate such difficult territory?

Many Cooks

In business they're called stakeholders. In football we might call them interested parties. Whatever we call them, they have always been there – since the beginning of the game there have always been those on the sidelines with an opinion.

A traditional snapshot of the game in say the 1970s would reveal the principal groupings as the chairman, the players, the fans, the press and the public. (There were always the governing bodies too, but with little direct impact on the daily life of the manager.) Today the groupings are much the same. What has changed is the degree of influence and leverage they have. Take the chairman, for instance. In a game where cash is often king, the man who holds the purse strings has massive influence. He is, after all, the person ultimately responsible for hiring (and firing) the manager, and with the rise of the new all-powerful owner, these leaders are becoming public figures in a much more dramatic way than ever before.

Other groupings have also become more powerful in their own right. Top players whose predecessors would nervously approach their manager for a rise now get their agents involved in contracting stand-offs with millions of pounds at stake. The public who used to confine their conversations to bars and pubs now exert influence through social media. And members of the press, who used to be the guardians of footballing standards, are now influential enough to get a manager fired. For the managers themselves, this means a tough, multi-layered and often frenetic environment. Never have the principles of centredness, self-knowledge, handling pressure and personal renewal been so important.

The Centre of Authority

The prevalent model of organisation in the world's leading football clubs sees the manager as the centre of authority. Hodgson relishes this aspect of the role and considers it a privilege: 'The reward for success in our profession as a coach is to reach a position where you are that focal point, where you are the person that everyone – from board to fans – is looking to for what they all require: a team that wins football matches. You're the man who has been given the task of producing that team and organising that team

– and it can't get much more important than that in football. What is more important in a football club than the team that goes out every week and wins or loses? Manchester United today are a worldwide institution and they sold for hundreds of millions of pounds on the stock exchange. But the bottom line is, it's still those 13 or 14 players who run out every Saturday in a red shirt who are the essence of the business. If Manchester United spiral down into the second or third divisions of the Football League, then all of this will fly out of the window irrespective of how good they are commercially. So Alex Ferguson was a key, key figure, because he was the man who governed the core of the business for so long.'

Sir Alex Ferguson as much as anyone embodied this principle of central authority over the last 26 years at Old Trafford. 'I always remember starting at Manchester United. [Chairman] Martin Edwards said to me that the guiding principle of our football club is that the manager is the most important person at Manchester United. Everything is guided by what the manager thinks. There has never been an occasion in my time that the board has overruled the manager at any point on how you control the football club.' His great peer and rival in north London, Arsenal's Arsène Wenger, goes a step further. 'I don't think it can be the future of the manager to have no control, because the quality of the manager is basically determined by the quality of his control. How can you judge a manager if it is not for the fact that he controls the club? I believe that the manager is a strong guide inside the club. His players must have the feeling that as well as establishing authority, he has complete control. If the manager is not the most important man at the football club, then why do we sack the manager if it doesn't go well?'

Whatever the model of governance in a football club, the manager is invariably the pivotal figure. Hodgson feels the same responsibility applies to the manager of national teams: 'Managing a national side brings its own challenges. The most obvious one is that I'm not with the players on the training field every day. I see them less often, and I have a wider selection pool [it's not about affordability]. My other big challenge, though, is the different demands on my time. I have time between matches, of course – the question is how best to use it. I like to give of myself and of my coaching experience to the federation and the country. I believe I should be involved in helping all interest groups through coaching schemes and programmes designed to produce coaches for the future.'

Whatever is going on – selection, injury, high achievement, low achievement, rumour – chairman, players, media and fans turn to him to make sense of it all. And not only is the manager key to the business success of the club – but as Hodgson points out, his influence can extend a long way beyond the current team: 'The manager's philosophy, if sufficiently clear and powerful, will filter down not only to his team, but also to other teams at all levels within his club's structure – and it might actually impregnate the whole club for a long, long period. We've seen lots of examples in the past of iconic football managers whose philosophy has actually led to the club adopting a certain style of football and projecting a particular image that the club itself is very proud of. This is true of iconic leaders everywhere, of course – great military leaders, great business leaders or political leaders whose character and philosophy can have a lasting effect on one or more nations.' Managers who started out as football coaches now find themselves at the very heart of a complex business. The coach has become a leader.

Gérard Houllier reinforces the point: 'There was a time when clubs thought that winning on the pitch was enough. Now times have changed and you need to win off the pitch as well – by which I mean commercially. If the commercial aspect works, the club generates good revenues, and from that flow better facilities, better staff, better players and then again better revenues for the club. Then it's important that the technical part is there too – and this is also based upon very good human relationships. I think that a good club is a club that looks after its players, looks after its people, looks after its employees, its staff and everything. Its human atmosphere is to me the foundation for success. And it is the manager who is at the centre of that.' The familiar lesson of putting people first translates directly to organisations in just about every sector and industry; the leader who can focus on his people even in the whirlwind of wider stakeholder relationships is set up for success.

The Man in the Chair

'The single most important thing for a manager is the relationship with the owner of the football club.' So says Tony Pulis. Is this simply a case of 'The man who pays the piper calls the tune'? Or is it that the owner has the potential to disrupt the smooth running of the club? Either way, if the manager can win the trust of the owner, then he will be given the space and resources to pursue his philosophy. If not, then the owner is likely to intervene. It is, after all, his club. If the authority of the manager is tested, then it is his relationship with the chairman/owner that will most likely present the greatest challenge.

The rise of the powerful owner

The acquisition of Chelsea in 2003 by Roman Abramovich triggered across a decade a series of high-profile football club takeovers. The emergence of Manchester City as a new footballing power in

Europe has been driven by the Abu Dhabi United Group led by Sheikh Mansour. Similar investments by high-net-worth individuals have taken place at Paris St Germain, Malaga and elsewhere. Other clubs in the Premier League, while not in the hands of a single individual, are owned by large organisations led by salient people. These owner-chairmen control the flow of funds around the club, including all that is needed for transfers and salaries. Sir Alex Ferguson represents many who have genuinely mixed feelings: 'In England, you had a generation of people who were fans who stood in the stand, and when they became successful their dream was to buy the club. That period looks to have gone and has been replaced by a generation of people coming in with different motivations. With some of them it is to make money, with some it is for the glory. To have more money in the league is good because you want to be the strongest league in the world. But it is very important that the structure of the game is not destroyed and that the pressure on salaries does not become ridiculous because the inflation pressure of too much money coming in at one time can be very destabilising for the players. For example, if a player is paid 1 and then is offered 5 somewhere else, he may want to stay but want 3. So then you go from 1 to 3, and the direct consequence is that all the other players go up as well – so it puts a huge pressure on the club's resources.'

As Sir Alex points out, huge sums of money can be destabilising. Yet, for the managers working with the investment, there is clearly enormous potential to create something special. Carlo Ancelotti describes the great freedom he enjoyed at Paris St Germain under the new owners: 'The owner had recently bought the club and they were changing everything. They changed 12 players. They had good ambition. We had to build a team, and the club wanted to be competitive in Europe. This was a very good challenge. The owner was young, very ambitious, very calm, not afraid or worried if you didn't win a game; he was looking forwards. They were very focused on their objective – to be competitive in the future. This was difficult to explain to the media, because the media were thinking if we didn't win there was no future. The first season's objective was to play in the Champions League. Then, in the summer, to buy some players to increase the quality of the team, to invest money for the next five years and to build the new training ground. The objective was very, very clear. If we won or didn't win it didn't matter. This is rare, and I hope that they will stay focused in this way.' At PSG Ancelotti and his club's owners achieved something important, which culminated in PSG winning the French Ligue 1 title at the end of Ancelotti's second season in charge: a truly shared vision, shared responsibility for delivering on that vision, and clarity around what success looks like. For a leader, this is extremely empowering. Because he has both clarity and trust, he can pursue his philosophy with confidence, and without looking over his shoulder. This gives purpose and stability to the organisation as a whole.

Roy Hodgson, while acknowledging the shift in nature of the high-profile, high-net-worth owner/chairmen of today, makes two significant observations. First, it remains a relationship game; and second, the onus – at least initially – is on the owner to get it right. 'In the past the chairman of a football club would be a local figure, a local businessman who would have been brought up with that club and had the club in his blood. But he had the capacity to have a good, bad or indifferent relationship with his appointed manager – just like any owner today. That hasn't changed. This is all about personalities, the personality of the owner and of the manager/coach. What has changed is the scale of wealth some owners bring. But if they are going to have success with their club, they must choose their manager very wisely, work with him and give him the support he needs. They will only get success for themselves through success of the team, and success for the team is going to come through the man who leads and manages the players. He is the one who will mould the team, i.e. bring the right players to the club and coach them to play in a way that brings success.'

So the powerful owner is very much a part of modern football, and he has a great influence on the game. But to be successful, he needs a manager who can share his vision, convey it with clarity and passion, take ownership for outcomes and deliver on all his professional responsibilities in the face of enormous expectation.

Agents

The nature of the chairman himself is not the only evolution of the last 20 years. Harry Redknapp believes that, for managers, the rise of the player's agent is threatening not only the sacred bond between them and their players, but also the critical stability of their relationship with the chairman. 'If a player had a problem, he would come and see the manager and speak to the manager: "Why aren't I playing, gaffer? I think I should be in the team. What am I doing wrong? Why don't you give me a chance?" But they don't come and see you any more. Instead, the agents ring the chairman and complain that you aren't picking their player! Very, very few players knock on your door – they all go through their agent now. So agents build relationships with chairmen, not managers. They aren't silly, they know that the chairman owns the club and that managers come and go. This can be very undermining – and it's happening all the time. More and more chairmen are choosing players in the transfer window. In the past, players were chosen and the chairman wouldn't know anything until the player arrived! It's very different now.' It's in this climate that the critical relationship between manager and chairman needs to stay watertight.

When it all works

The owner-manager relationship is absolutely critical and can create or destroy a club's chances of success. Gérard Houllier tells how it can have a direct impact on team performance: 'I remember one specific moment when I came to a club part way through a season. I wondered after a few months if maybe the team was not clicking, or maybe the players were not playing for me. Particularly in the Barclays Premier League, the players play for the manager in some ways, so I thought that maybe because I had changed a few things they were not playing for us. So I went to the board and I explained that maybe we have to take some action. One of the board members stood up and said, "Well Mr Houllier. We don't have the best quality in the world, but there are two qualities we do have: patience and trust. We are patient and we will trust you do what you have to do." So when I left the board I went to my staff and I said, "Now we are going to start winning," and we won. Because the more the board trusts you, the more assertive and the more strong you will be in your management.' This is an excellent example. Martin O'Neill agrees: 'The owner–manager relationship is of paramount importance and I don't believe that can be underestimated.' Above all others, this relationship can be the most painful one for managers.

Pain

For Neil Warnock, the pain comes most of all from not being understood. 'I said to Amit Bhatia [QPR Director] when I left, "You don't really know what I've done at the club." I don't think people understand what managers do. Yes, they are managers, but they are also fathers, brothers and friends to everyone at the club. The way QPR is run I was actually sort of Mother Superior to everybody, the cleaner included. I made everybody feel important and that's not easy to do. No disrespect, but you don't get that from a university. You can't put what we do behind the scenes into qualifications.'

And once the relationship between the manager and the chairman-owner is broken – as with many other relationships – it is hard to rebuild. Warnock says: 'I always work better when I work for one person who I trust totally. I have fallen out with a few chairmen in my career, but I only fell out with them when they lied to me. Once I felt that I'd lost trust in them, then I might as well have left. Once somebody lies to me or I lose trust in them, then I can never be committed to that same person again. When I left Sheffield United, the chairman – a friend of 17 years, I thought – came out and said on reflection he should have probably changed the manager. I had known this guy for 17 years and I rang him immediately and asked him why he said it. He said he was misquoted and he didn't mean to say anything like that. I told him I had heard it on the radio.'

The pain that comes from lack of appreciation and recognition is a significant challenge to managers. Many simply find they have to protect themselves. Sam Allardyce says: 'What happened at Blackpool taught me never to be sentimental and always get out when you're ready. I thought if I can get sacked by losing in the play-offs … The year I took over, the club had finished fourth from bottom, just stayed up, the first year we finished 11th, the second year we finished third in the play-offs. We missed out on automatic promotion by a couple of points, we got beaten in the play-offs and I got sacked. So I said to myself if I got back into management I would never stay when it was the right time for me to leave. I wouldn't get emotionally involved in the football club and get talked into staying. And I played that out at Bolton and Notts County.'

So pain doesn't happen only with the high-profile clubs and their high-profile owners. Allardyce is more concerned about the young managers trying to make it work in the lower leagues: 'Some of the conflict I have had with owners and chairmen – it made you want to leave as quick as you could. I had to put up with it because I was making my way in management. It was brutal. Most managers still suffer the same now: the brutality, the bullying, the interference, the threats. It's a cruel and hard, hard world trying to make your way up as a manager. You come through that, you generally end up being a good leader.'

As with most high-profile relationships in business, politics or sport, the one between football chairman and manager is at the same time combustible and essential. Many will become strong; some never will. All require mutual commitment and effort to make them work – and a basic acknowledgement that both parties are human beings, often caught up in the emotion of the game.

Stability ...

Across the domains of club finance, governance and personal experience, the chairman can create either stability or instability for the manager and the club. Tony Pulis speaks enthusiastically of a relationship that fuelled the unexpected rise of Stoke City: 'My relationship with owner Peter Coates was paramount to every-thing that we achieved. He trusted me and I trusted him. Being a local Stoke businessman Peter was massively important to our progress. He had a dream to put Stoke City back on the map but to do it in a way that also brought the community closer to the football club.'

Howard Wilkinson contrasts his experiences as manager of Sheffield Wednesday and Leeds. 'Sheffield Wednesday were fifth or sixth in the First Division when I was approached by Leeds, who were at the bottom of the second. The board at Sheffield Wednesday had dragged the club from the brink. But we got to the point when I said, "We need to invest now – I can't keep squeezing juice out of these oranges. All the juice has gone. They just can't come back next season and produce it again and again. We need to get better players." And they said, "Howard, you know what our policy is – we can't go down that road."

'When Leeds approached me, I met the chairman three or four times. Every time I met him it was a long meeting because I saw at Leeds the opportunity to go to a one-club town, with a chairman who was backing things with his own money. My message to him was, "I'll come here if at the end of this long conversation you say yes. So it's not me that's going to say yes – you say yes." So I put to him what I wanted to do and what I thought they could do. And it sounds ludicrous now, but the first part was five years and the second part was another five years and included everything – being promoted, winning the league, starting up an academy and so on. So by the time I'd got to that point I was starting to have very clear ideas about how I thought a successful club could be run. And he said yes. That was the start of an experiment, funded by him, which worked.' This rare example of a vision set for the long term and faithfully executed over the long term lent unusual stability to the club.

Sharing a long-term vision is a sure-fire way to secure a long-term relationship – and, with it, stability for your organisation or team. Former Newcastle United and Manchester City manager Kevin Keegan will never forget the inspirational phone call he took in Marbella from Sir John Hall at Newcastle United, who said: 'The two men who can save this club are talking to each other now.' Pulis found similar inspiration. 'I had just finished the season managing

Plymouth Argyle and was really enjoying it there. I was on holiday with my family when Peter Coates phoned me. He said to me, "I'm going to buy Stoke, but I will only buy it on one condition … if you come back with me." He described his vision for Stoke to me and what he thought the club could achieve if it was run properly throughout. A good few years before I was at the club the first time around, Peter hadn't been treated very well by certain sections when he had been chairman. So I thought if he's got the guts to do this then I should have the guts as well. In reality we were two really unpopular figures returning to the club – but I felt what he had outlined to me as the way forward made so much sense.'

Clarity of understanding and clear lines of responsibility make a big difference too. Allardyce's successful relationship with the chairman at Bolton was founded on clarity. In 1999 when his long-standing friend and peer Brett Warburton became vice chairman and Phil Gartside became chairman, they established some clear ground rules. 'Phil looked after the new stadium build and infrastructure; I looked after the football side. This wasn't as easy as it sounds. The club had got into severe debt, so the business needed major restructuring and a new board. They recreated the business; I recreated the football. And I learned to speak their business language – which was important when it came to getting across my requests for investment. It was about making a business case based on success and working within budgets. If I could show I'd added an extra £2.5 million of value in a year, then I expected them to reinvest in the football.'

… and instability

By contrast, instability at the top creates anxiety and additional challenges that a highly operational leader does not need. Walter Smith joined Everton from Rangers in 1998 but, pretty soon after, it all began to get tough. 'The owner–chairman, Peter Johnson, had one or two problems just avoiding relegation the year before I arrived. He told me up front there would be money to invest in the team when, in fact, the reverse was true. After about two and a half months he sold a player without consulting me. Shortly after, he put the club up for sale and then effectively walked away. Only then did we all realise what a chaotic financial situation the club was in.

'After he left, we had to sell nearly all the players that we had brought in. There was no transfer window then, so it was back and forward, bringing in players to cover for ones who were leaving. Then there was a new ownership. That new ownership was done on the back of a deal with NTL Communications. That fell through after two months, and we entered an unstable financial environment. That was where a little bit of anxiety crept in. I didn't really have the confidence to say it'll be OK in six months. I was there for three and a half years and it was pretty much a constant battle. Looking back on it just now I can say that I enjoyed it – more than I did at the time!'

Football stirs deep emotions for everyone involved. Players, staff and fans all feel pride and despair, strong attachment and over-whelming joy. They can also feel anger, resentment and pain. Allardyce recognises that owners and business leaders are suscep-tible to all of these feelings and more – and sometimes with difficult consequences: 'They get the bug as much as we get it. They get the adrenalin rush, love it, can't leave it alone, have to have it. High-powered businessmen find a new form that they have never experienced before in their life – and they can lose sight of where they were originally heading.' Maintaining clarity of thought, perspective and long-term vision with such emotions at play is a challenge for a leader in any field.

Living on the edge

When the relationship between owner and manager is working, life is good. But success can be fleeting. In his second full season at the City of Manchester Stadium, Roberto Mancini's Manchester City were in the Premier League's pole position for much of the season. In late March his team slipped up and the pressure on him – real or perceived – increased significantly. It's at moments like these that the relationship is truly tested. Speaking at that time, Ancelotti understood the pressure Mancini was under: 'Everyone says that Mancini has to win; if he doesn't win this year it could be big problems. But the owner one week ago said he is happy with the performance of the team. The problem is in football that only one team wins.' He himself has had his tougher experiences. At Chelsea – unlike at PSG – he inherited a team that was 'fully ready'. He was sacked after two seasons, despite winning the league and cup double. He is philosophical, while admitting the pain of the experience. 'I didn't feel good. I think that I did my best, but I had a problem with the owner because the owner wanted more. This is normal, but I cannot do anything more.' Successful leadership under such intense personal pressure is no mean feat.

The art of leading upwards

If a football manager is to play his part in creating the stability he needs to function properly, then, as in most organisations, he will need to lead upwards. Leadership is rarely about some heroic 'follow me' message – it's more often about inspiring all round. And an important component of that is inspiring confidence, trust, excitement and commitment in the person or people under whose authority you stand yourself. Hodgson believes it begins with respect and pragmatism: 'You have to work on the basis that the person at the top is there because he should be at the top, and even if he isn't, he's there anyway. It's a given. Then the three most important things he will need from anyone working together with him will be competence, diligence and communication. So when I have gone to football clubs, I have never really given serious thought to how I need to manage upwards – I've always concentrated on doing the job that I'm being paid to do. That's where the competence and diligence bit comes in. The communication point is all about speed of decision-making. We take a lot of decisions: every day the decision questions are flashed at you left, right and centre. The important thing is not to treat the club as purely your domain or to treat any questions about it as intrusive. The people running the whole show are responsible for the club surviving or not. They are entitled to ask questions. I have always tried to create a good line of communication upwards, provided the chairman wants that. You can't force it upon them, but I have always been pleased to get a call from the chairman asking how's it going and what's going on at the club because I think it's important for them to know.'

Choosing the right man for the job

Football managers like any other brand of leader all have their own style. Owner-manager relationships come in an infinite variety of textures, set as they are against variable and shifting landscapes. What is clear is that the successful owner will appoint an excellent manager, and one with whom he has natural chemistry; and the successful manager, once appointed, will devote considerable energy to making the relationship work – for the good of all at the club. 'Owners now are making massive investments in their clubs,' says Hodgson, 'so it is entirely reasonable that they may go for high-profile managers with track records, no matter where they were born. People now quite happily realise that being English is in itself neither an advantage nor a disadvantage [for Premier League management] – in the same way that being Italian or French or any other nationality is neither an advantage nor a disadvantage. A manager can succeed or fail whatever his nationality. There is some interesting variety though that comes from cross-cultural appointments. While the actual job of coaching and managing a football team in terms of the physical and tactical side may not vary much, what can vary from culture to culture are the leadership qualities and characteristics required, and with those the ability to lead a team of people to success. Bob Houghton and I both used our own style to get to success in Sweden in the 1970s and 80s; Wenger and Mancini have been doing it recently in England.'

While Hodgson positively encourages the arrival in British football of high-profile managers from other countries, he reinforces the absolute need for skilled communicators: 'Every day as coaches, we are in the communication business. In lower leagues we are also educators, but at the top end we work with people who know how to play superb football. I have been privileged to always work at the top end, so my work has been making sure that the skills and abilities the players have are blended together and are used purely and solely for the benefit of the team. And that's where you come to the major leadership challenges: some of your players whose abilities are important to the club and the team are going to be ego-driven and insufficiently team orientated to bring those skills to the team itself. They might even destroy the team ethos because they are only interested in their own personal gain – they are in effect using the team. There are two types of players: the players who bring what they have to the team to make the team good, and players who use the team to make themselves look good. When you encounter the second type, communication skills are absolutely critical if you are going to convince them that they are on the wrong road.'

The man in the middle of so many stakeholders needs excellent communication skills. The successful chairman will ensure this before he appoints a manager, and once he appoints, will trust his man and give him the space to use those skills to the full.

Governing Bodies

In addition to chairman/owners, modern football managers also have to deal with the governing bodies of the game. As a four-time national manager in very different geographies and 12-time club manager at very different clubs, Hodgson is well placed to address this topic.

First, the man at the top: 'The Football Association chairman is very much like the chairman at a club. But often clubs don't have large structures behind the chairman. Jack Walker owned Blackburn and had really set the club up as the Blackburn that we know today, Mohammed Al Fayed was the same at Fulham and Jeremy Peace the same at West Bromwich Albion. So it's a little bit different for David Bernstein than for those men who, as major stakeholders in a club, could basically bring people on board that suited them and could essentially do whatever they wanted. At the FA, David has to relate to a large board that represents the whole range of aspects of the game, and they have created a smaller Club England board who can deal rapidly with the operational issues as they arise, or form opinions to present to the main board in a formal way. Not unlike an executive team in business.'

So while the chairman can make a difference, it is essential that the structures around him be configured with the right purpose in mind. Hodgson pays tribute to the forward thinking of the Swiss FA: 'Switzerland was far ahead of its time in 1992 when I joined. As with other countries, the football association there is the governing body, so it looks after all aspects of the sport from refereeing to handicapped sport, amateur football and so on. The difference is that in most countries, there is a large gap between what the FA is trying to do and what the professional leagues are trying to do. Whereas in Switzerland, they ensured there was board representation from league football, pure amateur football and the professional lower leagues from an early stage. This worked extremely well, because these four important people and I would get together regularly, and determine together how to get the most out of my role.' This may sound like a minor tweak, until we hear the effect of the body on the wider game: 'The classic example of how it worked well for me was the time they gave me with the players outside of the standard days around qualifying matches and friendlies. I would get the team for five or six get-togethers during a qualifying campaign. So when the players had played for their professional teams on a Sunday I would get them until the Wednesday morning, which gave us a couple of days together regularly during the season. That's a very good example of co-operation between all the bodies working in favour of the national team. The clubs were asked to commit to it, and they accepted that between three and five times a year we would have access to their players. Then thinking more along PR terms, we took the players that I had selected to different venues around Switzerland. That's easier in a small country, of course, but we wouldn't meet in Zurich or in Geneva all the time – we would go to Berne, Basle and other cities so that people in the various regions felt the national team was engaging with them. The arrangement worked really well, and I got to know players so much better. So often I had to make decisions based on one or two sightings from a distance in the stand – do I want him or not want him? It fell down, of course, when some players built reputations and went to play in Germany and Italy – then I didn't get the same access. But overall it made an enormous difference.'

Hodgson's message is clear. Getting the governance structures right makes all the difference to the task of the manager. A leader cannot lead successfully and with authority without the right support and structures around him.

The Lifeblood

The Barclays Premier League is widely regarded as the most compelling football drama in the world. More than 35,000 people attend every one of the ten matches every week on average, with hundreds of millions more watching live coverage or highlights across the globe. It is estimated that 4.7 billion people watch Premier League football out of a global population of 7 billion. The true fans – those who pour enormous emotional energy into their chosen sides – will be gratified to hear the views of England's Roy Hodgson on them as the lifeblood of the game. He thinks of football supporters with great respect – almost affection: 'I've always worked on the basis of three very simple thoughts: that the fans know what they are looking for, that they understand what football is and that they want the best for their team. Then I add to that the simple fact that they keep our football going. It may not be their gate receipt money that keeps the current level of the game afloat – and they know that – but it is their presence. When you watch a Premier League game, you can't see an empty seat for love nor money. Then you watch a game in Serie A and you often see the empty seats everywhere, or you turn on to a League Cup game and there's hardly anybody there. Compare these and you realise that it's fans who are the lifeblood of everything we do. The reason there are such powerful sponsorships of football – everything from cars to soft drinks – is because so many people want to watch it and so many people care passionately about it.' From this basic understanding, he operates on a simple principle: as with all things, he focuses on the people he's with. 'At a football match, I focus on the team. I should not be the point of attention for the fans – that should be the players. The fans are wise enough to understand that you need a coach or a manager to look after your team, but he's not the one you've come to watch on a Saturday afternoon. He might be the one you get interested in when he's talking about the team, talking about his players, talking about his philosophy and plans.'

Hodgson's thinking here is valuable. Every business, every organisation has stakeholders whose voices are important and influential. But one of the traps of leadership is to believe you are the centre of the universe. Hodgson has both humility and pragmatism, not disregarding the fans for their emotional attachment, but honouring it with respect and thoughtfulness. And he's right to do so. The emotional power of supporters to drive the business of a club is unusually strong.

This emotional power can put pressure on an organisation, and considerable personal pressure on a leader. Wenger cites it as the single greatest pressure he faces: 'The biggest pressure you have is to drive home on a Saturday night having lost a game and to think that some people will cry because you lost that game. That is the biggest pressure, to let people down. That's a big responsibility and I feel that the longer you stay at a club, unfortunately, the bigger the responsibility becomes.' Wenger is right: the deeper the relationship becomes between manager and fan, the more burdensome that can feel for the manager. There is, though, one special case where this works for a manager, as André Villas-Boas explains: 'At Porto, I had one massive, massive advantage, which Pep Guardiola also had at Barcelona: we were both coaching teams we supported as fans. When that happens, you know exactly how your fans behave, you know how to touch people, you know how to move people, you know the channels. It's almost like every single word that comes out of your mouth touches people in a different way and moves your dressing room closer to what you want to achieve. The greatest managers are able to replicate these things at different clubs and in different leagues. José [Mourinho] is the greatest example of this kind of adaptability with maximum success. It is something that is not achievable for all other managers.'

For Warnock, supporters are both a pressure and an encouragement: 'At all my recent clubs – Leeds, QPR, Crystal Palace, Sheffield United – people have said, "Well, I've got to say you weren't my number one choice, but I'm glad you are here" and that's nice. They have heard or read about this Neil Warnock who breathes fire and smoke comes out of his ears and they don't want that – but when they actually get me working for them they understand how I work and they quite enjoy it. I think that's what I love – making ordinary people happy and lifting expectations. One of the best moments in my life was going back to Palace with QPR. I had left them when they went into administration – and I thought I would get some real stick. But as I walked out of the tunnel the whole ground stood up to a man and woman and clapped. I will never, ever forget that. Even talking about it now is giving me goosebumps. And I just walked down the tunnel and I have never felt as emotional as that, and the Palace fans were fantastic, and it was one of the best moments ever.' He also finds that supporters provide a very real reference point when the going gets tough: 'I knew the QPR fans were totally behind me and it's been fantastic to get the emails. If we'd been relegated and finished rock bottom, the fans would have been fantastic and wanted me to carry on. But we wouldn't have got relegated, we would have finished mid-table and every one of those fans knew more about me and the football club than any of the new owners. That's why I knew that the fans were right.'

Tony Pulis began his second period at Stoke expecting no great support from the fans, but he turned it around. He found that the fans were helping to define the club culture. 'When we got promoted in 2008 we were favourites to get relegated again. We used this to get the supporters on board with us. We said, "Listen, the whole country is against us, nobody gives us a chance – but we have got a chance if we stick together." The fans bought into that and they have remained very solid: we spent five consecutive seasons in the Barclays Premier League. We created history by being the only team in Stoke's 150-year existence to remain outside of the bottom six in top-flight football for five consecutive seasons. We featured in four major cup quarter-finals, an FA Cup semi-final and an FA Cup final. Furthermore we reached the latter stages of a major European cup competition only to lose out to Spanish giants Valencia. I guess there was a lot of psychology involved with me always beating the "us against the world" drum. The fans were magnificent, that siege mentality is still there and long may it continue. That togetherness permeates the club. When you go to Stoke's training ground, from the people who clean the dressing rooms out, people who look after the kit, the canteen staff to the players, everybody is together.'

This direct communication between fans and manager is almost unique to the large-scale performance sports. But it does carry a fascinating challenge to leaders around how to influence large groups of stakeholders directly. In the British Airways strikes of 2009/10, the CEO Willy Walsh personally wrote email messages to all reward card holders explaining the board's position and promising decisive action to end disruption. At the end of a season, Sir Alex has sometimes addressed the Old Trafford crowd through a vast speaker system. But perhaps the most delightful example in the pre-internet era of a manager communicating in this way came from Brian Clough at Nottingham Forest. He had noticed more bad language than ever coming from the home supporters. One day, arriving for a home game, the supporters were greeted by a hand-written sign: 'Gentlemen. No swearing, please. Brian.' The swearing is reputed to have stopped almost the same day. In the intense relationship between manager and fans, simple messages can have a massive impact.

Fans provide pressure, they provide encouragement, they are whom the managers do it for, they are the club's lifeblood. They are too many by far to speak with personally, and they can have a profound effect on a manager's career and on the fortunes of the club. In ancient Rome, the Caesars who feared the power of the people were the ones who kept themselves distant. Great leaders in football – and sometimes in business – use all the means at their disposal to engage with the wider audience, and they see it as a pleasure, not a chore.

The Voice

With only a few Clough-like exceptions, the voice through which football's leaders can engage their audience is the press and wider media. Unsurprisingly, Premier League football managers have a highly charged relationship with the media. Managers are as close to the action as it gets without (usually) playing themselves: they know things no one else knows (such as match tactics, players carrying injuries or the real state of team morale) and they are highly experienced and highly quotable. In short, if the manager is indeed the central authority at the club, then he is the one the media will want to speak to. From the other direction, the media provides managers with the single most potent connection to the public. Through interviews and press conferences, they can express their reactions, their thinking and even their vision. Hodgson values them as the single most effective way of communicating with the club's fans: 'All press conferences – but especially tele-vised ones – are very, very important.' The media needs the managers, and the managers need the media.

The challenge: intensity, intrusion, power and pressure

And the relationship is getting hotter and hotter. Where managers were interesting commentators 30 years ago, today they are central characters in the drama. Sir Alex is clear as to why this is: 'The media do this because today they are a beast that isn't interested any more in what happened in the 32nd minute of the match. If you go back in time, it was a chronicle of football. What you've got now is a dominant interest in reaction. It's all about how to sell a newspaper, and the manager is the focus of that because they know he is the one person that can be sacked. So there is a strong focus on the success or failure of a manager. It goes with the role as the most important member of the club.'

The media now have a direct impact on team dynamics. Kevin Keegan explains how it has changed since the 1970s at Liverpool: 'You might go to a player and have an argument – we had training sessions that could be quite feisty – but no one ever knew it outside the group. It was much easier to keep it in the group in those days. There was no Twitter or Facebook; the media was much easier to handle. I remember they used to travel with us from Scunthorpe on the bus! That changed incredibly, mainly because of the way the journalists were being pressured by their editors and other people penning the headlines, I guess, to get stories at any cost. That led to a breakdown of trust between players and the press. Even if the stories weren't that bad, the headlines could be bad, and the players would be saying, "Don't give me that – it's your piece, you wrote it." We moved to a siege mentality of, "We don't want to talk to them, we don't want these people around us."'

Allardyce is rueful at how the press can create a label for a manager, however undeserved. In his case, the label of employing negative tactics has created problems with fans, and even fuelled some discussion with peers: 'It's not actually about our style of football. It is a very unfortunate label that's attached to success. It started with fellow managers who were probably embarrassed by getting beaten by Bolton Wanderers. We knew we had a great team that could adapt to a different style … and play to win football matches … The unfortunate thing was that the press picked it up and because they said it, it had to be true. Mourinho didn't say it – he used that style to win the league! So we used to watch him and say he was playing like us. (They were better than us – we had good players, but they had *great* players.) It's a sad label that stuck. So now everywhere I go the first question they ask is always, "What style of football are you going to play?" It comes within about 30 seconds. So my answer is normally, "Do you ask every new manager that?" Many young managers are very aware of it now. They have understood that the last thing you want to do is get labelled. The only thing you can do about it is to create a label of your own.' As the banking sector (among others) will testify, shaking off a label or a reputation – whether personal or organisational – is a significant challenge for leadership.

Warnock is one of the most successful promotion managers of all time. He has a reputation for being tough, outspoken, unafraid to cross people – and with a hide like a rhinoceros. Only a part of this is true. 'My make-up is more complex than that. What the press say – it does hurt me, it hurts Sir Alex, it hurts all of us really. When I first started I wanted to ring up every paper that printed the wrong headline – pretend to be a source at the club. I had to realise, as I got older, that these guys have got stories to sell and I had to learn about people. I had to learn that this guy who is telling me he'll never let me down will stitch me up the second my back is turned. It's disappointing really and sad for the young managers nowadays that you can't have the trust that I had in the press people when I first started … I used to have our local jour-nalists on the bus with me going to games. Well, you wouldn't dream of that now. I remember in the last few months at QPR doing a press conference. There were six or seven there and this journalist said, "Could you just tell us, Neil – off the record – about so-and-so …" I just slowly took my breath and looked at everybody and said, "You are talking to me about off the record? Just look at every one of these f****** journalists here. Every one of them would stitch me up as soon as they look at me and you are saying off the record." That's how journalists are. They say "off the record", but if I'd said anything they'd have slated me. They all laughed – we all had a laugh about it, which was good. You've got to make it light-hearted. But they all know that I know.'

Wilkinson admits he felt under pressure in front of the media – largely because he liked to think about answers before giving them. 'When I was managing, my answers were never quick enough for the radio or the TV. The players would joke about how people would ask me a question and it would seem like there would be an eternity before I gave my answer. The press don't give you time – and it's under pressure when your weaknesses come to the surface.'

He also points to how much tougher it is now than 30 years ago. 'What's changed dramatically is the visibility. Everything now

is far greater and more immediate. In a strange way, I think sometimes it's less revealing for viewers and readers because managers
have all learnt to play roles. So when the interview comes up, it's
almost like you know what's coming. In fact, the media are happy
when you do lose it! When I went to Italy with Ron Greenwood
for the European Championships in 1980, there were about eight
or ten staff and we went out to dinner with a load of journalists
and TV people on three occasions. I would give the journalist an
answer to the question, but then I'd say but I don't want you to use
that and the reason is this and that. What they then wrote was a
more important piece and in many ways the piece that was nearer
to the truth and reality. Whereas now it's got to the point where
clubs have media offices. The very, very good ones have got pretty
much their own Alastair Campbell. It's a different world.

'Working with the media was like a dance where the judges are
walking round the ballroom tapping you on the shoulder and getting
rid of you. The reporters are the ones giving you the marks because
they are representing public opinion most of the time. When I was
chairing at Sheffield Wednesday, I would hear the local radio talking
about public opinion. Then I would go to the media department
and ask how many were on the blog in question – how many actual
names. I remember one figure of 28. After I'd been chairman it was
really weird walking round Sheffield – the number of people who
came up and said, "We can't thank you enough for what you did." I
felt like saying, "When all the s*** hits the fan, mightn't it have been
a good idea if one of you had got the other 90 per cent that think
like you and said to the others let them get on with it and shut up?"
It's a shame the way press relations have gone. I think the good
managers now exist in spite of the media – it's not part of their life
any more. What Alex [Ferguson] did was use it, and I think Arsène
is the same. The good ones use it rather than get abused by it.'

Cracking the code: acceptance, simplicity and keeping it all low key

At Arsenal, Arsène Wenger appears to have a stable and productive relationship with the media. So how does he do it? Most importantly, he acknowledges the job the media has to do and has a reputation for being dead straight in his dealings with them: 'This is because I am governed by two things. First, I have to accept their opinions. I respect that. I accept it if someone says I am a bad manager and I made the wrong decision here and there, as long as they keep only on the professional side. What I don't accept is when it goes into deeper [more personal] situations. Sometimes that can happen. Second, I think they do a job like I do – and they do a job that is not easy as well. In a competitive world they have to come out with articles that sell newspapers, and that becomes more and more difficult for them.'

Walter Smith had an excellent reputation as manager of Scotland for a low-key approach to the press. This was in direct response to the unusual, out-of-scale interest. 'In Scotland, the intensity of the media comes from being British. Being part of Britain, we have every national newspaper printing in Scotland. We have all the TV companies, we have the radio, we have everything there for a population of 5 million. So the intensity is out of proportion for a country of this size. I had to learn to handle that. I've always tried with the media to make sure that I never get too high or too low, especially in the Scotland job. I feel that that's important. It's sometimes a little boring for the media, and a bit boring for those who are looking in – but I always try to keep a middle line.'

Hodgson's approach to the press is typically positive and clearcut: 'First, I don't get concerned about myself. I find that if I start to concern myself too much about how I am looking to the media, and how the general public is perceiving me, then I will be diluting my real task: to coach and prepare the football team and to manage players. Always focus on the real task you've been given. But when the time does come to speak to the media, then I need to devote my full attention to them and to represent my organisation – club or national federation – in the right way. Finally, I take the opportunity of a press conference to speak to the supporters as the important people they are. I assume they have the same feelings about football and the same love and passion that I have myself. So the press conference is my forum, not the actual arena itself.'

Interestingly, managers find that media attitudes vary from country to country – which accounts for some of the variety in approach from non-native Premier League managers. Carlo Ancelotti actually prefers the English press to the more tactically aware Italians and French: 'I never had a problem with the press; usually I like to joke with the press. Sometimes we all take it too seriously. Football is a game, after all. I love the atmosphere in England for this reason. In England, football is very important, but the atmosphere is very good. The press in England are not so interested in tactics, so they don't put so much pressure on managers. They like the private lives – especially the tabloids. In Italy and in France they put more pressure on the tactics of the game. In Italy they want all the press conference to talk about the line-up. All the questions are to understand what the manager thinks about the line-up and which players are going to play or not. If they understand the line-up they can also understand the player that plays and maybe they can put some pressure on the players that don't play. In France they are the same. So in the press conference, I like to joke and keep it light.'

And, of course, there's always the language issue. Interviewers may push less hard on managers speaking in a second or third language, but as Hodgson has realised from his many years outside

Britain, it is down to the manager to have enough of the language to maximise his opportunity for public impact. 'While you can get around language barriers on the coaching field where a lot of what you do is technical, dealing with other stakeholders – not least the media – can present a major problem. You have to develop at least a working knowledge of the language when working abroad.'

Football's leaders generally have, it seems, genuine respect and appreciation for the press and media – although the divergent interests of the two camps will almost inevitably lead to pain in the relationship at times. Intention seems to be the key. Leaders who look forward to meeting the press as an opportunity to share their insights with the public, who respect the work they are engaged to do, and who approach the interactions with positive intent will generally come off well.

The Leader at the Centre

In the maelstrom that is top-flight football, the most successful leaders are intentional in their dealings with their stakeholders. They know how to approach them, and they spend time getting it right. Five mindsets and skills emerge as valuable.

1. Relish your role at the centre:
    It is tough being the man in the middle, but it also brings great privilege. It represents a great challenge, and great leaders relish great challenge.

2. Get your priorities right:
    Best practice seems to be first to ensure the relationship with the owner-chairman is in good state, then devote focus and energy to the team. In other words, understand your key stakeholder then do the job you're paid to do to the best of your ability.

3. Establish and communicate a shared vision:
    The relationship with the owner-chairman tends to flourish
    where there is a shared vision. Once that is established, the
    manager needs to convey the vision to his people – and so the
    owner needs to be sure to appoint a good communicator to
    the role.

4. Accept readily that other parties are involved:
    Far from resenting the involvement of genuine stakeholders,
    the top managers welcome it. They realise that owners,
    governing bodies, supporters and the media not only have a
    right to be there, but also have an important role to play. This
    mindset drives strong relationships. They *intend* good for the
    other party – be it a great performance for the fans, a return on
    investment for the owner or even a good story for the press.

5. Focus on each relationship in turn:
    From that intention comes an ability to focus on the rela-
    tionship in question, to take real time to connect with the
    people in front of them. It takes real leadership to do it and is
    not always easy. But the leader who can suspend the natural
    frustrations and come to every interaction with genuinely
    good intent will find himself with the strongest, most
    supportive relationships on every level.

PART TWO

Creating a Winning Environment

CHAPTER TWO

THE ART OF ONE-ON-ONE

THE BIG IDEA

At the heart of leadership lies an ability to inspire people. We hear powerful speeches and rallying cries, which might convince us that inspiration is all about motivating great crowds. For sure, that can be part of it. But at its most basic, inspirational leadership starts with individuals. Leaders are only leaders if they have followers, and followers – real followers – are inspired most of all by personal connection.

Think for a moment about the great leaders of recent generations. Nelson Mandela is good with a crowd, but it's when you meet him that you know you are in the presence of greatness. Former US President Bill Clinton is a man who has inspired millions. But according to all who have met him, his power lies in his ability to inspire one-on-one.

The challenge in football is no different. For football's managers, the players are the most significant expression of their leadership. One inspired player can lift a team. Remember David Beckham playing for England in the critical World Cup qualifier against Greece in 2001? More than his sublime skill, his sheer energy proved decisive as he covered every inch of the pitch from one penalty area to the other, desperate for victory, an inspiration to his teammates. The individual is key to the team.

Equally, a disenchanted player can drag everyone down. With the pressure on and the minutes ticking away, one player dropping his head can hurt the whole team effort. And off the field, football teams like any other kind of team are undermined when cliques form.

Great football managers know how to deal with disappointment and resentment in their team, with cliques and with open revolt. And, as most will tell you, it begins and ends with individual relationships: the one-on-one.

THE MANAGER

Carlo Ancelotti is best known to the English public as a highly successful but short-lived manager of Chelsea, whom he led to the famous English league and cup double in 2010. But that is only a part of his story. His playing career spanned 16 years from 1976 to 1992, during which time he represented his native Italy in the 1986 and 1990 World Cups, and was a mainstay of three great Italian clubs: Parma, Roma where he won a league title and four Italian Cups, and the legendary Milan side of the late 1980s with whom he won two league titles and two European Cups in five years. Since then, his achievements as a manager have surpassed even those great honours. Growing in experience over five years at Reggiana, Parma and Juventus, he struck gold at Milan. Beginning in 2001, he led them to multiple honours, crowned by two Champions League titles in 2003 and 2007. By the time he arrived at Chelsea, his credentials were beyond any doubt. His move to Paris Saint-Germain in 2011 placed him at the cutting edge of one of club football's biggest growth projects, and June 2013 saw him appointed as manager of one of the global games's biggest clubs, Real Madrid.

His Philosophy

Carlo Ancelotti is a man with a simple philosophy: understand every player. He practically defines the art of one-on-one. This is the foundation of his leadership, and he sticks to it like a terrier. It's obvious, he says, 'In football you may have an idea. The only way to bring this idea to life is to explain the idea to other people, and they have to go on the pitch and show this idea. For this the relationship between manager and players has to be the best.'

The Challenges

Football is a strangely territorial business. We, the fans, make it so. We define our club by our commitment. And for many, the club defines us. People look at you differently when you declare which club you support. Similarly, when a player joins a club, he takes on a kind of mantle. The club pays him well, and in return demands not just skill, but loyalty. Fans at clubs around the world hold up banners demanding passion and commitment from their players who they see as 'one of us'.

Capturing the players' loyalty

The manager is a key focal point for player loyalty – or player dissatisfaction. And rarely does a manager get to build this from scratch. Except for rare instances of extreme team rebuilding, managers inherit a going concern. They step into a club to take charge of a team-in-being, with its associated track record, its expectations and its attendant maze of relationships. The players on the team – as well as the fans – will invariably represent a wide range of opinions and expectations of the new man, from high hopes ('he's exactly what we need and he'll get us out of jail') to resentment, based often on change ('he's no better than the last one' or 'he'll never match up to his predecessor').

A defining moment for Ancelotti was his arrival at Roman Abramovich's Chelsea. José Mourinho had left in September 2007, despite leading Chelsea to successive Premier League titles. In the two seasons that followed, three managers of significant professional stature had taken their turns in what was proving the hottest seat in European football. Neither Avram Grant nor Luis Felipe Scolari survived a full season, and Guus Hiddink, despite huge popularity and an FA Cup trophy, had a prior commitment to Russia. The playing staff that Ancelotti inherited had in the main a deep-seated loyalty to the inspirational Mourinho, and a sense of loss at the departure of Hiddink. Many of the players had loved José Mourinho – and still did. A less secure man than Ancelotti might have tried the 'new broom' approach: change everything until the place looks like me. Or he might have decided to transfer-out the big Mourinho fans, to ensure no direct comparisons could be made. Or he might have distanced himself from the day-to-day running of the team, taken on the aura of a demi-god. Instead, Ancelotti chose a different path: he would get in amongst it. He would invest time in his playing staff. He would get to know them as professionals, but also as people. 'It is not easy to build these relationships – but it is important. I needed to stay on the same level as the players: not above, but not behind. I believe that players are real men with real problems, and I think to have a good relationship is the best way to have results.' Eight months later, Chelsea were champions of England.

They are people too

Ancelotti makes an excellent point. Players are not just assets – they are human beings. Human beings have emotions, priorities, beliefs, perspectives, needs and fears. Just uncovering these can be a serious task; working with them is another thing entirely.

Take an example from Milan. One usually very successful player was off his game. There was no apparent reason – but Ancelotti knew that something wasn't quite right. 'Then he came to me and said, "I have a problem." The player "had" to go and get married – but he was saying he didn't want to go! We talked about it, and in the end I said he had to decide what he felt and do that. I was very happy that he could come to me. In the end, he didn't marry this woman, and we are still friends today.' Ancelotti made himself approachable, and it worked. Simple advice and availability made the difference.

Ancelotti treats each player as an individual, and respects the way they like to operate. 'All people are different. John Terry is very open, Frank [Lampard], Ashley [Cole] are more conservative and quiet. My relationship with Frank improved during my work there. At the beginning it was more conservative, but at the end it was good. At the end of my time with him, we had dinner together – we had a party together, we had a very good time together. It was very good.'

The football cauldron

Leaders the world over – in business, politics, sport – find their greatest challenges lie in relationships. Building them, maintaining them, growing them, saving them. Most business leaders will tell us that their most pressing and time-consuming challenges are human ones. The main difference in football is that these challenges are frequently lived out under intense public scrutiny. A conversation between José Mourinho and Cristiano Ronaldo over the player's contract becomes international news. Carlos Tevez appears to refuse Roberto Mancini's instruction to warm-up in Germany and it makes headlines in Singapore. Sir Alex decided to leave Beckham out of a crucial match against Leeds in 2000, after the star player had failed to turn up for training on the Friday. With masterful understatement, he comments in his autobiography *Managing My Life* that, 'Because of the hype that constantly surrounds David, my decision to leave him in the stands became a bit of a drama.' It is difficult to nurture relationships in a goldfish bowl.

For Ancelotti, the tougher relationships work when the manager is fully supported by the club. 'It is very difficult. Sometimes a player causes problems for his manager. But if he doesn't understand what his manager needs, then he knows he cannot play at the top level. We managers have a possibility to leave players out. But if you take a strong decision you have to have the support of the club. If you don't have that support you are dead. If you make a mistake, you have to have the support of the club and until the last day you have to be the number one. The players know if there is no good relationship between manager and president or owner. It's very easy to break the dressing room. I had a good example when I was at Juventus. I felt that I was really the number one, and the club had a lot of trust in me. Eventually they sacked me because I wasn't good enough. This was OK, but until the last day, there was no problem. The players knew this very well. This is the key to keeping good relations when times are tough.' The board's actions and statements can either accumulate or relieve pressure for a leader. The same is true of almost any governing body in business or sport, and a resilient leader will be prepared for it. With their every decision being scrutinised from all angles, support from the board gives managers a stronger platform on which to build their one-to-one relationships with players.

The world around is changing

Leading footballers is increasingly difficult. The generation gap between most managers and their players is no new thing – indeed it exists for leaders and their teams in most walks of life. But the automatic respect that age commanded in the days of Shankly, Busby and Mercer is no longer there. Leaders have values and behaviours that their players don't necessarily share. Neil Warnock illustrates the issue perfectly: 'When I get off a bus – Premier League or Championship – players will go into the dressing room, big earphones on, music blaring, walk past the crowds. I get off last and when I get off I take my own pen out and I go round the bus and for 20 to 30 minutes I sign autographs. I'm happy doing that, rather than going into the dressing room and listening to that head-banging music which I've no time for. I'd rather talk to people.'

Without deliberate mentoring, footballers are unlikely to model something better than the society in which they live. Sir Alex Ferguson points to societal changes that have reduced resilience in players. 'The human beings that we deal with now are more fragile than they ever were. They are cocooned – brought up differently. They are often protected by parents who live their lives through the success of their kids. Then we have kids and parents wanting more and more, so they turn to agents much earlier. We are seeing more and more agents getting involved in a footballer's career at 16 or 17 years of age. I know there are some cases where they have an influence at maybe 14 or 15 – even direct access without parents, which is not allowed. So I found that when they got to me they were certainly more fragile because they are cocooned in a different way.'

Tony Pulis echoes this observation and its impact on professional football: 'From when I first started out in management to where I am now, the characteristics of society have changed enormously – and my own leadership approach has evolved accordingly. I spend a lot more time now speaking individually with players. When I first started and I had to say something to a player in front of the rest of the team, then I would just say it without flinching, even if it was detrimental. Today 90 per cent of the times when I need to sort out an issue with a player, I will take a player out of the group situation and talk to him individually. I think players – possibly reflecting society in general – take things more personally than they did 20 years ago, and it's important as a leader to adjust your skill set accordingly.' The art of one-on-one, according to Pulis, is now more important than ever.

Solution Part One: Understand Your People

When it comes to understanding people, Ancelotti is a master. He is warm, generous and compassionate. 'I believe that every experience can form your character. Your relationship with your parents shapes you as a person because your parents are your most important teachers. They form your character and, as a manager, it is important to have character.'

This runs deep for Ancelotti. He grew up on a farm in rural Italy – a safe and nurturing childhood, much loved by his parents. 'My family were very quiet and calm, I grew up with a very good family, small family: mother, father, sister, grandmother and grandfather. It was very good; I understood a lot of things. My father never shouted; he was very quiet and calm. I had a beautiful childhood.' The result is a centred leader who – for the most part – exudes calm. And this calm is at least part of the reason why his players will run through fire for him.

The loyalty challenge

In the bestselling book *The Seven Habits of Highly Effective People*, management expert Stephen Covey quotes St Francis of Assisi's famous principle: 'Seek first to understand and then to be understood.' And it's not hard to see why investing in understanding people grows loyalty. But where to begin? People, after all, are complex. One good place to start is with a player's strengths – understanding where they lie, focusing on them and using them to the greatest possible effect. Neil Warnock's philosophy is to make average players good and make good players great. In fact, he regards it as something of a personal challenge: 'I enjoy getting the best out of people where other people say don't touch them with a barge pole. When everyone tells me, "They can't do this, they can't do that," I look at what they *can* do. I also look at *who they are* – their temperaments and personalities. I like creating a team of different characters. When I first started at Scarborough in 1986, we were betting certainties to be relegated – supposed to be the worst team in the league. I took about 20 players up to Scarborough to show them the set-up. All of them were free transfers, all cast-offs – but I just felt that every one of them had something to offer. They all had plusses. I think you can get carried away looking at what they're not good at, but I think if you can work on what someone *is* good at you have more opportunity of progressing than you have if you focus on their faults.'

It is not always easy to see gold when everyone else is trying to dissuade you. But the rewards can be huge. Warnock continues: 'When I was at Sheffield United, I was looking for a wide player. I had seen Michael Brown at Portsmouth. He was on the books at Manchester City and had a bad-lad reputation. He was on loan at Portsmouth, who wanted to send him back because they didn't like his attitude in training. He didn't play out wide at Portsmouth, he played up and down. We went down there to watch him, and playing in front of me I saw his attitude. He was like a little terrier – I just liked something about the lad. City didn't want him, Portsmouth didn't want him, so I took him on loan and then I signed him in the summer about two months later. In the end I think he scored 23 goals and got us to the semi-finals of the FA Cup and the League Cup.' By understanding a player who wasn't even on his own staff and then by focusing on his strengths, Warnock had done what he believes in. The player had become greater than he himself would have believed possible. 'In the end he got a move to Tottenham and became a multi-millionaire. It pleases me when he'd been cast out, not going to go anywhere and then I make a star out of him.' Warnock teaches us a good lesson here. A leader should be prepared to back his own judgement, even in the face of contradictory advice from those close to him.

Understanding a player can be very fulfilling for the manager. And Warnock believes it generates loyalty: 'Brown came back to join me at Leeds United, and he played his socks off.' But it doesn't stop at understanding. It also takes acceptance. Acceptance is about taking the player at face value – not damning him out of sight for perceived limitations or weaknesses. This may involve giving him a chance that perhaps many feel he doesn't deserve. It is also about openness: football managers who are prepared to be proved wrong have a greater chance of succeeding. Walter Smith concurs with this observation. 'One noticeable aspect that you observe as a manager when you join a new club is the reaction you get from some players. Players can certainly turn around a preconceived view that a manager may previously have held about them from a distance. A new manager can sometimes invoke a very positive reaction from a player that exceeds expectation.'

Players as people

Seeking to understand the person beneath the behaviour is a critical act of leadership. Sam Allardyce is committed to it: 'Most of the problems for a footballer who goes off his game lie outside the training camp – they don't generally lie inside if you've got it right. Ian Green was the manager who taught me this as a player. Looking back on it now, he was a real man manager, a real motivator. It was his personality and his knowledge of when and where and what to do … We all thought, "How does he know that?" and we put it down to his experience. He would ask what was happening at home. Are you not sleeping? Little things, but important.'

So point one for a leader is to make yourself aware of what's going on – to spot the symptoms and have the courage to delve deeper. Point two then is to address the individual challenge. How to do this though depends again on understanding. Ancelotti is committed to this; he invests time in understanding every personality he is dealing with: 'In Milan, I had a report to help me understand what kind of player I was seeing, for each player. It was very interesting. So when they make a mistake yes, you have to speak to them individually. But also you have to understand what kind of communication players like because there are some players who don't like to be spoken to in front of the others, there are others that don't have a problem with you speaking in front of the others. Sometimes you have to speak in front of the others so the others can understand. This is a leadership challenge. But it's important to know which type of communication to use with each different player. There are players that are focused on what you say, but there are other players, for example, that like to be touched – a hand on the arm – when you are talking to stay focused. Others are not so bothered about touch. You have to understand each one, to get the most out of him.'

Football managers like Ian Green or Ancelotti add to their raft of skills the all-important art of listening. They understand that to listen fully requires considerable effort and application. Empathetic leaders don't just catch what is said – they listen for what is *not* said, and actively search for underlying meaning, scanning conversations, facial expressions and body language for clues. The result is that players like the young Sam Allardyce feel they have been taken seriously – and they respect their manager all the more.

This works in all areas of life. Take the example of a young American professional working some years ago in London, out with a group of colleagues for dinner in a small restaurant. A few minutes after they arrived, the table next to theirs was taken by a small party including Bill Clinton, who was in town while visiting his daughter Chelsea at Oxford. During the evening, the two tables got talking, and Bill Clinton – recognising a fellow American in London – spent some time speaking to his countryman, also called Bill. The young Bill was an out-and-out Republican voter, and had precious little time for Clinton. But his opinion changed after the encounter: 'That evening I was listened to for half an hour like I've never been listened to before by anyone – let alone a former president of the United States. He gave me all his attention, and I was the only person in his universe for those 30 minutes.'

Brendan Rodgers sees 'four magic words that people have on their foreheads: "Make me feel important."' This was very much the source of Clinton's strength as a leader. He could have leveraged his status as a former president, but he did not. Instead he had an enormous and lasting impact on Bill through his deep listening. Leaders who listen like this command not just loyalty but affection from their people, which in turn means that employees or players are willing to work harder for them, leading to more success for the organisation or on the pitch.

Understanding in the cauldron

What Ancelotti or Ian Green display is empathy. A much misunderstood idea, empathy is cast aside by too many leaders as 'the soft side' when, in fact, it is incredibly hard for most of us to practise. Empathy has two components. The first idea is that we put ourselves in the shoes of another person, to better understand their mindset and thus their worldview. Once we understand this, we can work much more productively with them. The second idea is that we show our awareness of their situation by some clear acknowledgement. Again there is a productivity bonus: he is happier to work with me because he feels I understand him.

A moving story emerged in the UK press around 2007. A father was taking his young son to Cambridge for cancer treatment at the world-renowned Addenbrooke's Hospital. He decided to turn the visit into something memorable by staying in a top-quality hotel for a few days and seeing the beautiful city at leisure. The evening before the operation, the head-waiter at the hotel noticed the boy was anxious, and asked his father about it. He explained that his son had had to shave his head for the operation, and was feeling self-conscious. The head-waiter expressed sympathy. The next morning, when father and son came down for breakfast, the restaurant staff had *all* shaved their heads. This story of empathy in practice shows its power even in the most difficult of circumstances. It also reminds us how costly it can be to get it right.

Like the head-waiter, Ancelotti believes in a costly version of empathy. And it is all tied up with the fundamental need for leaders to show their human side. 'I think that you have to show the player your character, because in a group it is normal to have a better relationship with one and a different relationship with another. By showing your character, you build trust – and in this way, I was able to keep friendships even when making tough and unpopular decisions.' Ancelotti has never been afraid to share his own fears and concerns, and his players sense in him an openness and a centredness that they find easy to relate to. Ancelotti is comfortable crossing boundaries that others do not: 'Provided a player respects my job and my decisions, he can still be a friend. This is important, because when the jobs have changed, the friendship can still remain.' However, this is a risky and hugely difficult line to tread and most leaders struggle to get it right. Get it wrong and a leader can lose respect, results can drop, professional relationships and reputations can be damaged beyond repair.

Solution Part Two: Build Steel

Empathy does not equate to softness. There is a steel common to all the leading football managers that marks them out from their peers. Ancelotti gives an example: 'I was a manager of someone who had played with me. How could I break the relationship that we had when we were players? We stayed friends, but they have respect because my role was different. I was no longer a player – I was a manager. They have to respect my decisions. Sometimes that is not easy. I remember dropping players who came to me after my decisions to ask me, "Why did you take me out? We are friends!" I would answer them: "Yes, we are friends – and we can continue to be friends – but you have to stay on the bench today."' In stepping up to lead your peers, the art of one-on-one – specifically *how* you deliver the message – is critical.

Perhaps the absolute master of steel is Sir Alex Ferguson. His resolve stems from a profound belief in his ability to make decisions, and originates back in the dockyard unions of Glasgow. 'In the trade union I was a shop steward. I had a strong sense of responsibility about looking after or protecting people who were vulnerable, and I had to make decisions and stand by them. In an era when trade unions were very, very powerful, very influenced by communists, there were still two or three times that we took strike action – for the right reasons. I had a great mentor as a shop steward – a guy called Cal McKay, who was this fantastic, down-to-earth man and very intelligent. He could talk the length and breadth of any subject you could name, but he would never force his beliefs on you. It was obvious that he had strong communist beliefs, whereas I was socialist and that was it, but it was his strength of character that had a serious influence on me. I learned how to make decisions and had the strength of character to take me into management.' Steel, then, can come from professional knowledge, decision-making ability and self-belief. It is a hugely important quality in a leader.

Steel can build loyalty too

Football managers value loyalty – perhaps above all else. When the chips are down – either personally or on a wider scale – they want their players to come through for them. We have seen how under-standing builds loyalty when allied to acceptance and openness. But can steel do the same thing?

Mick McCarthy was finishing his playing career at Millwall in 1992: 'It was Sunday night and Millwall had lost 6-1 – I think it was at Portsmouth. I was in the pub with a good mate of mine, John Colquhoun. We were talking about our game the following week, at home to Port Vale – which team would you pick, and so on. We weren't involved in team selection but after all, everyone knows better than the manager. And it was particularly interesting because there was talk of Bruce [Rioch] getting the sack. Our conversation went something like this:

> Me: My team is, so and so, me, so and so, back four … and you at right wing. What's your team?
>
> John: You'd be in at centre half … and Paul Stevenson at right wing.
>
> Me: What? You're not playing in your own team?
>
> John: I know I should play, but I've been struggling a bit with my back …
>
> Me: That's interesting – not playing in your own team …

On the Tuesday I woke up – St Patrick's Day, 17 March – I was looking forward to it. Then I get a call to go and see Mr Burr, the chairman who told me that Bruce had been sacked. I was called to another meeting next day. On the way, I met my mate Ian Evans, who would become my assistant for a long time. I said to him: "I think they are going to offer me the manager's job." Straight away he asked: "Do they owe you any money? They might want to pay you up – you haven't played for a while …" So I'm going into the meeting with two different thoughts in my head: new job or heading out. Next day, Wednesday, I get the job. I've broken into football management. Thursday we come in to train. Friday we're training again and I have to select the team. I pick Paul Stevenson on the right. John Colquhoun came to see me to ask why he'd been left out. I said, "You didn't pick yourself in your team and you want to play in my team? Not a chance!" So I'm a player in the dressing room on Tuesday, and I'm the manager on Friday, making team selections and leaving out personal friends. Not easy.' McCarthy makes light of it, but, beneath the easy-going nature, there is steel in abundance. And the loyalty? 'John and I have been friends for years – and still are. Very much so.'

So what did Colquhoun see in McCarthy that commanded his ongoing loyalty despite being dropped? Two things. The first is reliability. We often think of reliability as being on time, or playing a solid, constant game – we talk admiringly of reliable goalkeepers, for example. However, being a good leader is more about whether or not they keep their promises – or, put even better, whether they make promises they cannot keep. Tempted though he must have been to promise Colquhoun a place back in the starting line-up as soon as he was fit again, McCarthy did not take the easy route. Beyond reliability, he acted with integrity. For a football manager with integrity, what he thinks, believes, says and does all align. McCarthy knew Colquhoun wasn't fully fit – and Colquhoun knew that McCarthy knew. In not selecting him, he behaved with integrity, and he and Colquhoun remain friends to this day. Integrity and steel can build loyalty.

Steel works with real people

A common issue – especially for less experienced leaders – is a nagging belief that steel can hurt people. But this does not have to be the case. The critical act is to separate the problem from the person. In football, a common application of this principle is around leaving players off the team sheet. In other fields, an example might be delaying someone's advancement or promotion, or passing over a candidate for a specific task. No one enjoys dropping players, but the needs of the organisation or the club and the team are almost always greater than the needs of the individual. If you keep your eyes on the bigger picture, then the tactical decisions become much easier to make.

Great leaders make tough decisions, and still build powerful relationships. The first big challenge is the mindset of the manager. It's important to recognise that tough decisions don't have to damage relationships – on the contrary, they can build them. The most powerful relationships have mutual respect in their foundations. A losing mentality is: 'He'll never forgive me for dropping him.' A winning mentality might be: 'If I select him, we're not going to win. The right team for this match looks like …'

Walter Smith sees steel as an essential for dealing with players. 'In football we don't deal with products, we deal with people. And these people are not daft. They watch what you do – that's life as a manager. At Rangers in my first year they would have been looking at me asking: "Is he going to weaken under the pressure of having to handle this situation or is he not? Is he going to be able to lead us out of this?" I realised I had to try and show all the time that I was going to lead us out of a tough place. There can be darker moments on your own when you are making an assessment of the situation, where you think, no, this isn't going to work – but in front of everyone I think you have to show that you can be up front and handle it.'

Managers also have to have clear reasons underpinning their decisions – even if, like Ancelotti, they tend not to share them: 'Usually I don't want to explain to the players the motivation, because here we have 28 players and before the game I have to explain which 11 play and which 17 have to stay out. I don't have the time; I don't want to explain. But if one player came to me and if he wanted an explanation I would have to give it. Sometimes it's easy; sometimes it's not so easy because some decisions that you take are based on little details. So it becomes difficult to explain this. And it is sometimes difficult to tell the truth, because you can't say to a player, "You don't play because your teammate is better than you." It's difficult to say this because the risk is he will lose motivation to play so you have to find a different way to explain, while still behaving with integrity and, of course, not lying.'

Again, how you deliver the decision is critical. A famous negotiation tactic taught at Harvard Business School in Boston is the idea of Yes-No-Yes. It runs something like this: 'I need to say No to you. Why? Because I am saying a bigger Yes to something else. Once I have that clear, then the No becomes much simpler to say. I can now move past it, and offer you an alternative Yes.' This plays out for football leaders on a weekly basis. It might go: 'I am leaving you out of the starting line-up for tomorrow. That is because you have not been at your best this week in training. The match is tough, so I have to field the best team for the task. On current form, this other player has earned his start. Next week, I am offering you one-on-one time each day with our defensive coach, so you can work toward getting your place back.'

In the final weeks of the 2011–12 season, Roberto Mancini hit on an unchanged line-up that carried Manchester City to the title. He was profoundly aware of leaving great players out of the team, but needed the momentum that was emerging from his successful starting eleven. In effect, his proposition to the rest of the squad might have sounded something like: 'I know this is not easy or rewarding for you right now. But if we do this, we can all become champions. You will have played your part every bit as much as the others. And then you will have a champion's medal, with all that that entails.'

The work of a football manager – as with most leaders – is to balance the needs of the task, the team and the individual. There are times when the greater needs of the team or the greater demands of the task (for example, beating the team in front of you) simply have to take priority. Working with this principle, transparently, allows many football managers to make tough decisions well.

Steel in the cauldron

Professional football at the highest level is, at best, a defining experience for managers. At worst it can be brutal. Steel, if you don't already have it, becomes a major priority.

After Brendan Rodgers' disappointment at Reading, his move to Swansea already had a real sense of last-chance saloon: 'I came in and now I had to show my character. My career as a manager was almost over before it had begun. I didn't know how much of a chance I was going to get, but now I knew the rules. I had learned from my experience at Reading, and now I knew I was in the business of winning. My philosophy had been tested at Reading – the first time in all my years that it hadn't worked out. I had gone away for a six-month reflective period, so that when I arrived at Swansea, I again had great belief in my philosophy – maybe even more so than before. I was also stronger and more realistic. I had to be more clinical in my decision-making and get to the end point much quicker than I had done before.'

Rodgers realised that he needed steel mixed in with his natural style: 'Because of my caring background, I was always about giving people the opportunity and the chance. I have not lost that, but I have tempered it. I was simply giving people too many chances for too long. So I went in with my personal philosophy unchanged, but then I did three things differently. First, I became much more open in my communication. I started speaking to players like men and not boys, and I expected them to speak to me like a man. I became straightforward with them – not waiting six months to tell them something that I know now. Secondly, I committed to provide more quality in my work. I'd study, I'd prepare, go into detail in my planning and preparation to ensure that the players were as prepared as possible. And thirdly I would be much more ambitious: for the club's success, for the players' success and for my own success – in that order. So now we have both style and steel. That is the phrase the team uses – it is true for them, and it is true for me.' Rodgers' shift to steel expressed itself in his one-to-one dealings with players. He was still investing in them – indeed he took even more time to think through his messages and his interactions, linking them to his vision and his personal preparation. But the messages were clearer, stronger and with no room for ambiguity.

Changing times: steel expressed through values

It is not uncommon for leaders to regard values as stakes in the ground – anchor points against the seemingly endless change of the environment around them. And that's all very well. But living out these values in the face of criticism requires a steely commitment from a football manager to his deeply held beliefs. Since joining Arsenal in 1996, Arsène Wenger has seen huge shifts in the very foundations of football. He reflects on them from a player's perspective, as a good leader would who understands his people. But there is an underlying steel also to his words: 'Let us say honestly they have gone from a very normal world to a very privileged world, today all the players are in a very privileged situation. So how players are perceived has changed. Some people believe now that because they make a lot of money, they just have to produce. But it doesn't work like that. No matter how much money you make in life, you are a guy who wakes up in the morning with a pain in his neck or his knee, who feels good or not so good, and you are first a person, no matter how much money you make. At this club – as at a number of others – we manage to keep traditional values at the foundation of all we do. These include respect for people, solidarity when people are in trouble, supporting players' families, keeping our word. Basically old-fashioned qualities are still respected here and maybe that is why people have fond memories of our club.' This understanding and these qualities are at the heart of successful one-to-one leadership.

The Graphic Equaliser

There are four challenges to great one-on-one leadership: capturing the loyalty of your people, understanding their humanity, the extent to which the environment you're in is one of high pressure and high visibility and the changing nature of the world around. In response to these challenges, football's leaders must deliver a mix of empathy and steel.

1. Empathy:
   The master of empathy builds loyalty through understanding, listens to his people at a profound level, shows a human side that speaks louder than the external noise and transcends the changing times through personal charisma.

2. Steel:
   The master of steel builds loyalty through clarity and objectivity, makes good decisions with clear rationale but without apology, takes time in the high-pressure environment to get to the clarity and holds fast to his deeply held beliefs.

There are no hard-and-fast rules for what the mix is. Instead, the leader needs to see it like a graphic equaliser. With sound, the settings are adjusted to give the right effect for the music, the venue, the audience and the occasion. With leadership, the context is defined by the organisation and its values: the business challenge (the competing needs of task, team and individual), the person involved (does he prefer a gentle approach to feedback, or does he value head-on confrontation) and the natural style of the leader himself.

Individual managers will also have their own preferences. Leaders are unique too, and have a bias toward empathy or steel. The best ones can dial up either dimension when needed. Gérard Houllier says of himself, 'I think I'm tough, but I'm a loving person – and you need tough love to win. I can be extremely ruthless, but at the same time I can be extremely generous, indulgent and patient.' Ancelotti is high on empathy – but there is real steel. Sir Alex is high on steel – but there is real empathy. This is a case of 'both-and', not 'either-or'. No leader will deliver real success without mastering the two.

CHAPTER THREE

BEHIND THE SCENES

THE BIG IDEA

Time spent on the field is short. How players live their lives off the field – what they believe and how they behave – shapes them as people and ultimately determines the quality of their performance. Players of integrity build great reputations for themselves and their clubs.

Creating the environment for success is an essential component of a leader's role. Being able to engage with people one-to-one is, of course, a part of the answer, but there is more to it than that. Having set a vision, a leader needs to ensure his people have a fighting chance of fulfilling it. He needs to address his team's behaviours since right behaviours will assist on the journey where poor ones won't. Deeper than that, he has to establish some values which will help his people become self-determining. Deeper still, he may have to address some human needs or risk losing his people along the way.

These are important issues for leaders. Employees and even directors leave businesses when their basic needs are not being met – sometimes with serious consequences for the organisation and those who remain. Players leave clubs when they are not playing – their need for growth and for belonging is not being met.

Great football managers meet their players at all these levels. It is a rare skill indeed.

THE MANAGER

In the world of football, the name of Arsène Wenger stands for consistency and quality. An eight-year playing career in France included a league title with Strasbourg in 1978–79, but it is in football management that he has really found his purpose. He made his mark during eight years at Monaco, where he built a reputation for developing young talent and led the club to a league title and cup victory. He left the club in 1994, wanting to broaden his horizons, and sought new experience in Japan, where he led Nagoya Grampus Eight to league and cup trophies.

In 1996, after the departure of Bruce Rioch, Wenger was offered the manager's role at Arsenal. Eighteen years later, he has established himself as the club's longest-serving and most successful manager ever. Before Wenger's arrival at Highbury, Arsenal had finished in the country's top four places on 16 occasions. In the subsequent 17 seasons, Wenger has achieved that status every time. He is one of only six managers to win the Premier League, which he has done on three occasions – twice as part of the coveted and still rare league and cup double. Most notably, his team of 'Invincibles' in 2003–04 won the title without losing a single match – a feat unprecedented in the modern era. Wenger is the longest-serving manager in the Barclays Premier League. He has an excellent reputation among his peers, who admire him for his breadth of knowledge, strength of mind and commitment to his values.

His Philosophy

Wenger is known for many clear principles and beliefs. He is committed to internationalism, to youth, to fairness, to high-quality nutrition, to sustainable transfer and wage policies, to entertaining and attacking football and to the purity of the game. That he should embody such rounded and progressive views is especially notable in the light of his small-town origins. Born in Strasbourg in 1949, he grew up in the village of Duttlenheim, south-west of the city, where his parents owned a spare-parts business for cars and a bistro. The region was still emerging from the pain of the war, and Wenger grew up amidst distrust for internationalism, Europe and Germany in particular. However, the young man had a mind of his own, and an accepting spirit. 'I was always very curious and when I crossed the border [into Germany] I realised they had the same problems as we did. They wanted to enjoy life, they wanted to be happy; they go to work, they go home, they enjoy life like we do. In this way I got an interest and tried to discover more. I realised no one is completely good or completely bad and everybody wants to be happy in life.' It would not be until 1994, at the age of 45, that Wenger's work would take him out of his native France, but he soon showed the greatness of mind and breadth of worldview that would define his Premier League years.

The Challenge: Individual Behaviours

In Euro 2012, two sides are believed to have been undone by behaviours. Both were powerful, skilful sides packed with top players. Both were regarded as having a good chance of success at the tournament held in Poland and the Ukraine.

The power and the danger

The Dutch national side arrived at the tournament with very reasonable expectations – they had won nine out of ten of their Euro qualifying matches, and had been runners-up in the World Cup of 2010. But they fell at the first hurdle, losing all three of their group games and finishing bottom of their group. Winger Arjen Robben subsequently suggested there had been 'issues' in the squad – and that he was not surprised: 'Of course, there were some internal issues – but we will keep them indoors. We must all look in the mirror.' From outside the camp, Ronald de Boer, winner of 67 international caps for Holland, was clear on what he believed the 'issues' were. He told the BBC website: 'There were too many egos on the pitch, players who had great seasons, van Persie, Huntelaar and Robben, and overall too many who wanted to be the star of this tournament. Huntelaar and van Persie are not only the top-scorers at their clubs, they are both top-scorers in the Premier League and the Bundesliga, but they're not playing well [for the Netherlands]. Football is still a team sport. You have to do it together and we didn't see unity at this tournament.'

In that same tournament, France reached the quarter-finals – but also appear to have been undone by disunity. Like the Dutch, they arrived in Eastern Europe for the finals on a wave of optimism founded on a 20-match unbeaten run, but something went wrong in the pressure environment of the tournament. Speaking in a French newspaper, and reported by the BBC, then national coach Raymond Domenech (himself no stranger to team disruption) commented to the BBC: 'A major tournament reveals the strength of a group, a generation. The most glaring [weakness is] their inability to see anything other than their navels.' Two years previously in South Africa, striker Nicolas Anelka was banned from the camp for insulting Domenech, the players revolted and refused to train, and France finished bottom of their group.

Managers ask their players to perform on the world stage, and self-belief is a prerequisite for success. But managing the behaviour of a squad of players who believe that they have what it takes is no simple task.

Howard Wilkinson argues that talented players now stand in more danger from themselves than at any other time: 'It has become more difficult as the rewards have got greater. The genius now has more opportunities to abuse himself than ever. There's just no limit. If I've got two bob in my pocket and I've got ego what am I going to do? What am I going to say? How many people is it going to affect? Who's going to notice? Nowadays I can finish a game, get on an aeroplane and fly to New York, act stupidly in a nightclub there, get on another plane, fly back and have it YouTubed immediately. Then we've got a big game on Wednesday night ...' As Wilkinson points out, 50 years ago the same player would have gone out on Saturday night on the bus with his mates. 'He might have had too much beer, might have got in a fight – but unless it was really serious it wouldn't get in the paper. The manager would ring the newspaper and say, "Don't use it, I'll do you a favour next week."'

Not only have the dangers increased, they've also become more public. Creating the environment for success – and the behaviour that allows it – has never been so tough.

Human icebergs

A simple and popular image is of the human being as an iceberg: only a small part of us is visible at first sight. These are our behaviours – the things we say and do. The huge part below the waterline is our mindset: the things we think, feel, believe, value, need and fear. As we go deeper into our icebergs, we discover the things that drive us. Our behaviours are driven by our thoughts and feelings, in turn those are driven by our values and beliefs and, still deeper, these are driven by our needs and our fears.

Meanwhile, above the iceberg are outcomes and behaviours. An individual's behaviour has consequences for himself and others and is a constant preoccupation of managers. If one player behaves badly, it can upset the whole team. Bad-mouthing the manager, squaring up to a colleague on the training ground, drinking too much one night and reporting late or not at all for training the following day – these things all cause ripples in the team. They are at the least distractions – and at the worst, serious upsets. And distractions lead to preoccupation, anxiety and eventually reduced performance on the field. Conversely, good behaviours can have a profoundly uplifting effect. For this reason David Moyes rates former Australia and Everton midfield player Tim Cahill as one of his best ever signings. 'We had a meeting with him in the chairman's office at Millwall in London. His character was superb – he was bubbly, hungry, energetic, his eyes were sparkling at the thought of coming. We were all taken by him – his gratitude and his desire to try and do well – and he went on to be a great servant for the club and a good Premier League player over many years. He was a really positive influence in the dressing room.'

If a manager wants to create great outcomes, he needs to address his players at every level of the iceberg. The most obvious level is at the top: addressing the behaviour head on – 'Don't do that again.' But unless the circumstances were truly unique, the player is unlikely to change. If he is tempted to drink too much one night, he will be tempted again another night. What the leader needs to address is the *why*. Why did the player drink too much? Because he was angry. Why was he angry? Because he was left out of the team. Why did that make him angry? Because above all else he values playing. Why does he value playing? Because he needs to be appreciated. And so on. When we change what's below the waterline, we also shift the visible part.

The challenge to the manager then is to get at the stuff that is below the surface for his players – to address them at the level of emotions, values, aspirations, needs and fears. This is how he will get real shifts in the individuals and the team. This is why Wenger is committed to working with emotions, identifying beliefs and motivations, and embedding practical values.

Getting Below the Behaviours

The many behavioural challenges are clear. For the leader who can address them, the prize is a smooth-running ship – or at least a club where he can concentrate on the real business of the day: delivering results on the field. We know that behaviours are best addressed below the iceberg waterline, but how?

Level 1: Build people, not just players

The iceberg works at multiple levels – and this is how Wenger thinks about the challenge. At the emotional level, he believes players have a huge opportunity to influence society: 'You can show emotions to people without even talking to them. I can remember a whole period of my playing life when I had good passes from a Russian without ever speaking to him and we shared exactly the same emotions. In the same way, you can dance with somebody without ever talking and you are on the same wave-length because you can feel the music. Sport can be fantastic for that. It lets people share emotions without having the absolute necessity to communicate with words. Emotions can then create inside the desire to communicate afterwards: I would like to know more about this person because I had a fantastic feeling.

'In this way, I think sport can show how the world can live together. In the world of tomorrow, we will all have to live together more and more – and football and big sports can be in advance of society. Seeing 18 nationalities work together at a club, trust each other and create something powerful together – this is very exciting.'

Wenger's experience in Japan influenced this thinking: 'It made me believe that everyone during their education before the age of 14 should ideally try to spend six months or a year in a different culture, because it makes you realise that the way you see life is not the only way. It made me more open-minded. We all need to discover for ourselves that other cultures have other advantages. You will always feel completely at home within your culture, but you know as well that's not the only way to live. Sport can do that.'

Wenger's skill is in addressing the whole human being. He shows his players that he is interested in them as people – not just because they have ability with a football. And at the same time he inspires them with a call to use their gift to help reshape society. We can point to players who have responded to his deeper leadership – and to those who appear not to have done. But the critical point is that he stands by these powerful beliefs and achieves undeniable human and sporting success.

Wenger's firmly people-centric approach to leadership sits well in the modern era. Howard Wilkinson gets playfully reminded by ex-players of his traditional style: 'I get players who used to play for me saying to me now, "Gaffer, you can't say to them now what you used to say to us!" Now, one answer to that is: "Why not? Is it suddenly not right to tell the truth?" But the smart answer, of course, is that footballers have changed with the society around them. They are more sensitive – so the letter has to be delivered by a different postman. And the good managers do that. It's not about you enjoying yourself and having a good rant – it's about the result and how best to achieve it. Today that means more one-to-ones.'

Wilkinson is undoubtedly right. The more enlightened modern leader sees the need to address the emotional component of his people. But addressing emotions is only the first step.

Level 2: Establish your values

In a world where values are constantly in flux, Wenger is known for steering a steady course. He is a clear advocate of the principle of the three musketeers: 'Sport is about trophies and spectacle; it's also about values. And in team sports, solidarity is very important. You can see this when individual sports are turned into team sports occasionally – like the Ryder Cup in golf. It becomes a different sport. It adds something by being together, the emotions, going for something together, and suddenly the interest becomes bigger, suddenly it is about "us" and not "me". Human beings subconsciously understand that alone I am nothing, but in a team I can achieve great things. So a leader helps people understand at a very young age that "together" can give them more than just "me". It is in a period of your life when your ego is massive – if you are 20, 21, 22 the world turns around you – and that's a normal developmental thing for a person. But at that age I believe that a leader has a big part to play to give this understanding that, OK, you are important but all together we are even more important. That's the joy of a team sport.'

David Moyes is admired as a strong leader but his strength comes from inspiring a value of self-discipline, rather than imposing rules: 'Discipline has to come from within. If that were not so, I wouldn't have it myself. I treat people with respect and I expect the same respect back. If someone lets me down at any time, then it makes the relationship harder to work with.'

Howard Wilkinson picks up on this theme of setting the tone yourself and inspiring through values: 'At its best, a football club is a greenhouse, where you can really create a culture. As I watched people, I realised that group behaviours have a massive influence. In football, the manager is the culture. I need to embody what I want to see – in training and elsewhere.' Like Moyes, Wilkinson found that modelling values reduced the need for rules: 'My rule was to have as few rules as possible. We worked on the basis of respect, trust, fairness, honesty – and team spirit. Team spirit is acting in a way that gives us all the best chance to succeed most of the time.'

Wilkinson recalls a moment when he knew that team spirit had really taken hold in Leeds: 'Four players came to me one Monday – almost a delegation, led by the team captain. I'd been a bit tough on our fantastic goalscorer, Tony Yeboah – all about sharing a responsibility for working to get the ball back. They were saying: "Gaffer, we think you should leave Tony alone. We know when we give him the ball in a goalscoring situation, he scores – so we're happy with him. We know that the most difficult job is scoring, and he does that."' Wilkinson was so happy to see the values permeating his team that he did not mind at all what a less confident leader might perceive as a challenge to his authority.

The values message is clear. If a leader can both articulate and embody a clear set of values, then his people will not only police themselves – they will eventually stand up and be counted for something they believe in. Achieve this, and there is inspiration for everyone.

On a lighter note, the importance of setting tone and embodying values is amusingly illustrated by Alex McLeish in a story about Ferguson at Aberdeen: 'I was never really scared of Sir Alex, but I had great respect for him. He took the game seriously, and so did we. We had a multi-gym for players to use when they were injured, but there was a snooker table in the same room. Players used to use both at the same time – kind of, "Right, you play a shot while I do the multi-gym and then when it's your turn I'll go in the multi-gym." We could always hear him come down the corridor so it was fine! One morning, they thought Fergie was away training, but sometimes he would hang back a bit and do some administration stuff. It was 20 minutes into when training would start, and this day he caught them red-handed. The lad had the snooker cue in his hand ready to pot when Fergie put his head in the door! Superb moment – the lad was absolutely brilliant – he put the cue around his neck and started doing squats! Fergie loved it, but he never let the seriousness of the football slip.'

Level 2 again: Work with beliefs and motivations

Also sitting below the level of thoughts and feelings is the question of beliefs. These are the things we hold to be true – about ourselves, our work, our colleagues, our purpose. Ultimately they determine our priorities, and Wenger is a master of them.

He begins by identifying his own: 'What keeps me going is my love for the game, for doing the job I do and for football. I have that internal desire to be as good as I can, refusing to be average. Unfortunately sometimes in the job I feel very average when I don't deliver results, but there is something in every individual that pushes him to try and be excellent. That is my petrol.' This combination of pure love for the game and striving for excellence naturally influences what he looks for in players: 'If you want to make a career at a big club you must be capable to believe in your abilities, and keep them in perspective off the field also. You can have players who appear quickly to have a big talent, but if they cannot handle keeping their feet on the ground and continue to improve, they will be eliminated. So always the people who last are those who can handle that kind of pressure and that kind of approach to their life. When you go out there [on the pitch] with the ball, it must mean something to you. Of course, you make mistakes at any age, but what basically always brings you back on track is that deep love and deep motivation to be as good as you can be.'

Once a player has that motivation, he must stay focused on it – against all the obvious distractions: 'The consistency of focus around an individual's motivation is an underrated quality. This is what sets one talented player apart from another with similar talent. And if you analyse people who have been successful, they don't remain successful automatically. Their standing goes up and down, and to come up again you need a huge level of consistency in your focus. So, for example, if a player is only motivated by money he will not go far. Players are made rich very quickly, so if he has the money and is only motivated by money where does he go? The players at the top are people who have a very strong internal need to be the best. We are all motivated by that. Strikers may love to win, and defenders may hate to lose; but the final focus is the same.'

Of course, for a player this deep motivation brings with it a flip side. It is down to the manager to provide a valid channel for that motivation to express itself. Wenger makes the point that this challenge surfaces weekly: 'One of the difficult things of being a manager is to sack 14 people every Friday morning – and then re-employ them on a Monday morning and say, "Right, we start again – I take you back on board." This, of course, is extremely difficult. Somebody who doesn't play or who is injured feels useless. The difficulty of our job and the key for the club is to take care of these people. And the nature of elite sport is you can be number five or six in the world in March and be number 500 in November. So if a player isn't playing, he is feeling in danger and is asking how he can get out of that. Therefore inside the club it is important that we give respect and credit to people who for a while aren't really in situations where they can show how good they are.'

Level 3: Create belonging and fulfilment

At the bottom of the iceberg, Wenger sees the need to create belonging for his players – both individually and as a team: 'I believe in creating an organisation where every individual believes that he can exploit his full potential, and as well that he contributes to the goodness of the club and team. We have a sense of belonging and a sense of wanting to realise what we are capable of doing. In an organisation you can get these two things right: I feel I belong to it and I feel I can get the best out of myself by doing that. You have a chance to be successful. Unfortunately that's not always possible and some of the aspects of our game are completely the opposite of that. When you have 25 players and on Friday morning you filter them out, you turn those people into unemployed people and the sense of belonging diminishes ... the sense of being able to show what you are capable of doing disappears.' The danger here is that a demotivated player can lose his appetite for the game, descend into a victim mindset and even begin to drag others down with him.

Leaders in whatever setting need to create belonging in their teams: belonging to something special, something intimate, something big and something lasting. Being part of the first-team dressing room at Manchester United is a good example of something special – and not least because Sir Alex maintained a strict confidentiality. He saw it as essential for his players' well-being: 'You've got to have a system in your club where it stays in the dressing room. Anything that we have to say remains there. That was true for me right from the start, from 32 years old. I never ever would talk about what happened between me and the players. I've always held that confidentiality. By doing that I am laying a foundation of trust – a sense they can depend on you. Human beings need that because they are fragile. In fact, the human beings that we deal with now are more fragile than they ever were.'

Intimacy is important for a sense of belonging too – and it does not have to be incredibly profound to have a positive effect. Kevin Keegan would create an easy sense of belonging simply by being there with the players every day: 'I would be there all the time, make sure the staff and I are first in and last out: looking around trying to feel what's good, what's right, what's not right, sitting at tables when the players are eating – not actually listening to the conversations, just getting a feel for the mood. When the players train I'm there, when they're doing their fitness I'm there. Then people know this guy is full time, he's serious, he's committed.' Keegan is serious about relationships, but pragmatic about how deep to go: 'The secret is to get people to believe in each other. Once you've got that, you've got a chance – because you won't beat the opposition if you're beating yourself. But they don't all have to love each other.' He gives the example of his excellent working relationship with John Toshack at Liverpool: 'John Tosh and I were a great partnership. We weren't *great* friends; we were good friends. I never went out for a meal with him, we never socialised together other than at club functions, but on a football pitch we were *best* friends. Everything I tried to do was to make him a better player, to make him score goals, to help him – and vice-versa.'

The something special also needs to be something purposeful. Thoughtful goal setting helps turn that sense of belonging to something worthwhile. Howard Wilkinson is a big believer in this: 'The first thing I did before my first full season at Leeds began for real was to sit down with my players and talk through some facts: "to get out of this league you need that many points, to win this league you need that many points, to do that you need to score that many goals, you need to concede no more than this many goals, and looking back over the last ten seasons, the number of players we need to use is 16 (or whatever the right figure was). So now what do you think we can do? What do you want to do?" I'd have my own view and I'd throw that in at the end, because players in that situation out of bravado always think they can win it. Then it's hang on a minute, let's think about this and what it means. It was very important for me to get them to commit to goals.'

Finally, the something special should carry some sense of the long term. David Moyes recruits for that: 'I've always looked for players I feel could go on a journey with me, not just do a job. I try and sign players who I think could go with me for four, five or six years if possible. I always have to believe I could work with them in the long term. I've got to say I've met quite a few players and chosen not to take them, some quite well-known players I've not chosen because I've felt that what I heard wasn't quite what I wanted to hear. A lot of them have turned out to be top players, but I just felt there was something missing, so I've stayed away.'

When we think of human needs, we often think of the basic stuff: food, shelter and so on. The reality is that the people we lead will have pretty developed needs – and belonging and fulfilment are at the heart of them. Football is no exception, and the great managers meet those needs head-on.

Back to Level 0: Set (and enforce) boundaries

For all the need to work lower down in the iceberg, the simple act of agreeing boundaries at the least makes it clear to everyone what is acceptable behaviour and what is not. Gérard Houllier cites it as one of his four foundational values, saying players should: 'Be a pro, on and off the field.' He stresses both: 'A player has to be a top pro in terms of looking after himself, and doing the job properly – because he lives for that job, which is different from other jobs.'

The challenge to managers is only very rarely about the high-profile misdemeanours we read about in the newspapers. David Moyes says the more common issues by far are around personal commitment: 'It's much more likely to be someone turning up late for training, maybe somebody saying something through the media which they shouldn't have done, maybe a tweet, maybe while they are away on international duty which causes you problems. The overall discipline of the players is much improved against previous generations.' Hope Powell, manager of the England women's team for 15 years, also finds it's about timekeeping and personal discipline: 'I'm very strict on time, as in turn up for breakfast on time, turn up for meetings on time. And players are very good. Just now and again they might just need a gentle reminder.' And is it ever more than a gentle reminder? 'Oh yes, and sometimes it's innocent really and they say, "I didn't mean to," and the response is, "If it happens again it'll be the last time it happens." And that's it.'

The women's game is different from the men's – with less media profile and different group behaviours. But, regardless of gender, David Moyes believes societal trends allow leaders to be much more empowering in their approach to discipline: 'The style of leadership is different to what it was in years gone by. Maybe leaders needed to be stricter then. In the world we are in just now, players can't really step over the mark because there will be so much to lose – their work is worth too much to them. With camera phones and instant media, players have to be much more self-disciplined than in the past.' The approach now from football leaders at the top of the game is about role modelling, self-discipline and appealing to a player's sense of responsibility. André Villas-Boas decided early on that he could 'only be a leader with open-minded leadership – open-minded in the sense of implying responsibilities in people and making sure people are made accountable for the mistakes that they do instead of me reprimanding them hard for what they are doing wrong.' Moyes adds: 'There are the basic ground rules that most football players have to abide by, and one or two which are important to me which I might mention to the players, but I really want them to discipline themselves. Good leaders don't have to be too heavily involved in it all the time. Only in extreme cases do they need to come in and take action.'

Essentially, the leaders set the environment for self-discipline. It begins, of course, by hiring people who are likely to embody your own values. Moyes would only sign players who 'display self-discipline, honesty and respect'. For Gérard Houllier, respect is the second of his four foundational values: 'Respect means that the player cannot say, "I should play," because if he says "I should play" in the press, he lacks respect to his teammates who he is playing with, or to the institution, or to the manager who picks the team. He must have respect even to the kit manager, not just to throw things away. He must respect the facilities, everything. Respect is a huge thing.'

As important as respect is boundary setting. When Hope Powell got her team together for international duty, she would think about it as a duty of care. 'It's more for their own protection. So I do lay down the boundaries – this is what you can do, this is what you can't do. But they are adults – I'm not their mother – so I want them to take the responsibility, take the ownership. It's quite a childish thought, but when you say you can't do something, all of a sudden everybody wants to do it! But the players are really good – they generally ask. We negotiate, but I make it very clear that my word is final.' Finally, it's about enforcement and sanction. Most of the time, this is understated. As Powell puts it, 'I have to just gently say, "Hang on a minute, what are you doing?" and just bring them back.' Moyes also believes in keeping it low-key where at all possible: 'I personally don't believe in fining people if I can help it. I've had to do it, but I'm not a great believer in taking money away from people – it's not usually the best solution to indiscipline. I would rather just remove the players from the environment – I think in its own way that's a bigger punishment. It can cause other difficulties through the media with internet reporting, but by removing a player from the situation I'm sending him home to think about what he has done. He will have to explain to his family why he is not training.'

Martin Jol confirms the need to maintain the boundaries once set: 'You need to have certain arrangements before a match and before a season, and certain rules and regulations, and I always say I won't let anything slip. For example, you have to be on time. I won't let them be late for a minute because I will say these are our standards. Another example: everyone wears the same clothes and the same socks. One player, he was always coming on the pitch with black socks. I thought, "It's not about you, it's about the group." So you have to tell them, although they can be pretty sulky, but you have to be firm and that is what I have learnt.'

Even when confronting behaviours head-on, both Moyes and Powell favour an empowering approach. Not surprisingly, Wenger takes a similar tack. He is constantly inviting his players to take ownership and look at their own standards – both off the field and on it: 'To every quality player, I ask him how well he thinks he has done and I listen carefully to what he says. If he has a fair assessment of his performance you can think that this guy has a chance in life. I also ask them to consider their level of ambition. This is very important to show how much you want to be the best and what kind of price are you ready to pay for it. Of course, in football you do need special talent, but when a player passes the age of 20, what is in his mind is more important than the rest and that's what makes a career.'

Howard Wilkinson remembers clearly a moment of confrontation that worked well when, even in the heat of the moment, he got the player to look inside himself: 'I got a player to think about the lack of respect he was demonstrating for his colleagues by turning up late. It was a case of, "Right, you've turned up ten minutes late. There's 30 of us on this training ground. We are all paid this much per hour so you've cost us that much. We have work to do."'

The important message here for any leader is that behaviours need addressing, one way or another. Strong leaders grasp nettles when necessary. Of course, there are times when this is not immediately appropriate – other people are present, other matters are pressing, or the moment is just not right. (After all, 1-0 down with ten minutes to go is no time to address a player's behaviour.) But when a difficult behaviour is left unaddressed, it still needs dealing with – it's just harder to do after the event.

Have the tough conversations

Tough conversations are part of the job – and successful leaders have them. In part, that is why they are successful. When things go unsaid, resentment builds. What was a small misunderstanding becomes full-blown conflict. It is an act of strong leadership to address the root cause of the problem.

As a manager, Glenn Hoddle often had to hold tough conversations. He recalls one especially difficult instance as England manager: 'The problem with being England manager is the players are not yours – you are only leasing the car – so you're not with them on a daily basis. Paul Gascoigne was one of our best players. I could see that he had too many injuries, and he was such a good player so I wanted him fit for the 1998 World Cup. I gave him so many opportunities. I said, "Look – you've got to get fit, your diet has got to change …" But I wasn't hands-on. He kept coming back a bit injured, missed a few games … We got all the way to the moment of choosing the World Cup squad, and Gazza was still not fit. I had to play him in a pre-tournament game in Morocco. He was a genius as a player and I wanted him in the team and it was almost down to the very last game whether I was going to put him into the squad or not because of his lack of fitness. It was the saddest decision, but the toughest decision I had to make because the whole nation wanted him, I wanted him. He got injured after 20 minutes, he got caught on the ball because he had been too slow and in the end I turned to my assistant and said, "John, we can't take him." So I had to sit him down in the hotel one-to-one and I spoke to him with the facts. "Listen, Paul, for a year I've been telling you if we get to the World Cup it could be magnificent for you, you're at your peak – but you haven't listened and now I have to make this decision." And it was a tough, tough decision.'

The key to tough conversations lies invariably in the preparation. David Moyes takes the decision rationally, then prepares emotionally: 'I remember the tough conversation when I changed the captain. Like any leader making big decisions, I looked for the best way to do it, tried to be fair and did what I believed was right. It was a long thought process – I don't make these decisions lightly. Then I worked out how to give him the message in a way that would keep him completely engaged and playing well.' Glenn Hoddle uses quite detailed preparation. 'I use role plays [getting someone else to play the character] and visualisation, which I find very powerful. But because I'm dealing with a human being, there is a reaction that I can't predict – so I have to be ready to go somewhere I didn't expect.'

Howard Wilkinson's direct style lends itself well to tough conversations. It also inspired his team at Leeds to be direct in their dealings with him, and with each other. In the League Division One (then the English top flight) title run–in in spring 1992, Wilkinson's Leeds side looked to have lost all chance of winning when they conceded four goals at Manchester City, leaving Manchester United ahead on points and with games in hand. 'I went in on the Monday and said, "Here's my plan for the next five games. We can win four; we've got to draw the other one, at Liverpool. On the penultimate game of the season we play Sheffield United in the morning, and Manchester United have to go to Liverpool in the afternoon. If we do what I say, we may just put pressure on them to get a result from that game and I don't think they will. So I'll pick the same team every week, unless we get injuries, but against Liverpool I'll make one change." The next morning Gordon Strachan, who was captain, came in and said to me, "I've come to save you the embarrassment and tell you to leave me out when we play Liverpool. Don't give me any bull**** about you want to keep me fresh for the home game. We need one point there as you say, and you're right I'm not the best person to get one." Wilkinson had been direct with the team, and Strachan had been direct with him. The clarity was inspiring, and all was well in the Leeds camp. Strachan was on the bench for the Liverpool match, they got the draw and Leeds won the title.

If for any reason it becomes impossible to have the tough conversation, matters can spiral rapidly out of hand. Martin Jol describes such a situation. 'I always try to speak to my players individually. Sometimes I don't like a player because I know he doesn't like me – but I still invite him into my office. With one player it went:

Me:	Come into my office ...
Player:	I won't come into your office.
Me:	We have to talk about the situation.
Player:	I don't want to talk about the situation.

He basically stopped talking to people, and if you stop talking to people you can't play any more.'

Direct clear feedback given in the moment is a light form of tough conversation. It prevents something festering and growing into a bigger problem. Wilkinson appreciated the way his great goalscorer, Lee Chapman, went about his business: 'I used to use statistics in my feedback. Lee Chapman is an intelligent man, and he knew how many crosses we needed for him to get a goal. So he was red hot. He'd come in at half-time and he'd be saying to a teammate, "You should have crossed it. If you'd have got it in, I could have scored. I need more of those." This created trust in the dressing room. The player comes back with, "No, actually I couldn't" – and he explains why, or he says, "Yes, you are right – sorry." Fine ... end of argument. The two agree. You need that level of honesty in order to be able to conflict and resolve. Because then he's dealing with the problem – otherwise it's left to fester. For me, that's Lee Chapman taking hold of his own career a little bit and saying, "I've got ownership. I know what I need to do, but I also know what others need to do." And then they by their token can say, "I know what I need to do but I know what you need to do, Chappy." This sort of live feedback is gold dust to a team.'

When the manager gives feedback, though, the key is to remember why you're giving it. Dario Gradi is committed to the growth of players and uses his feedback for this purpose: 'When managers talk to players, they should make sure it's the players that feel better for the conversation and not the manager. The manager has got something off his chest and he's pleased, but if the bloke feels attacked then he is worse off. When you shout a name and the player responds, he's effectively saying "I want the knowledge – what are you going to tell me?" It might be that he's playing too far up the pitch or needs to play a bit quicker. You don't say "What the bloody hell are you doing that for? You've just given that away!" He knows he's given the ball away, and shouting at him is not going to help him at all.

'That's the key thing: can you say something of benefit to the player? That's very difficult to do. It's a very passionate game, and when managers are leaping about on the sidelines, I don't think it helps their players. Commentators say, "Oh, he's showing great passion, players must be impressed by that." Actually, a lot of players pretend they haven't heard the manager when he's shouting from the sidelines! They've done that to me. They don't want to hear me, and I've spoken to them about it afterwards, but I've got past that. I think most of them now appreciate that I'm trying to help them, which perhaps I wasn't in the past. We all still get it wrong sometimes, but at least if we're conscious of the fact that it's not the best way of behaving, we might be able to do something about it.'

Build a strong dressing room

Feedback helps to build a strong dressing room. This is a place where players feel at home, can speak honestly, are unafraid, don't get beaten up.

Wenger is committed to a strong dressing room – through a strong captain: 'The captain is basically the messenger of the manager. I always think that when a relationship between a captain and a manager is strong, it makes the team stronger and it makes the manager stronger. When that relationship splits, the club is in trouble because there is nothing worse for the team than to get two different messages from two different leaders. That's why I believe that for a manager it is important to spend time with the captain. We speak about what he thinks the team needs, and about any special difficulties inside the dressing room. He mustn't tell you everything, and usually they don't – there are normally some things they don't want to tell you that belong specifically to the dressing room and I respect that. However, there needs to be trust and that trust is built by going through a season together. That relationship is the difference between losing six games on the trot and only losing two or three – with that solidarity, they get together to turn it around.'

David Moyes admits his gratitude to former Everton captain Phil Neville for strong leadership: 'I found him an incredible leader behind the scenes with the players. He's somebody who I could speak with. I could ask how he thought things were; I could ask him personally what did he think about what we'd done. But more importantly he is the one who would keep the players in line; he's the one who would lead from the front of the training. He trains every day, does his best every day. So there is an example being set by this player for all the young players to look to and say: "This is the standard and the level I have to train at and the level of professionalism if I want to play inter-nationally. And if I want longevity as well, I have to look after my body, make sure my training is correct, listen, and learn."'

Martin Jol builds a strong dressing room by creating a team spine: 'It can be the goalkeeper – it doesn't have to be but it could be – it's always at the centre at the back, it's in midfield and it's up front. So it's a spine, and in my spine I always try to have strong, experienced players. In the perfect world I would get my spine of players in for a conversation every three or four weeks. (Last year it happened only twice!) Then, of course, the captain is important. You can't always choose your own captain, of course. In Germany I could, but at Tottenham, Ledley King was already the club captain. He's a very good guy, so I absolutely didn't want to change it – but I can imagine that if [the existing captain] is a strong fan of the former manager, you could end up with a problem in creating a new, different football culture.'

The Guide

A lot of work is done behind the scenes, and the world will see only a very small part of it. It is no surprise that – just like complex organisations – human beings are more complex than the small part we get to see. But how should a leader work productively with that complexity? Wenger's answer to the problem is clear and simple: 'For me, being a football manager is being a guide. A guide is someone who leads people somewhere. That means he has to identify what he wants in a clear way, convince everybody else that is where we go together and then try to get the best out of each individual. Overall if you want to be a guide you have to question yourself, be somebody who can get the best out of people, and be convincing.' While the watching world is seeing the outcome, guides take time to think and work at all levels of the iceberg. Here are the lessons from guiding leaders in the world of football.

1. Think first of the root causes, not the behaviour itself:
    When seeing a behaviour – especially a disruptive one – it is easy just to confront it at face value. Far more powerful is to work below the water line of the iceberg.

2. Work with people on an emotional level:
   As Wenger says: 'There are times when words are not important – it is like a dance.' Too many leaders dismiss emotions as time-consuming and irrelevant. But emotions are a powerful driver of behaviour. And the leader who can tap into them can inspire feelings of contentment, self-worth and even elation.

3. Establish your own values:
   A leader who can articulate and act out strong principles from an early stage will find that they permeate his organisation, providing clarity and meaning. People have stronger radars for values than we think. They pick up on a leader's values, and know intuitively when they are pursuing or departing from them.

4. Know your own motivation and seek it in others:
   Wenger is motivated by the game of football itself and by a personal quest for excellence. He looks for the same thing in others – and those who share these beliefs are drawn to him. Perhaps more strongly than anything, this is at the heart of Arsenal's success.

5. Address deep needs head-on:
   A leader who can create belonging and fulfilment in the work of his people will affect them at the deepest level, get the most out of them and inspire deep loyalty.

6. Set clear boundaries and empower people to live within them:
   Back at the top of the iceberg, a leader establishes guidelines in the spirit of creating clarity and expecting personal ownership. As Hope Powell says: 'I'm not their mother!'

7. Have the tough conversations:
   When values are ignored and behaviours are getting out of hand, the organisation will be in danger of disruption. The guiding leader then needs to have the tough conversation that will clear the air and get the team back on track.

CHAPTER FOUR

BUILDING HIGH-PERFORMING TEAMS

THE BIG IDEA

In football – as in business, government and all places where significant tasks fall to teams of people – leadership is a complex challenge. Tactically, the modern game is in continuous change; physically, mentally and emotionally it is ever more demanding on teams and individual players.

In many businesses today, more and more is demanded from existing (or even declining) resources, and in times of great economic challenge, the need for transformation is overlaid on the daily round of business as usual.

The senior professionals do not do it alone. They build, develop, nurture and sustain a leadership team, and together that team leads an organisation to deliver against the demands of the business. Whether that team is in football or a global corporation, the core leadership challenges remain the same.

THE MANAGER

Sam Allardyce began his professional football career in the Bolton Wanderers defence in 1973; and it was back at that same club that he came of age as a manager. In the eight seasons from 1999–2007, Bolton were transformed under his leadership from a small but proud club to genuine European competitors. Fielding such luminaries as the World Cup-winning Youri Djorkaeff, former Real Madrid Captain Iván Campo and the excellent Jay-Jay Okocha, Allardyce's side regularly defeated their more illustrious English neighbours, finishing sixth in the Premier League in 2004–05 – level on points with Rafa Benitez's European Champions up the road in Liverpool. After Bolton, Allardyce managed at Newcastle briefly and then at Blackburn Rovers for three seasons, before joining West Ham in 2011. In his first season at Upton Park, he guided the Hammers back to the Barclays Premier League via a play-off final victory at Wembley against Blackpool.

His Philosophy

The man they call Big Sam is truly a big man in every sense of the word. Big frame, big heart, big vision, big ideas. Surprisingly self-effacing, he is nonetheless rock sure in his opinions. He knows where he wants to take a club, and will pursue his vision with passion and determination just as long as his employers will back him. Perhaps his most telling attribute, though, is the manner with which he welcomes change. From new technology to new psychologies, Allardyce wants to be at the cutting edge. And far from feeling concerned about how leadership teams seem to have grown, he brings expert colleagues on board with eagerness and expectation.

The Battle

For the manager, the day-to-day can feel like a battle royal. Forces are amassed against you. Opposition tactics, media challenges, public expectation, disciplinary issues, a hectic schedule, uncertainty, anxiety, injuries and exhaustion. It raises the question: why would you try to deal with all this on your own?

Allardyce sees his work very much as a battle, and his core response has been to establish a close-knit leadership team around him that he can rely on without hesitation. At Bolton, their headquarters was known as the 'war room'. 'We had our dreams and our war room; and we established a siege mentality, with an aim to break out of the Championship while everyone was trying to stop us. We turned the challenge to our own advantage, and the confidence of the club grew.' As we shall see, Allardyce's approach to creating a high-performing playing team is to create a high-performing leadership team.

Like Allardyce, Tony Pulis looks to close colleagues to support him in bearing the burden of enormous expectation – especially in the heat of the battle. He says of his time at Stoke: 'I was very fortunate to have had my coaching staff with me for quite a few years. I trust my staff and if I were to miss anything I would hope that the staff would see it and pick up on it. That 90 minutes is a very emotional time, and when I watch myself on TV on the touchline sometimes I can't believe what I am doing! I just get so wrapped up in the game. I want to win so badly for everybody, and the weight of expectation for the city of Stoke was enormous. Sometimes I feel as if it comes down to just me to get the result that everybody wants. I have to be able to control the emotion, work with it, manage it and stay focused. My staff help me a great deal.'

Football managers speak of three core areas of challenge where teamwork can have real impact: complexity (problem-solving leadership), technology change (expert leadership) and people (values-based leadership).

Complexity

There is a great deal of complexity in the modern game. Governance, stakeholder interest, societal pressures – all are significantly more demanding and harder to unravel than in any previous era. And right at the heart of the manager's trade, the game is evolving too. Changes to rules, attitudes and information mean that football – much like the world around it – is constantly shifting. Howard Wilkinson is excited by the changes: 'Since 1992–93, when the Premier League began, there have been many gradual changes in football. There have been changes to the rules, starting with the back-pass rule, then the tackle from behind, then the offside rule. At the same time, standards of fitness and preparation have gone up; in tandem with that the quality of players has gone up. Even the pitch has got bigger. The whole game is tactically more complex. Teams can outperform the competition for a short time, like Chelsea's finish to the 2012 Champions League – determination, a solid organisation and a smattering of luck. But you couldn't play like that for a season.' World-class teamwork is essential for real success in such a changing and complex environment.

Allardyce's own experience at Newcastle United is a salient example of complexity. Fresh from his long-term success at Bolton, he signed a three-year contract for the historic and passionate Tyneside club in May 2007, but a series of poor results led to his resignation just eight months later. Reflecting on the experience, he says: 'Newcastle United was the right club at the wrong time for me. I wanted to build something like I'd built at Bolton – to take the same long-term view. But I knew that 95 per cent of my energy would be spent convincing the Newcastle supporters that this team was going to improve. They'd finished 14th the previous year – when I left Bolton, we were fifth. That's why I got the job – because they had Michael Owen and other quality players and should have finished higher.

'In the initial stages I did win over the fans, but then it went downhill. Newcastle had always blessed their manager with a decent transfer budget, but had never really achieved expectations. Then they have 52,000 highly motivated, but also highly critical fans every week. So it was going to be a big challenge, and I knew I needed to restructure everything on the football side. Most of the staff from Bolton wanted to follow me, and we knew we could attract the balance with good recruitment policies. Then we needed to improve what was already a relatively good side, adding players and creating a high-performing team. But as we were getting started, suddenly the club was sold and then the transfer budget of £30 million came down to £14 million due to the club's debts at the time of sale. European football had recovered, transfer fees had gone way up and you have to pay foreign players a lot to attract them to the location – Newcastle isn't as attractive as Manchester and Manchester isn't as attractive as London. That became a very difficult thing to deal with and in the end, Mike Ashley took the line of, "I never picked him anyway – he wasn't my manager." So in the January, that was it.'

Historic context, soaring expectation, change of ownership, short-termism, macro-economic changes, personal relationships: in the end, the problems were too big and came too fast for Allardyce to solve.

Technology change

With the increased demands of the game has come a balancing increase in the availability of information and technology. These channels can greatly benefit managers, but they also need managing. Allardyce remembers keenly the shift as it happened at Bolton: 'When I arrived in 1999, there were two computers – one for the physio and one for the academy secretary. By year four we had so much technology – data and the means to crunch it – we knew there was no turning back.' Wilkinson is another manager who has watched the growth of technology in football with interest. 'The information available to managers has grown over the years, and it's good that it's grown. People ask how we make good decisions, right decisions. The first thing we need is fact. We need as much objective information as we can get. It doesn't make decision-making any easier; but it does help us come to a higher-quality decision.' Harnessing the raft of new technologies available is a complicated and demanding business. Progressive leaders are surrounding themselves with experts who can do this and interpret the data for them.

People

While all of this has led to significant shifts in the task of a manager, Wilkinson makes the case that the underlying people-focus of the profession has not changed. 'The job's changed, but I don't think the best managers have changed fundamentally. I think they still have knowledge and a thirst for knowledge, they are prepared to move and change with the times, but not fundamentally to change what they believe is important and not to change what they expect from players. No matter what culture or background you come from, the best managers are still interested in your being a better person when you have passed through their door and leave. They see that as part of being a better player.'

No business leader would dream of dealing with all his organisation's people issues alone. Among his close advisers will be at least one HR professional, and beyond that he will typically discuss critical people issues with other close colleagues. Chris Hughton finds his staff colleagues hugely valuable here: 'As a manager of course you always want to be liked. But I know I am going to upset players from time to time. The advice of my staff is very important here, and they often help me think things through.'

A story from the USA convinced Allardyce of the value of people focus: 'Mike Ford [Performance Analysis Manager] came back with a great story of an American football team that won the Superbowl. When he asked for the key success factors, they were clear that a major contributor was a woman who we'll call Alice Smith. Everybody spoke about what they did in their department to win the Superbowl, but they all acknowledged Alice Smith had a big part to play. So he's going around from the CEO to the head coach and he keeps hearing the name Alice Smith, and he didn't know who this Alice Smith was. It turns out she was the ticket office manager and travel organiser! She was so good that the players didn't have to worry about a thing. Every ticket, every family, everything was sorted. All the players had to do was run out, wave and play. In football, things move on – but leadership is still all about people.'

Building the High-performing Leadership Team

Leadership is a lonely task unless you are surrounded by people whose character, opinion and expertise you can trust. So convinced is Allardyce of the need for support from his staff that he considers it the heart of his work as a leader: 'Daily leadership looks like leading the team behind the team, and making sure that the team behind the team is delivering on a daily basis. It's about preparing them for the battle ahead. We call it "managing the madness". The best way to manage the madness is your staff, the team that works with you and their heads of department. The staff that we recruit in each department is the critical side of delivering to the players. We have to earn their respect.'

But if your staff team is this important, who should be a part of it? Carlo Ancelotti took his assistant Paul Clement with him from Chelsea to PSG and then to Real Madrid 'because of his player knowledge and his knowledge about football, about training. He has a lot of experience, knowledge, charisma, and personality. He would probably be a very good manager, 100 per cent.' Great leaders are not worried about having people around them who might outshine them; in fact the contrary is true. One of the acts that distinguishes a strong leader is deliberately seeking close colleagues who will stretch him, and who have strengths that complement his own. Allardyce would agree: 'I recruit excellent people I can delegate to. I trust them to do the job better than me. I add to that the experience of many years in football, and I always listen very carefully to them about the job that they do and how they do it. Again from sheer experience, I have gathered a little bit of knowledge about how everyone's job works so I can speak to them on their level: knowing what the words mean and how they think.'

The principle applies also on the field of play. Kevin Keegan looks for 'the area of expertise where I'm not strong. I'll take a defensive coach with me nine times out of ten, because I was a forward and I can see how to score goals, I can see how to make goals, but I was never a defender so I don't think from a defender's point of view.'

The team also need to be people you can intrinsically trust. Keegan points out that players now easily make friends among the staff: 'They have a favourite physio; the doctor has different relationships. It can be more difficult where it should be easier, because you should be able to delegate. At Newcastle I had probably about six or seven too many staff for the way I wanted to run a football club.'

Support and challenge

Martin O'Neill has built up a core of talented staff he trusts. When he arrives at a new club, the trick is to fuse them together with the existing team, and to craft a new leadership team dedicated to the task ahead. 'I started out in management at Grantham – it was really what I wanted to do, and I needed to find out whether I could manage at all. I got in touch initially with John Robertson, who had been my playing partner at Nottingham Forest. My idea was that John might be able to play a bit for me even though he had left the game at that time. He did play a number of games for me, but by now was much more interested in joining me in management. We forged a relationship then.

'When I moved to Wycombe Wanderers, I reconnected with Steve Walford who had played with me at Norwich City. He dropped down to play at Vauxhall Conference level for me at Wycombe, and he and I built a trusting relationship there. Steve's fascinating – a quiet man, but a totally different person when he's on the coaching field! He is a very, very good coach. We were all at Leicester City, Celtic and Aston Villa together, and Steve was with me at Sunderland. Steve is remarkable: he is as good as any of the coaches out there, but never promotes himself. We also had an excellent goalkeeping coach in Seamus McDonagh who was with me at Leicester City and at Aston Villa, and a terrific fitness coach called Jim Henry that I met at Celtic. This is the small team I brought with me.

'Joining a club in a mini-crisis, it was important to me [at Sunderland] to have these particular people. Apart from that, I didn't make any other changes. At the same time I also embraced what was happening at the football club. I've never gone in with a scattergun approach of relieving people of their jobs – I go hoping that I will be able to work with these people in time. I think the staff are very, very important, and I always hope that eventually I can build the same levels of trust that I have built with the other people. There will be the occasional person at the football club who's been involved with the previous manager who might want to leave of his own accord or because he wants to go with the other manager who has gone to another club, and I understand that fully.'

Of course, great leaders want to know that they will get challenge as well as support from their leadership team. As O'Neill says: 'We have differences of opinion in the team, which is good. But when we get to the field, we are all of the same mind.'

The art of delegation

Like Allardyce, Glenn Hoddle also thinks of his leadership team as close allies to whom he can delegate: 'I can't have my eyes everywhere, so I want people around me I can delegate to. For example, I want them to tell me if they can see a problem coming up with a player. I remember once I was left out of a team. I was 20 years of age and I thought I should be in the team every week. I went off and did my sulky bit and the manager left me for about two weeks, when I think if he'd had left it a day and we'd had a chat I could have been straight back in to the team. So I learnt from that you have to communicate quickly – and a good team of staff help you to do that.'

If you buy into the value of delegation, then there is a very simple way to think about who you need. For any individual in any area of effort, there are two dimensions involved: skill and will. For example, I might be excellent at clearing up my kitchen, but having done it a thousand times, I am not excited to do it again. In this situation, I am 'high skill' but 'low will' so I might decide to pay someone to do it for me. Keen to earn the money, he is very happy to do it – but has no idea where anything goes. For the time being at least, he is low skill but high will. Both these things can be improved – skill through training and will through coaching – but in the final analysis, the leader wants people allocated to tasks where they are both high skill and high will. To these people, he can delegate with confidence. And delegation means you can almost forget about the task until it is done – or at least be checking in only occasionally, to encourage and be informed.

O'Neill admits that, like a surprising number of leaders, delegation isn't something he always finds easy: 'The people around me would probably tell you I am not the greatest delegator in the world. For me it's a matter of trust – and part of that trust is in their sheer ability to do the job. Delegation has always been difficult for me, but I've learnt over time to trust especially my close colleagues, Steve, John and the team, to do in my absence a job in a way that I would be happy with.'

A lot of a football leader's daily delegation is done in the specialist areas: logistics, medical, analysis. Hope Powell puts it neatly: 'I trust them to do a good job and if they say to me, "Hope, I think this," then I will listen. I'll make the final decision, but I trust their knowledge enough to take it very seriously. If a medic says that a player should only play for 60 minutes, well – I'm not a medic, so if he's telling me that's the case then I have to respect that.' Acknowledging your team's expertise that complements your own skill set is important for the smooth running of your leadership team and for your own successful decision-making.

Another component of the art of delegation is knowing what *not* to delegate. There is an economic principle that translates into leadership: that leaders should 'only do what only they can do'. In other words, focus on the things that no one else can do. This principle allows Allardyce to delegate effectively to his team of experts: 'I employ coaches to coach, not to carry balls and put out bibs and cones.' He defines his own role as leading his team of close colleagues, and making selective coaching interventions: 'I spend my time meeting with other members of staff and making decisions on a daily basis, then going out working with the coaches and still doing some coaching myself. I refuse to be a megalomaniac and do their jobs as well as mine – so I make a sacrifice and let go of what I like doing the most, i.e. working with the players. But I won't sacrifice that 100 per cent. I still think it's important to keep that personal link with the team.'

For O'Neill, results are what a manager lives or dies by, but just as significant is ongoing recruitment and watching potential new recruits for the squad: 'Getting young players through from the academy might take three, four or five years, and in the meantime you have to be on the search for improvement in the playing side. No matter how many times somebody would report that this player is really good and we should do something about it, I need to see a player at least once in a live game before I make a decision on him.' Alex McLeish also takes pride in his deep knowledge of players' skills – and not just his own players: 'I've always been a bit of an anorak in knowing my players, but since I've come to England [with the bigger league] I've learned to trust the advice of other coaches and scouts. However, I still find it important to take a good look myself at any player before he joins the team. If we're looking at a player individually and I've got a scout or assistant manager I trust and he comes back and says to me "sign him" – I've done that in the past and I've regretted it. Unless it's a household name like a Zidane, then you have to know what you are taking in.'

Expressing your personality

An important observation made by many managers is how their leadership team essentially bears their signature. A team is known by its leader – just watch how the press and cameras pick out the manager at every significant moment in the life of his team. The leadership team should be intimately involved in formulating the vision and goals of the team, but once the leader's philosophy is articulated, they need to faithfully convey it. Martin Jol is clear on this point: 'Half of my work is on the pitch, and the other half is with the staff. So it's important that the staff understand my philosophy. I want them to deliver their expertise, but that must be in line with my philosophy.' His former close colleague Chris Hughton echoes the principle: 'It's really important that we have a coaching staff that leads by example and creates an environment around my personality. My style is to offer people some flexibility. So if a lad runs out two minutes late with his boots undone and gives the excuse that he had to go to the toilet, then we look around the rest of the players and ask, "What do we do? Do we fine him or let him off?" We are being professional, but also creating warmth between the players and the staff.'

The special case of the captain

The captain is an appointment made by the manager and a position often held for a long period of time – typically more than a single season. Managers vary as to how they use their captain – the responsibilities they assign and the performance they expect. But invariably they select someone with leadership qualities, who can act as a decision-maker on the pitch and an authoritative influence in the dressing room. In this way, some managers see them as a full part of the leadership team. Roberto Mancini defines the captain as 'the player who has respect from all the other players; who creates a team spirit'. He also points out that he seeks six or seven players with a captain's mentality. Hoddle agrees almost word for word. Even when he was player-manager at Swindon and Chelsea, he appointed a team captain. 'What I want is five or six good leaders, one of whom has got the armband. The captain is important to the rest of the players because they go through the captain to the leadership team. When you are a manager and not a player-manager, that captain has to be an extension of your management. He goes on the pitch while we go to the sidelines. But you need a character, you need the players to respect him.'

For the leader of a complex team facing a daunting challenge, the high-performing leadership team needs to be made up of people you can trust and will probably be founded on a core of people you know well. They need to support you and challenge you, you must be comfortable delegating to them, as ultimately they will carry your signature.

Building the Environment

Once assembled, the leadership team needs to create a high-performing playing team. This is why Allardyce calls it 'the team behind the team'. The work is a combination of art and science – some things can be prescribed, others are intuitive. At its essence, it involves role modelling and coaching the mindsets and behaviours needed from the playing team. But even before the leadership team can fashion the playing team itself, they must first focus on building an environment for success.

When British swimmer Adrian Moorhouse arrived at Berkeley, California in the mid-1980s to begin training for the Olympic pool, the first thing he saw was a large sign, high up, that read: 'This is an environment where success is inevitable.' Allardyce believes creating this environment is very much the role of the leadership team: 'The team has to deliver the philosophy you have so as to create a successful environment that people enjoy working in and that people don't want to leave as quickly as they possibly can. I want an environment where they want to stay and improve themselves as much as possible.' Gérard Houllier agrees: 'In creating the environment in which you are going to work, the first thing to get right is the staff: make sure that the team behind the team is competent and that they have a very positive attitude because that attitude will influence the players and create the atmosphere. The leadership team needs to infuse confidence, trust and positivity into the club.'

If the leadership team is to take on the responsibility for inspiring the players, then they need to be inspired themselves. Allardyce does this through dreams: 'I believe in living your dreams. I won't call them goals – that undermines what a dream is. Not too many people in life can actually fulfil their dreams. We are very fortunate in professional football. If you get into the game as a youngster, you have already started to fulfil one of your wildest dreams. And although there is hard work – you are getting paid for it! When I moved from playing to managing, I felt like I was putting something back into the game that I loved. I wanted to dream dreams for others, and inspire them to pursue great things. I had to make sure it was reachable, this dream – and I wanted to share it with just a close family. This family for me was the group of staff I assembled at Bolton.'

The Bolton story

Allardyce's reign at Bolton was an extraordinary time for all involved – from chairman to fans. Inheriting a team in mid-table Championship anonymity he made an instant impact, leading them to the play-offs and two domestic semi-finals. In his second season they won the play-off final in handsome fashion (3–0 against Preston); and thus began a period of top-flight success not seen at the club since the heady days of Nat Lofthouse in the 1950s.

Inheriting a club with a proud history is rarely an easy task. Expectations are either ludicrously high ('here at last is the man we've been waiting for') or depressingly dismissive ('why should he succeed? – no one else has'). Allardyce felt a mixture of the two on arrival at the Reebok Stadium. But the story was to become a shining example of how high-performing leadership teams can deliver high performance at the front line. 'In 2000 we had a dream that was short term–long term. The short term was to get to the Barclays Premier League, but the long term was to become a successful Premier League football club, to develop a winning environment and then to take Bolton where it had never been before: the Champions League. We set up a war room, which was named by Fordy [Mike Ford], and the room was our room and only our room. Normally, it was for core members of staff only, sometimes it would be all of us right down to the kit man – one of the most important people at any football club.

'Three or four years later, the challenge became: "Now we have to win something, now we have to achieve something that's not been achieved before." We got to the Carling Cup final and lost it, then in year five we got into the Europa Cup, something that had never been achieved in the club's history. Then I realised it had all changed – that, in fact, we didn't need a siege mentality.

What we needed as a staff was to understand our own potential, and what it would take to live up to it. Our players were extremely high quality – international stars mixed in with home-grown talent – and if we were going to get the best out of them we would have to live up to their standards.

'So we set ourselves a goal to get above even their standards and ask them to live up to ours. I was doing a lot of thinking about current reality and what could be. Our squad between them had won in the region of 30 championship medals throughout the world of football. The clubs that many of them had played for had demanded performance from them just by their nature. But Bolton couldn't do that. Bolton is a 28,000-seater stadium. It's got its tradition, but it's not Manchester United, it's not Arsenal, it's not AC Milan or Real Madrid or Bayern Munich, so it doesn't demand an awful lot out of you. So we realised we were going to have to demand it ourselves, drive ourselves on – because that's the only way we were going to be really successful. And that's where we earned respect from them, coming from AC Milan or Real Madrid to little old Bolton.'

Allardyce and his team created magic at Bolton, finishing level on points with Liverpool in 2004–05 and securing a UEFA Cup place – just five years after a standing start in the Championship. 'That was a lot faster than we first imagined, and I think that there were probably four key people responsible as well as me: Phil Brown my assistant, Mark Taylor head of sports science and physiotherapy, Mike Ford performance analysis manager and Jack Chapman in recruitment. He was an old-school scout – fantastic eyes to spot a player, then later on we added all our technical scouting approach. That group all went out to add to our team, and went through a serious recruitment and interview process to put it together.'

Complexity

How do you know when a leadership team is truly adding value? In football, it appears to revolve around the three overlapping challenges already framed of complexity, technology change and people.

In the daily running of the club, the leadership team brings a welcome routine, cutting through the complexity. At the start of each day at Sunderland, O'Neill would meet with his team of four or five colleagues, assessing medical reports and getting player updates: 'In the run-up to a match, we would maybe take a look at some video and we might agree we want to introduce some new things into training.' Then the players would begin their warm-up in the gym: 'This is something that has come into the game in the last couple of years. Working in the gym suggests that the players are lifting weights but it in fact refers to the agility work they do in preparation for the work about to take place on the practice field. I would know that the warm-up would be done very, very well by the fitness coach and I wouldn't have to concern myself too much about that. Then we would get out on to the field together and begin the training session, and we would all know what we needed to be doing.'

Howard Wilkinson points out that how much a manager makes use of a leadership team to help resolve complexity remains very much a personal choice. 'A lot of teams will have someone in the stand to give an overview, and some managers want to know the stats even before half-time. So there is a range of people now feeding in to decision-making processes. Some managers will even take a member of staff in to the half-time team talk from time to time to make a point. It's not that common, but for sure the manager's role is more flexible now, and if you are going to have a staff team then you have to use them well. Generally, though, the manager remains the voice that delivers the message.'

Expertise, of course, can create simplicity for the leader, cutting through the complexity. At Fulham, Martin Jol was very happy to rely on an excellent medical team: 'Within my staff we must have had the best medical team in England. These guys had worked for Sam Allardyce at Blackburn, where they created excellent procedures. Then they worked with me at Fulham. Post-match and pre-match we had all these procedures and Mark Taylor – not a doctor but a former physiotherapist – was the head of my medical team. He was a big part of what we did, and I talked to him every day.'

People

One of the key areas of complexity for the leadership team is recruitment – in football as in business, the organisation stands or falls on the quality of its people. The war for talent needs fighting well – and it's another battle that no leader of a complex organisation can win on his own. Twenty years ago the war was fought more simply, but no less ferociously. Kevin Keegan recalls the scouting organisation at Liverpool: 'They'd have a couple of guys who Shanks really trusted who he thought had a good eye for a player and they would be despatched off to watch Bury play – or Scunthorpe, or Doncaster or whoever with a view of watching a player like myself. That's all you had – it wasn't rocket science in those days, it was very simple.'

Thirty years later, it was beginning to move faster at Allardyce's Bolton: 'We started by watching games in the traditional way, and then would file an individual report on anyone that stood out. Then as more technology came in, we could make great use of this data. We added to our own scout reports some information from a scouting organisation that we bought in. In that way we could scout for the ones we could afford, and keep an eye on that top player because one day we might be able to afford him. The secret was to persuade the club leadership to recruit bright young people coming out of university who knew their IT. They liked doing all this stuff that footballers and ex-footballers don't like – research and data entry on a laptop. We went as far as hiring interns so the critical staff didn't waste time doing it. Through the interns they could play the numbers game, i.e. if you look at enough information you eventually find something that's worth going for.'

Allardyce's first golden nugget was none other than French World Cup and Euro winner, Youri Djorkaeff. 'We were desperately short of a quality front man in year one of the Premier League. We were beginning to evolve our recruitment practice, when Youri came up. It's an interesting story because people said we would never get him. He was in Germany, not really playing. We knew that people in Europe wouldn't know much about Bolton Wanderers, so we had put together a club profile – and we had agreed that if a European player was worth going after, we would travel to and meet him on his turf. Football in general says don't meet them on their turf, bring them to yours – if they really want to play for you, they'll make the effort. I thought, "No this is Youri, he's won the World Cup, European Championships, played for AC Milan …"

'The word was that his national coach had called him in the January and with the World Cup coming up in the summer had said, "Look, Youri, you're not playing so you aren't going to be in the squad." So we went out and said, "Youri – this is Bolton. We're in a dogfight because we are bottom of the league, but we're a great club. Then we put the video on: Reebok Stadium, Manchester Airport, 40-minute flight to London, Premier League football, play every week with us, if you do the business you get in the World Cup squad. You can help us; we can help you. That was it. He said, "Right, that'll do me." Then the hard bit came because of money: we knew Youri would have a lawyer, an image rights lawyer, his agent – but in the end we had the upper hand because he needed to play football to get to the World Cup and he'd been dropped at Kaiserslautern, he was training on his own. It was a good discussion. It worked out pretty expensive compared to what we were paying for the rest of the players, but that was the start of the golden recruitment time. Other players and other clubs started to realise that we were recruiting some of the world's best.'

In 1983, the young Allardyce was playing for the Tampa Bay Rowdies in Florida when he met up with some of the American football players from the Buccaneers across town. Even back then, Allardyce was stunned by what he saw: 'There was one coach for the quarterback, probably four physiotherapists, qualified, at least ten masseurs, a dietician and a nutritionist. The food was laid on in the restaurant in the morning, at lunchtime and before they left along with the fluids and the supplements. And then there were the stats lads; the lads who used to make the play-book with the head coach ...' Allardyce saw how the experts in a high-performing leadership team have great impact on people matters: 'The sports psychologist and the psychiatrist used to do sessions with the players on a weekly basis. The sports psychologist would do the group sessions, whereas the psychiatrist would literally sit with the players on the sofa one-to-one. There was this monstrous organisation ...'

Glenn Hoddle is a great believer in scientific expertise: 'I always used psychologists with the team. As a player I saw how it broke down barriers and made us purer to go on to the football pitch and perform as a unified team. When everything's going well and you are playing well, life is easy. The real test of the leader of people comes when things are not going well. That's when people turn on each other and they say things that have built up between themselves. It's almost like an invisible wall starts to build. Using experts helps prevent the sort of problems we heard about in the Dutch squad in Euro 2012.'

Soon after his arrival at Newcastle, Keegan and his team had immediate people impact with a simple example of creating an environment for success. 'We won our game on the Saturday and I gave everyone the Monday off. I asked for the training ground to be fumigated and painted. We spent about £5,000 on it at that time, which wasn't a fortune but was still quite a lot of money, and when the players came in on Tuesday the reaction was unbelievable. The place was spotless – everything was clean, everything was repainted, the physio's room was immaculate, the baths had been cleaned, it had been re-tiled, and it looked like a different place. I spoke to the players before training and said, "I want to change a lot of things here, but you've got to help me."' A leader getting his team's working environment right can provide an excellent platform on which to build success.

Technology change

In the modern game it is widely accepted that good use of technology can give a team a competitive edge. In Shankly's Liverpool era, tactical data was pretty limited. As Keegan recalls: 'They had a system that consisted of maybe two people who would watch the opposition. That was the job of a guy called Reuben Bennett when we first went there – and he was also in the boot room. People don't mention him very much, but he was a great guy and very important. We used to do tactics on a Subbuteo board! It's a bit more high tech now ...'

Much of the mindset and technological capacity that Allardyce saw in Tampa has now landed in Premier League football. While it has the power to reduce complexity, it does need to be in the hands of experts the leader can trust. As in the matter of recruitment, Allardyce eagerly embraces all the technology he can find: 'I like the language of sports science and of sports medicine. There is an accuracy that shifts people's thinking. Instead of "he's broken a bone in his foot," they explain about the metatarsal – what it is, what it does, how it works. It puts it all on to a new level.' The point is significant in any leadership setting. Imparting a new language and using it to share accurate information is an act of empowerment.

O'Neill is delighted by the advent of video technology, but points to his and the staff team's role of filtering the information so the players aren't overwhelmed. 'In Clough's time [at Nottingham Forest] the tape machine was in its infancy, but I don't think we ever had a session with him where we actually watched a game on television, stop-starting the opposition. I do believe that in the modern game it's a good thing for players to see how they've performed, both individually and collectively, as soon as possible after the match. A day or two after a game we use video to bring some condensed, thought-through points at a time where the players' concentration is at its height.

'Before a game there's only so much a player can take in and, no matter how intelligent he is, if you give him four or five new instructions just before he goes out, he's unlikely to take them all in. Even after a game, going into something for more than an hour is counter-productive. Our job is to make good use of the brief time of heightened concentration. These moments are vitally important.'

Gérard Houllier is also enthusiastic about technology – and sounds another interesting warning note about how best to use it: 'It is nearly 15 years since we started to have match analysis in Clairefontaine [the French national training academy]. Systems like Prozone helped me a lot when I was in previous clubs because

I could assess the effort and the technical achievements of the players in the game. But I never use technology for negative reasons. I've never shown a player "You've done wrong, this is where you went wrong" – I never show that. I prefer to enhance the positive aspect of his game. I would say, "You've done that before and there is no reason why you can't repeat that." The image is very important – the image gets into the mind of a player. So if you want to show something, make it something positive.'

From recruitment and routine through technology to personal issues, a high-performing leadership team creates the environment for a high-performing playing team to emerge.

Creating a High-performing Playing Team

Establishing the ideal environment is essential – but in itself is not sufficient. A high-performing leadership team goes on to model and coach the behaviours needed from the playing side to achieve their shared vision.

The war room and the boot room

People are much more likely to imitate what they observe than to do what someone tells them. If a leadership team wants to inspire high performance among their people, then they must themselves display the behaviours and set the standards they seek. In Allardyce's war room, he and Mike Ford fashioned a leadership team that modelled what they needed to see from the playing team. Allardyce was especially struck by Ford's thinking on sports psychology, disputing the then commonly held belief that those who sought it were weak. His commission to Ford was focused primarily on building the leadership team: 'I told him, "We don't need you mainly to work with the players – we want you to work with the staff, and we want to build these goals and dreams that we want to aspire to achieve." We planned it out while we were growing the staff in each department, so everybody understood where they wanted to go in five years' time, what they wanted to be – collectively and individually.' As well as planning, the leadership team modelled renewal and learning. 'An important piece was looking after their own development. Too often in football the people that work for the players are not in a position to go out and improve the job that they do. I made sure the team were given enough time to go and learn about leadership and other subjects – and they come back refreshed and much revived, instead of the 24/7 that they so easily get sucked into. There is a lack of development in football while you are working at team level: the 24/7 is looking after everyone else, but not looking after yourself.'

In many ways, Allardyce's war room is a successor to the famous Liverpool boot room, where successive managers at Anfield somehow combined warmth with mystique, modelling excellence and creating an environment for high performance that spanned a quarter of a century. Keegan recalls that the boot room 'was nothing to do with the players! It was Shankly, Paisley, and their team. Someone told me – and I believe it to be true – that they had a book in there where they wrote down the training they did every day, every week, before every game and the results of every game. And if they ever lost two games on the trot they went back to look for patterns. I've never seen that book though I'm 100 per cent sure it existed. It was kept as a close-guarded secret.'

The mystique was there all right, but the legendary boot room leadership style was about role modelling and human engagement. Shankly, Paisley, Fagan and many great managers at many great clubs since have led teams around a set of core principles. There is no definitive list, but there are seven that are commonly talked about:

1. ## Collective belief

    When Keegan arrived at Newcastle United in 1992, the famous
    Magpies were in the lower reaches of the second tier of English
    football – a worrying place for a club of its history and stature.
    He describes a dangerous downward spiral that had taken place:
    'We had players that didn't even come through the front door
    – they were parking their cars at the back and coming in that
    way. I had to change pretty much everything really. What
    happens at a football club when things go wrong is people start
    to punish each other. It's like "we aren't staying in hotels any
    more, they don't deserve that, we'll travel down the day of the
    game, three and a half hours … We're not washing the kit any
    more, they can take it home and wash it …" This is where
    Newcastle had got to: some of the players were in black and
    white stripes and some were in grey and white stripes. The club
    was pretty much saying, why should we do anything for them
    when they're not performing?' The collective belief had disap-
    peared and the overriding mindset was one of negativity.

    André Villas-Boas strives for collective belief by emphasising
    the equal value of every individual to the team: 'My European
    background has taught me that players should be treated
    equally, because the club is always more important than any
    single individual player or employee. In the European model,
    the executive board actually comes to training sessions with the
    manager, and represents the club with him. I've always based
    my leadership on collective values rather than individual values.
    At Chelsea and at Tottenham I had to explain that when I
    encourage the group it's not because I don't want to praise an
    individual – it's because you want the players to understand that
    the group is more important than anything. Within that, I want
    them to understand they are all important. The person who

scores the goal and wins the game is only as important as the
third goalkeeper who never gets to play – and this value runs
very deep for me because it was the way I was educated. Give
everything that you have to give for your club, and the club will
give everything back to you.'

2. Selflessness

In a high-performing team, the players play for one another.
Keegan puts it like this: 'There has to be selflessness. All the
top players in teams will tell you that you can't win European
Footballer of the Year on your own. You need five, six or
maybe seven good players around you. It's not an act – you
genuinely say thank you for making me be able to score goals.
They are working to make each other successful.'

This applies also to going the extra mile for one another,
which for Sir Alex Ferguson is at the very heart of a high-
performing team: 'The essence of a good team is recognising
the qualities of each other, and the weaknesses of each other
too. And on a given day I always think if eight players are
playing well, then you've got a great chance of winning the
match – and sometimes maybe you've got to carry one or
two players. To ask or expect a footballer in today's world to
play 50 games a season at 100 per cent performance is impossible – there will always be off days and bad days. Pulling
together when that happens is the essence of teamwork.'

Teamwork is another of Gérard Houllier's four foundational values. He uses it to guide his players' approach towards
one another and the club: 'I need to think team first! It's a
collective sport – the team is more important than me. Not
just the club, but the team. So that means, "What can I do for
the team? How can I do better for the team?"' It is also

Allardyce's number one value. He very frankly sees teamwork in his playing team as the most crucial contributor to his own success: 'If you are going to have a long career in this game it's all about results. It's not about how much money you make or save. If the results don't back you up they won't stand up for you – if the crowd get on your back, you'll be gone. So it all depends on the players and how they play as a team. So the biggest value that I communicate to the players is how we should come together to be a team to enjoy what we are doing and deal with the pressure and be all in it together. That way we can achieve what we all want to achieve.'

3. Excellence

When Keegan arrived at Hamburg as a player, he had a tough beginning. But he was struck by the club's commitment to excellence: 'I was 27 years of age and I just relished the challenge. It was massive. Everybody says but you were so successful, and I say the first six months were horrendous. The players didn't really want to know me. I couldn't understand why because I couldn't speak the language, so I couldn't ask them. The coach was brought in because he could speak English – they didn't like him and they blamed me for that. I got sent off and suspended for about six matches for punching a guy in a mid-season friendly, and I had to go back and apologise to the guy. Plus I was on a big wage there compared to other players, and the president put it in the papers – here is the guy who will save Hamburg! It was too much about me, and the players just downed tools and said right go on then.

'It wasn't easy. But I knew I could play, and I knew I would get through once I was given a fair chance. But when you win a battle like that, it's like a juggernaut – once you turn it around, wow! I learnt the language so I could communicate and have a laugh with them – I could swear at them if I wanted to! Then I saw it was much more professional even than we were at Liverpool, believe it or not … The players would do *anything*. Some of our training was ridiculously hard and I think at Liverpool Tommy Smith would have gone in and said, "Hey you're killing us!" There they just did it. The German players were very disciplined. The players would run through a brick wall for the coach, almost to the point where it took away some of the individual. If the coach says it, it is right. So I got very fit, and we won the championship!'

4. Motivation

Excellence becomes in itself a motivation for leaders and their teams. Gérard Houllier is driven by a quest for excellence: 'If that winning mentality is in you, then once you have won something it becomes like a drug – you want to win again, and again, and again. I remember when I was managing at Lyon and we knew halfway through the season that we had won the title. No team had ever won La Ligue in France with more than 80 points. We managed to do it in two consecutive seasons.'

For Houllier at Lyon, the classic upward spiral of high-performing teams kicked in. 'When you win, of course you create an atmosphere: people work hard, they enjoy their work, they work for each other. This is the most thrilling experience. It's more than just working together – it's truly working for each other.' Motivation and selflessness would appear to be closely connected.

5. Personal commitment

In a high-performing team, individual commitment to the team is strong. Keegan sees it as one of the great indicators.

'What's the commitment? Are they here for the benefit of the team or are they here for the journey? Are they here for the money or do they really want to win something?' More than this – in a high-performing team, they show it. 'You sometimes think: "This kid's not committed," and then you find three months later actually he is very, very committed; he just hasn't shown it. [In great teams] players show a bit more – actually state their case why they should be in the team, why they shouldn't be sat on the bench.'

Allardyce is single-minded on this issue: 'The leadership team would sit down and ask, "What does our group look like – staff and players? In the playing team we would have a good number of what we call Players. These are people the leadership can look to, people who will lead others. Then there are the Followers – people happy to commit to the team and go with the Players. But then there would be a couple of Saboteurs. These are the ones we had to be careful about – or else they begin to recruit some of the Followers and cause problems. Generally I am a bit more direct and abrupt with these people. If I find I have one or two recruiting other people, I know I have to get into them to turn them back. Generally the Saboteur is a good player who just has a bit of a problem. Maybe I've left him out for a while, or for some reason had a contract fall-out. If you can't resolve that, you have to get the board to get rid of him as quickly as you can. If you can bring him back, then you are doing OK.' Keeping everyone committed will prevent these disruptive behaviours.

6. Clarity

Great teams have clarity of role and process. Keegan again: 'Everybody needs to know what's expected of them, where the parameters are, what they're expected to do. At Liverpool it was so easy because you knew what you could get away with and you knew what you couldn't get away with, so you knew exactly what your job was and what your fitness levels should be.'

They also have clarity around responsibility. Martin Jol encountered an interesting challenge during his time in England: 'Just recently I told a right-footed player [player R] to play on the left, and a left-footed player [player L] to start in the centre of midfield. I did that with a purpose because player L can be very good on the inside with his left and player R is right-footed so he can change play to the right. And then they changed it from the start! Player R played on the right and player L on the left. So after two minutes I thought what are they doing? If you leave it, if you let it go, you've got a problem – they will do it for the rest of the season. So at half-time I said, "Never do that again, OK? If I tell you to play on the left, play on the left. Don't change it!" And he said, "Yes, but player R prefers to play on the right!" I said, "Everything I do, I do with a purpose. So if I studied the opposition, if I tell you to play on the left, then you play on the left, OK? And maybe at half-time or after a game we can talk about it, and maybe in the next game I could do something else or change it – but never do it on your own, don't take these sort of decisions." I don't want them to take those sorts of decisions. Players are very black and white. If you leave it and if you won't explain why you are doing things, they will think, "OK, this is a manager where I can express myself," and that is not want you want.' The strong leader needs clarity in his message – both in delivering it and in enforcing it.

7. **Positive response to pressure**

Great teams respond to pressure as one. Glenn Hoddle recalls the 1981 FA Cup final where Spurs took Manchester City to a replay. 'We had to learn from that first match – we knew we had to change. We had a real open discussion from that; we all spoke individually. It was this dream and it was too big. All of us had gone through it and we wanted it so badly. We got there as a team, we played well as a team, but at the big occasion we started to fragment. We all wanted to be the man of the match, and in a team sport that won't work.' Spurs took the pressure on board as a team and won the replay 3–2.

So there they are – seven mindsets and behaviours needed in a high-performing team, football style. All seven need to be both coached and role modelled by the leadership team, though, if they are to take hold and truly create a high-performing team at the front line.

The High-performing Leader

The leader of a high-performing team in a complex and changing environment needs to inspire both directly and from one step removed. He can curse complexity, technological innovation and societal change, or he can choose to embrace them. He can be fazed by the scale of his team of staff, or he can create it himself, building trust and leading it to high performance in its own right. In doing so, he can infuse it with his own personality and leverage it to tackle successfully all the challenges that present themselves.

High-performing leaders create high-performing teams – in football just as in other arenas. While individual priorities vary, most leaders will agree on the four major tasks to focus on:

1. Understand the nature of the battle and the need for close allies:
    Some will use the war analogy more readily than others, but high-performing leaders recognise the gravity of their task, and happily admit their need for support. In that vulnerability lies a strength that will bring them success.

2. Create a high-performing leadership team:
    This is a group of close allies – normally not more than eight to ten – in whom the leader has trust. He trusts them to both support him and challenge him, and he knows he can delegate to them in their areas of expertise. They will bear his signature, so he needs to express his character through them. And he may wish to have as part of the leadership team his playing captain, who takes his leadership philosophy right to the front line.

3. Build the environment for success:
    The leadership team adds real value when it fashions an environment where success is inevitable. It does this by dealing with the pressing issues of the industry in which it is working. In football these include complexity, technology and people; in business these three might translate to strategy, operations, IT and HR.

4. Create the high-performing playing team itself:
    Finally, a leader's focus should be on the people at the front line. The leadership team – from their war room, boot room or executive team room – need to model and coach the key behaviours and mindsets they expect to see from those people. In football, these distil down to seven critical principles: collective belief, selflessness, excellence, motivation, personal commitment, clarity and positive response to pressure.

As with many leadership arenas, football leadership has become a whole lot more complex. But the leader who can use his team of staff to bring simplicity out of the complexity will win the day.

PART THREE

Delivering Results

CHAPTER FIVE

THE FIELD OF PLAY

THE BIG IDEA

Leaders establish a way of being in their organisations, through what they think, believe, say and do. They impart some sort of fingerprint – some DNA – that is intimately associated with their character, which drives the behaviours and performance of their people and leaves a clearly defined legacy. Think of almost any society from any era. England of the 16th century, for example, is associated with seaborne trade, commercial flourishing and religious reform. All these were driven by the character of the leader, Queen Elizabeth, and the era is naturally called Elizabethan. But she clearly did not do it all herself.

Leaders at all levels are judged by the performance of their people. From captains of infantry companies to heads of schools, leaders need their people to perform at the front line if they and their organisation are to achieve their goals. In professional football, nothing is more public or more defining than the team's results. From technical areas and half-time talks to technical reviews and training sessions, every intervention counts. So how do football's leaders ensure they inspire their teams to deliver world-class performance on the field of play?

THE MANAGER

Roberto Mancini established himself as a 17-year-old attacking footballer at Sampdoria where he won multiple domestic trophies and the club's first-ever European competition. Fifteen years later he left for Lazio where, under Sven Göran Eriksson, he again won multiple trophies, both domestic and European. As soon as his scoring touch began to desert him, he announced his retirement and moved seamlessly into coaching as Eriksson's assistant.

Mancini was an almost instant success as a top-tier manager, winning trophies at both Fiorentina and his former club Lazio, and working with a huge array of world-class talent. At Internazionale, he led the club out of the shadow of their Milanese neighbours, rebuilding the Nerazzurri's reputation over five years and taking them to an unprecedented three consecutive Italian league victories.

In late 2009 he accepted the enormous challenge of revitalising Manchester City under its new ownership. His first full season in charge brought FA Cup victory and Champions League qualification. The following season, he won the Barclays Premier League after the most dramatic of season climaxes to end the club's 44-year title wait. September 2013 saw Mancini move to Turkey's biggest club, as he became manager of Galatasaray.

His Philosophy

Roberto Mancini is a charming man with a core of steel. His philosophy is very straightforward: assemble great players and work extremely hard. By 'great players' he means players with both the skill and the mindset needed for the task. 'I have good players because you can't win if you don't have top players. But if you tell me they all look like top players, then I tell you with some we need to work on mentality. You can look like a good player, but not have the mentality to win at the top level.' And by extremely hard, he means a relentless pursuit of excellence. As his assistant and former Sampdoria teammate David Platt comments, 'Even winning the league did not alter that. After a break, it was straight back to work.'

The Dimensions of the Task: Skills and Mindsets

Roberto Mancini was installed as Manchester City manager in time for the 2009 Boxing Day fixture against Tony Pulis's Stoke. Presenting an immaculate and calm image, he oversaw a 2-0 victory – and so began his journey to club success. It was not a simple journey though. To begin with, Mancini has some unshakeable views of how a team should work: 'When I started to do this job I wanted players with good mentality ready to understand my view, my mentality.' David Platt observes a single-mindedness that alienates the less committed: 'He has a very strong work ethic. There is an Italian way of doing things which is professional, strong and committed, and he brought that with him. When he arrived at Manchester City he didn't say, "Well, I'll hang around and look and see what's happening and maybe change the odd thing." He said, "I am going to come in and do it my way and that's the way we are going to do it and it's as simple as that – because in the end, I am responsible for team performance."'

Mancini may have felt he knew little of English football, but he wasted no time in getting to grips with the challenge. 'It was difficult because I didn't know this championship, I didn't know the English players, I knew only David. In Italy it is different. I had to adapt a bit to the culture. Sometimes this is not easy and the first six months were difficult because I changed the training sessions, the method of training; and for the players it was also difficult for the first few months. However, in the first six months we improved a lot as a team, and we fought until the last game against Tottenham for the Champions League place.'

Mancini had made a fair start, with City finishing fifth. But for his first full season in charge he started shaping the team in his image: 'In the summer when I changed players, and bought players that were for me good players, that month we start to work on their mentality and their attitude.' There's that word again – mentality – the mindset of commitment and hard work. Mancini attributes it in large part to his small-club origins: 'I had always this mentality even when I was a player and I wanted to play always to win. And from my colleagues too I wanted 100 per cent because only by this can you arrive on the target. I didn't always play for a top team – this was my choice because I wanted to play for 15 years for Sampdoria and then three years for Lazio. I started playing for Bologna when I was young, but they were all small teams and with these teams who never won, we won everything. And I learnt this: that if you are in a small team and if you want to win, you work hard and you can do everything. Also if you are not the top team, it is important that you have players with good mentality – that you have teammates who say they want to win, they want to work, to improve.'

Mancini's early work paid off: he managed to shift the mindset of the squad, and City's trophy drought ended with the FA Cup. In Mancini's view, that was a turning point: 'I think we changed our mentality after the FA Cup. We started to believe in ourselves. When you arrive in a club that has not been winning, you need to win one title. It's not important [if it's the] FA Cup or Carling Cup – it's important to start. When you start to win, the mentality changes. And the players are human beings – if every day you work hard and if you still don't achieve your goals after one or two years the players can go down. If instead you work hard and in the end you win a title, your job becomes easier. It is never easy to do this job; but when you win your car is full, everybody is with you. When you lose you are alone.'

Preparation is everything

Football matches themselves are intense bursts of activity in the flow of the work that the manager, staff and players do together over weeks and months. Getting the pacing right is all-important. Mancini's approach is to even out the workload: 'Before the game we spend a lot of time together. I believe you should work every day during the week to prepare the game, because the day of the game the players have pressure. Usually I speak ten minutes with the players before the game and maybe another five minutes in the dressing room. The day of the game I don't think they need a lot of this because if you are a good manager you explain everything during the week on the training ground.'

In the run-up to the match, one of the manager's tasks is to help his players into the right frame of mind for their burst of high performance. Much of the preparation is personal. Glenn Hoddle recalls his own preparation as a player, involving getting detached, listening to music and using visualisation techniques. Then he'd drive to the ground, visualising how he was going to play. Where his manager really helped him was in two areas: guidance on his tactical role on the team, and helping him to stay positive: 'I would also have to think about positive things. You can learn from your negatives, of course, but people don't learn enough from their positives. As a player and as people we always analyse when we play bad or when something goes bad. We don't analyse enough when things are going really well – we take that for granted. I've found with experience how to deal with those fears and those anxieties I had when I was younger, and I've tried to hand that on to my players as a coach and get them to learn that early. If you haven't played that well in a match – well, there must have been one or two things that you did well because you are back in the team again. So, an hour before kick-off, focus on the strengths that you have got and learn from the good things that happen to you. Grasp hold of them, then step back into the arena and play again.'

Hope Powell reinforces both Mancini's view of the flow of preparation and Hoddle's commitment to the positives. She adds to that a clear message of ownership: 'We have meetings every day with players where I give them ownership. We do a lot of group work, scenarios, what happens if? what would you do if? We have a lot of unit meetings – the back four and the goal-keeper, the midfield and the front three – and for each unit we ask what's your role within the overall philosophy? Then I get them to share it with each other. What I am trying to do more and more is get the players to own their performances rather than leaving it all to the manager. They own the game. Then when we're leaving for the stadium, it's just about reinforcing the work that we've done in training: a gentle reminder of what the job is, remember what we're good at, remember what we can do, what your role is, what your responsibilities are.'

One thing the managers all point to is de-emphasising the Big Event. All the preparation is done before. The well-prepared team arrives at the field of play confident in its ability to deal with whatever comes. Such a team has no need for pre-match hype; they are professionals, out to do their job to the best of their very considerable ability.

The Training Ground

Training is not just about honing footballing skills. At Chelsea, Carlo Ancelotti built great rapport with the players through the professional setting of the training ground: 'I gave to the players all my experience, everything because I found a fantastic group. The English players were the symbol of the team: Joe Cole, Ashley Cole, Lampard, Terry – they are great professionals. The English players surprised me because on the pitch they are really professional. Outside the pitch I don't know, but on the pitch nothing compares, not the French or Italians, because you have to push the French to work hard. The same is true with the Italian players – you have to push them too. The English you have to push to stop! I felt really good about the group, we had a very good relationship.'

Brendan Rodgers accepts the implied compliment to English footballers, and builds on that on his own training ground: 'The English players have a will, and that goes back to part of my philosophy, about integrating into their football their other qualities. Decision-making is the big one. I build their decision-making capabilities. We practise this. Get intelligence working alongside that natural fight, that willingness the English player has, and you get a big player.'

The training ground is an ideal environment for building the team and for the manager to assess the quality and state of his players. Many issues can be addressed and opinions formed. Howard Wilkinson found a need to address head-on a poor behaviour before a match: 'I had a player who didn't like doing set pieces in training. Every time we were practising them he would be mucking about. So one morning I went out with a ball with his name on it and said, "Here you are – this is your own ball – you go and play with that, and we'll get on with this!" I wanted to keep it light, but give him a clear message: what you are doing is at the expense of everyone else. Carry on doing it by all means, but understand that while you may think it's funny, it's actually disrespectful. We've all actually said that there are certain common goals and common ways of doing things and processes that we think have to be there, and we have committed to them. We all agreed that this is the best way to do it, so you are being disrespectful of your teammates.' And did it work? 'Just about. There was a laugh because he had got what he wanted, but he was suddenly not with the team. He wanted his own way, but he wanted to be included too. At least we got to a greater awareness.'

Sam Allardyce uses the training ground as a place to build on what's going well. 'I do put my hand on the shoulder of a player and have a conversation when times are tough – just like my managers used to do with me when I was playing. But it's even more important to say, "You are playing really, really well – don't start slipping up! I don't want to be coming to you when things go bad, don't let them go bad." I tell them don't start practising when it's too late. Most players start practising when they are going bad. Practise while it's going well, because it's easier then.'

Training is about preparation on every front: both skills and mindsets can be assessed and addressed. Neil Warnock vividly remembers his first encounter with a player whose position was unclear, but whose mindset was excellent. 'Craig Short was at Scarborough when I started there. He was a bank clerk earning a small wage and he had such a great attitude. I was only a young manager then. They told me he was a right-winger and I played him everywhere: right-winger definitely not, midfield definitely not, striker definitely not. One game I told him, "Look, you've played everywhere else – just go and play centre half." He was marking Peter Withe, who was one of the top players at the time, playing briefly in the reserve team at Birmingham. I told Craig to mark him, wherever he went: "Just go with him everywhere. If he gets subbed, you go down the tunnel with him." He was all over him like a rash, and after about 20 minutes Peter came over to the bench and said can someone get this so-and-so off my back! In the end he made a great career out of it – and he's such a superb lad as well. To see people like that, that's what makes me proud.' Warnock stuck with a player whose mindset was ideal, and coached him through the technical challenges.

Football managers are at home on the training ground. We'd expect that. For the former players especially, it is a second home. The great football leaders push themselves and their team on the training ground, and fashion team spirit, character and a winning mindset.

Team selection

When Ancelotti played for Fabio Capello at Milan, he got angry with his manager for leaving him out of the team. 'He took me out. I didn't play and I didn't understand the reason because I wanted to play, and I was really angry with him. Capello told me, "One day you will understand, you will be a manager." And when I became a manager I understood that it's not easy.'

Team selection – picking those who will start, those who will be on the bench and those who will not appear – is one of the toughest tests of a manager's leadership. Few if any find it an easy task. Mancini is no different: 'It is difficult because if you are a player you know that when the manager says we need to play [in this particular way] that you will be on the bench. This is my worst moment as a manager because I understand their feelings in that moment and this is difficult. I would like to change this, but until they change the rules to play with 14 or 15 players then 11 players will be happy, the other players will be upset. If you are a top club you have maybe 20 top players and I think that moment can be difficult.' Mancini feels this keenly. David Platt recalls the dream situation where City had a settled, winning 11 for the six-match run-in to their title in 2012. A dream on paper – but a real pain for the leader. 'He really does not enjoy having to leave players out. That run of games meant that good players were on the sidelines, and that gave him great personal concern.' But when Mancini finds the winning mentality he so keenly seeks in his players, his selection task becomes less painful. Kolo Touré was not always a first-choice defender under Mancini, but he does embody the winning mindset. He reflects: 'It's not easy to not always be the one who is picked by the manager. But my attitude is always to keep going and give 100 per cent, and put pressure on the manager to give me time to play as well.'

Actually playing – bringing their skills, capabilities and flair to the big stage – is probably the greatest single motivator for true professionals. The top managers agree that this dwarfs the question of money for pretty much everyone. And it is the very mindset that Mancini promotes at all levels of his squad: the desire to play, the desire to win. Small wonder then that there is a disconnect when players are asked to take a back seat, however temporary. And with a squad of more than 20 players vying for 11 starting places, it is a leadership challenge. How then do the managers deal with it?

Most football managers do three things. The first is to be up front, clear and personal – without prejudicing team morale. Mick McCarthy tells people individually, but picks his moment carefully: 'If I'm leaving a player out I speak to him and tell him. I never pin a team sheet up or anything like that. It's a horrible one for them, but at least they are getting it from me. They all prefer to be told. I've never done any different. I've never shied away. I may have left someone off a subs' bench, but the subs get named just before the kick-off. If you tell the subs prior to the game, that will have affected them completely, so you need every one of the 20 to know they have a chance of being involved. The 11 starters will know either Thursday or Friday, so you get some of them feeling a bit disenchanted, but if you tell any of the rest of them they aren't going to be playing at all then they will come along heads down and that's unsettling for everyone else. Some will have an inkling, but they don't know. You have to keep everyone involved.'

Alex McLeish adds to that the need to be discreet with the modern football professional: 'At Aberdeen we would sit and have a pre-match meal and then we would watch *Football Focus* on the television. Archie Knox [the assistant manager] would come and tap somebody on the shoulder and say, "Gaffer wants a word with you." This would be about 1 p.m. before going to the stadium and you knew as soon as you got that tap on the shoulder, that's me dropped. It was fine for us, and Alex [Ferguson] was great – but I've found it really awkward in recent years trying to do it that way because all the players know, and I know that the modern-day guy is extremely sensitive. One or two players at Birmingham wanted me to tell them on the Friday – anything, but not getting that tap on the shoulder in front of their colleagues. After a few times, some players would even find the one-on-one approach disconcerting, when I thought I was giving them great respect. I now use the tap on the shoulder for other things like a tactical change – but for team selection I try and mix it up a bit to keep them on their toes.'

The second thing is to engage the players in the reasoning. This is not about consensus decision-making, nor about a leader justifying himself. It is about treating players like the adults they are, and cutting them in on your thinking. Many of today's managers have learned from less-than-perfect experiences as players. Glenn

Hoddle recalls: 'When I was a player, I *hated* getting left out and not told why. Too many managers do that. So when I became a manager, I always told people why – even if it was just a quick word. Then I'd say, "If you want to talk more, come and see me on Monday after the game." Lots of them did come. In fact if he *didn't* come, I would have a question mark over his appetite!' In short: a leader needs to be transparent with his people. If a leader has integrity, he has no reason to fear being open, and Hoddle's invitation to his people to 'find out more' earned him considerable respect among his players.

The third thing is to work with the players who are left out. Hoddle believes there are times when managing the ones that aren't playing is more important even than working with the ones who are. 'When I had a team I used to ask them which is the most important team: is it the one that starts the game or the one that finishes the game?' Games can be won or lost by the substitutes – they are very, very important people. And the ones that are out of the team remain crucial to team spirit – and might be tomorrow's first choice. So in the World Cup in France, we did everything to make the players who weren't selected feel part of the team – that at any given moment they could be called on – and they had a part to play in winning the World Cup.'

Selecting the best 11 for a given day is a technical, knowledge-based skill. Knowing your own mind, communicating your choices, and inspiring the rest of the squad to continue to give their all day after day – this is a real test of leadership.

The half-time team talk

The half-time team talk is the stuff of legend in football because of its potential to change the course of the game. Most fans will be able to point to the time their team staged an extraordinary turna-round – or suffered a reverse in the second half – but fans cannot really know what goes on during those few crucial minutes.

Half-time emotions can run high, but more often it is a prac-tical session, an opportunity for the manager to communicate clearly with the players in an oasis of calm before 45 more minutes of intensity. Mancini is honest about the variability of the talk: 'You can have different situations depending on the score, depending on the performance and whether we made a lot of mistakes, and depending maybe also on my confidence at that moment.' Regardless of the content though, his players know to expect a standard pattern: 'During half-time it is important for the players to have a 10-minute rest and to recover because they spend a lot of energy. After, we talk for five minutes on specifics, tactics for the second half.' It's interesting – though unsurprising – that Mancini's focus is clearly on the needs of the players: hearing their experience and offering them rest.

Most managers make time for encouragement – for the whole team and for individuals. Hoddle would always finish on the posi-tives, making sure they walked up the tunnel with a positive mindset. As he candidly admits, 'Sometimes as a footballer they switch off during a talk – the last thing that they hear is probably the only thing they remember.' Mick McCarthy agrees: 'Sometimes I just encourage a player at half-time – say something on the way out, just a little word to say how much you love him, I guess. That's what we do. You have to. One of my philosophies is love them for what they bring to the party, try and make them better, practise, but you actually bring them in and love them for what they've got, don't loathe them for what they haven't got.'

Of course, there are times when tough love is the right approach – and some characters respond well to a stern word. Martin Jol admits he can become 'autocratic' if the situation merits: 'I can remember being really angry in the dressing room when I think we [Spurs] were 2–0 or 3–0 down away to Middlesbrough. The second half we came back to 3–3, so it helped. But if you do that all the time, I think it loses its impact on players.'

Alex McLeish remembers vividly his encounter with the young Alex Ferguson at half-time in Aberdeen's celebrated European Cup-Winners' Cup final against Real Madrid in 1983. 'We were 1–1 and I'd had a hand in both goals! We had been 1–0 up and well worth it. It was a sodden night, torrential rain. I had been quite meticulous in my warm-up – I'd checked conditions and everything – then I'd said to the lads in the dressing room before kick-off, "Look if you are trying to pass it you need to try and chip it a bit because it's going to stick in the water." Of course, the ball came to me and in those days the goalkeeper could pick it up. Instinctively between myself, Willie Miller (fellow centre back) and Jim Leighton (goalkeeper) we had a really fantastic understanding. But I was a victim of my own teaching. I was under pressure, I struck one back and under normal circumstances it would have just run safely back to Jim, but it got stuck in the water and although I shouldn't say it, big Jim was a bit slow off his line! The Real Madrid striker – a famous name at the time, Carlos Santillana – rounded Jim; Jim brought him down and they converted the penalty. I just wanted to bury my head in a hole in the ground.'

When McLeish arrived in the dressing room at half-time, the boss was ready for him: 'It wasn't a calm "what were you thinking about, big fella?" It was the famous hairdryer treatment. I was equally vociferous and Archie Knox had to calm things down. Nowadays we can beat players up with TV coverage, HD, slow motion, super slow motion – you can kill players if you choose to. In those days coaches just had to remember exactly the detail of the moment something happened – a goal scored, a goal lost or a mistake and, of course, they could dress it up in those days because you didn't have the benefit of looking at 20 replays. Sir Alex said it and you just had to accept it. That was the kind of motivational powers that he had in those days and we thought he was just like any manager! But in that second half I knew that I couldn't put a foot wrong; I didn't want to let him down and I didn't want to let my teammates down. It was a kind of fear probably – there's a fear of failure that drives you – but with that comes the determination and I've always had that trait and character.

'The second half went to plan; we won in extra time. We must have played really well in that second half and I was so glad at the end when we had won – but there is that individual thing where you still think of the mistake. We'd just won the European Cup-Winners' Cup and still my mistake was uppermost in my mind. Alex came into the showers and I was last out – I was kind of reflecting and thinking the newspapers are going to kill me. It was a massive overreaction, but that's what it's like, that's what the mind does. He came in and I always remember the shower splashing on his trousers because I was looking down and I was kind of laughing to myself thinking he is getting soaked here and he said, "Really proud of you. A lot of people would have crumbled tonight, but you stood tall and it was superb."' Sir Alex knew how to get the best out of his man, and played it to perfection – great leadership in action.

Half-time talks then are a mixture of the standard pattern and the variable content, depending on the player and the circumstance. But, whatever the circumstance, dialogue rather than one-way communication is becoming the norm. Hope Powell begins her half-times with no management staff – just the players and medics – and five minutes so they can have their own dialogue. Then she comes in with clips of the game. 'I'll bring those clips in then my first words to the players are: "Right, what do we think?"

and I give them a voice. Then I'll go through and the clips hope-fully marry up what I'm saying with what they are saying and I'll visually give them some feedback. Half-time is a really powerful opportunity and they embrace it.'

Hoddle goes even further on the dialogue point: 'I used to like it sometimes if two players had a confrontation in the dressing room. If they had a bit of a spat, verbal not physical, I didn't mind that – it showed to me that they cared.' The dressing room is almost unique in this regard – outside of sport, probably only the military in liberal societies allows for this level of head-to-head confrontation. Hoddle would use it for good though: 'I'd always say "Right, give me your input – you're the ones out there and let's see if we can work this one out." Some youngsters wouldn't say a word and then you'd get the captain and a few others saying things, but it's good to entice them to bring out their thoughts.' But even the great dialoguers reserve the right to resort to a one-way conversation in a crisis. Powell admits, 'If we are having an absolute shocker and we are not doing the things we say we were going to do, I don't show any clips. I let them have five minutes, but I know when there is silence they know they aren't performing well and then I say, "Right, you need to do this, this, this and this and that's how we do it."'

In the heat of the battle leaders must choose carefully how to inspire their people. They use silence, listening, asking, telling, even shouting; they use calm reasoning and, from time to time, emotional appeal. There is no simple formula – a great leader will know what works best for his team in the particular circumstances.

Tactical change

One of the most dramatic ways in which a manager's craft is judged is by the substitutions he makes during a match. Some will be reactive, driven by injury or as a response to a red card and the enforced change of formation. The most interesting ones though are the substitutions a manager makes when he perceives that something needs changing. Something – or someone – isn't quite working out. His team needs fresh impetus.

Mancini's Manchester City were neck-and-neck with Ferguson's Manchester United all through the dramatic run-in to the 2011–12 season. With two matches to go, United were behind on goal difference alone. City needed to win both remaining games to be sure of clinching the title. The first was away against a talented Newcastle side brim-full of confidence after an excellent run of wins themselves. With 30 minutes to go, the match was still goalless. All eyes were on Mancini. What would he do now?

His response was to send on a defensive midfielder (Nigel de Jong) and withdraw a world-class goalscorer (Carlos Tevez). To some observers, this might have been a surprising substitution, although by anchoring the midfield, de Jong would allow the powerful Yaya Touré to move forward and pose a new threat to the Newcastle defence. But used to seeing him play deeper, the home team were caught out. Yaya Touré scored twice in the last 20 minutes, and City won 2-0. The fans were delirious; the press praised Mancini as a tactical genius and City were firm favourites for the title going into the last match one week later.

The vastly experienced Martin O'Neill outlines his approach to substitutions. 'There is no question that substitutions can turn the course of a game. We see endless examples of this every weekend and the art or fortune of making these decisions can impact greatly on the result. I suppose there is a science that can be attributed to this, but it is really down to intuition and obviously an element of good fortune if it works.'

This demonstrates the power of a decisive intervention. O'Neill would be the first to acknowledge the element of good fortune involved; but there is science too – and intuition. 'First, you have to know your players pretty well. You're then looking at the state of play with 20-something minutes to go: (1) whether you are chasing the game or holding on to a lead, and (2) whether you think the energy levels have dropped considerably. If you're chasing a game, you may need a bit more forward play, you might have someone on the bench that you think might be capable of doing something. If you are holding on to a lead, it's important not to drop back too deeply, but maybe you can get a bit more solidity.

'When you know your players well, you get a feel for how they play at certain stages of the match, and how they're doing. You may have a good player playing in the team, but that particular day is not going right for him. You know that on another day he could turn it – so at what moment do you decide that because he's a good player, you just forget about what happened in the last 25 minutes and believe he'll turn something for you? If there is someone there that might be able to do that then maybe that's worth the gamble of keeping him on; then another time you might think he's run his race, and know that no matter what happens, he won't find that energy and determination and you make the substitution accordingly.'

The tactical substitution is another real test for the leader. The stakes are high personally and professionally, since the match outcome can turn on the choice; and the world will have as long as it likes to review the decision afterwards. In big matches it requires deep knowledge, clarity of thought and conviction against the backdrop of noise, drama and emotion, and leaders facing these tests need intuition and self-belief to carry them through.

The fallout

After the 90-something minutes are done, the leader's primary task is to take the team forward. Whether the result is cause for celebration or upset, there are lessons to learn and then a future to play for. When Mancini's men lost at Arsenal with six games of the season left to play, it appeared to most onlookers to be the end of their title chances as United were eight points ahead of them. Mancini chose not to dwell on what had gone before, but to focus purely on the final few games. 'At that moment we had a lot of pressure and the players had a lot of pressure around them and we decided with the staff to take off this pressure from the players. I told them we did a good game, we are a top team and now we need to finish our championship well. If we win all our games, we will finish second.' While publicly declaring it impossible to go on and win the Premier League, Mancini privately thought it merely difficult. His public declarations had the desired effect: 'Once we took the pressure off, the players started to play calm and controlled and we started to win the games.'

Where Mancini tends to be calm and phlegmatic, Sir Alex tends to be direct and crisp – and yet there are similarities between the two. Sir Alex says: 'I think it's black and white. If they've had a bad performance, I would tell them. I wouldn't hold back. And once it's over, we would never revisit it. I would say my piece on a Saturday after a game and that's it finished, we wouldn't go over it again. I'd have no time to go over it again, I'd have next week to consider.' This is the core of Sir Alex's philosophy: 'There is no point going back. Suppose you have a game on the Saturday and you give them the Sunday off. You come to the Monday training session and you've maybe got a Wednesday game – two days to the next match. There is absolutely no point whatsoever raking over old ground.

The other important thing is always to tell them the truth. You have to be black and white about it. There's no softening for one player over another player, they've all got to understand what black and white means, and they'd also have to understand what I am. Once they accepted that, we'd have absolutely no problems.'

While the need to move forward is paramount, leaders give more or less vent to their emotions depending on their character and the circumstances. Mick McCarthy is not prone to shouting in the dressing room, but admits from time to time emotion carries him away: 'I did it twice in my last year at Wolves. Once was at Manchester United when we lost 2-1 in the 93rd minute. We had the ball and all we had to do was take the draw – don't try and win the game, just take the ball to the corner and keep it there – job done at Old Trafford. We come on the inside, give a bad pass, concede and we lose. I went mental; I threw stuff around, I booted stuff. I was very close to lamping the bloke who gave the goal away, but I didn't.

'Bolton was the other one. There was a throw-in in the 94th minute, we were drawing 0-0, he throws it, little back-pass and it goes to Sturridge and it's a goal. I apologised afterwards for it. It wasn't calculated; it wasn't to shock anyone. I was waiting for them to come in, I was throwing stuff, I was incandescent with rage; I could barely control myself. I didn't do anything that stupid, but it was good for them to see it. I am calm generally and I think it shocked them how much it hurt me that we'd lost. I more often come in and sit them down and say, "Look, lads, let's analyse this: this happened, that happened, you could have done this better… " Discuss it and move on to the next game. Then it's done with. If there is an individual that has done something then I may point that out, and then maybe four or five things tactically with the team we might just have a discussion about.'

Even the serene Ancelotti can get riled – but only around poor behaviour. And when he does, it is calculated: 'Sometimes we play well and we lose for an individual mistake. Then I don't say anything. But recently we drew a game because the players were selfish and didn't want to pass the ball and wanted to score themselves. I killed the players for three days.' Ancelotti also makes sure the effect is not lost: 'After the game I spoke in Italian. Usually when I shout, I shout in Italian. I am more fluent in Italian. It doesn't matter if they don't understand the words – they understand the sense and the emotion. Sometimes in a foreign language it is very difficult to show emotion. This is not good, because sometimes you have to show what you really feel, and if you don't have the proper language it is very difficult. One of the most difficult things is to motivate the players. You have to use the right expression. Sometimes with a foreign language I don't have the expression – I speak like a computer. This is the most difficult thing. I show something with my volume and body language.'

The final piece of the post-match jigsaw is dealing with the individuals. As we know from McLeish's encounter with Alex Ferguson, this matters a great deal. Ancelotti's approach is to take his time: 'When an individual makes a mistake, I wait. I say nothing. Normally he wants to think for himself. If you say something like "it doesn't matter," or "you have to look to the future," – it's not good enough. It's better for me to stay a little bit back. I have to wait.' Keegan learned from the great Liverpool masters, Bill Shankly and Bob Paisley. 'When I had been sent off with (Leeds United striker) Billy Bremner I think I got an eight-match suspension and Phil Boersma had gone in and done very well. I'd also been injured and hadn't even played a match for the reserves. Then the first game I was available and the manager chose the team, I thought he might not play me. He announced the team and there I was and Boey was sub. I felt so sorry for him – but in some ways very clever from Shanks – because Boey had done well and in my mind he just said to me you're my guy, go on. I played a cracker – I had to!' Keegan the manager would in turn always persevere with key players: 'It's not about "I am just going to take you away for a little while." Unless they are having a desperately bad time, it's the opposite. Don't even question it, name your team and say his name first. I don't go to him and say, "You are having a shocker here but I am going to play you." I say, "There's the team – I trust that team to go out here today, I think it's the right team for the day and off you go." That way you put it back into the player's court. That is what I would want a manager to do with me.'

It is interesting how managers who are ex-players talk often about what they experienced at the hands of other managers. The power of empathy is transmitted down the generations.

In the matter of the post-match fall-out, it is clear that when the referee blows his whistle, the leader's work is not done. How he deals with his players in the hours and days that follow will shape their ability to perform in the next match.

The Solution: Command, Lead and Manage

Much has been written on the subject of leadership, and much debate exists around the difference between leadership and management. In England, we talk about football managers. In the rest of Europe, they more usually talk about coaches. Neither of these titles tells the full story. In reality, like most leaders, their work falls into three distinct categories, each requiring a different approach. Which approach depends on the situation in which they find themselves – and a little bit on their own natural preferences.

Leadership and management expert Professor Keith Grint of Warwick University defines these categories vividly. One approach is 'command'. We don't often think of leaders as commanders, except perhaps in the military. In fact, football managers quite often use command. It is the act of 'taking charge' and imposing a solution. It provides little or no room for discussion or disagreement, and is a sound approach in a crisis. When the going gets tough, people become worried and unsure. They look for direction – and commanders provide certainty and answers.

When the team is *not* in a crisis, the question then becomes: is this something we've faced before – something to which there is a clear answer? If the answer is yes, then it will respond to well-tried methods. It is a 'tame' problem. This is 'management'. The manager is about rolling-out things that have been done before, where the degree of certainty is high. The problem may feel like a puzzle – may even be quite complicated – but there is a solution, and the manager engages in a familiar process to solve it.

If it is not something we have faced before, and there might well not even *be* a clear answer, then we're into 'leadership'. Grint calls these challenges 'wicked problems'. In football, this could be about unusual individual behaviour, about a club near to bankruptcy, about a critical injury or about facing opponents who on paper are better in every department. The leader will need to ask questions. He will often hear himself saying: 'I've never seen this problem before; I need to get people together to work out what to do.'

Mancini is a natural commander. As a player he was known for his assertiveness with his colleagues. Sven Göran Eriksson was Mancini's coach at Sampdoria where he observed his young colleague's natural leadership: 'He wanted to be a manager even while he was a player. He was the coach, he was the kit man, he was the bus driver, everything. He wanted to check that everything was in place before training. Sometimes I would have to tell him: "Mancio, you have a game to play on Sunday. You'll be exhausted if you have to control everything." But he was like that.' Perhaps the young Mancini recognised this in himself: 'I thought this when I was 12 years old – that I wanted to be a manager. When I started to play football I thought I would want to be a manager. When I finished playing football this was still in my head.'

Arriving at a Manchester City starved of success, Mancini the natural commander simply said: this situation needs turning around. I know what to do here. If we do it, we will succeed. If we don't, we will fail. In the end the margin to win the title could barely have been smaller. But Mancini's strong leadership delivered success and, although he has since moved on and joined Galatasaray, his fans are now legion. Or, as he would put it, there are many people in his car.

The Gift

While the delivery of results in top-flight football is an almost unique challenge, there are interesting lessons for a wider leadership audience. Football's leaders, like business leaders, would agree that the underpinning dimensions of the task are the skills and mindsets in the team. Then there is a six-stage flow from preparation to fall-out that enables repeated success.

1. Preparation:
    By focusing relentlessly, day in day out, on the basics of the work, the leader does away with any need for pre-match hype. In a healthy organisation, teams encounter major hurdles with a mindset of 'all in a day's work'.

2. Training:

    By dry-running scenarios, football leaders foster team spirit, character and a winning mindset – as well as honing skills.

3. Team selection:

    Choosing the right people for the task is of critical importance. It must be done objectively, protected from the distractions of personal bias, preference and allegiance. For the leader, it involves knowing your own mind, having a clear rationale and communicating your choices.

4. Half-time:

    Most great football leaders use the mid-point check-in first to listen, then to speak. There is no formula for this: in the heat of the battle, they choose carefully how to inspire.

5. Tactical change:

    In the heat of the moment, great leaders can think clearly enough to make tactical changes – standing down one team member, introducing another, switching roles, and refining responsibilities. Preconceptions are dangerous. The game belongs to the leader who is bold enough to respond to reality.

6. Fallout:

    How the leader deals with the immediate aftermath of the big moment will contribute significantly to his organisation's chances of ongoing success. He must put the result into context, and with a cool head choose how much emotion to show, how much significance to attribute to events that may seem disproportionately good or bad and how and where to deal one-to-one with his people.

Above all of these, though, is an understanding of the problem. Does the challenge require management, leadership or command? There is something inspirational about Mancini. He is a commander in turnaround, a leader with conviction. He is a man who does not seek the approval of others, yet is genuinely concerned with the feelings of the players he has to leave out of the team. He is also a serial winner.

Success inspires – people follow winning leaders. Mancini knows full well that the more he wins, the easier it becomes to lead. But he also knows he has been given a gift: 'To be a top player means you have been given a gift. I had a gift from my Father. Then after, I need to work hard.' The world's most successful leaders all have gifts that set them apart from their peers – gifts of ability, strength, insight or just plain circumstance. The leader who recognises this adds to his qualities humility – and that is inspirational indeed.

CHAPTER SIX

HANDLING OUTRAGEOUS TALENT

THE BIG IDEA

Genius is a mystery. Why could Mozart compose at the age of five? Why could Albert Einstein see beyond the scientific horizon of his day? The debate may continue forever around what we are born with, what we are born into and what we are taught, but there is no doubt that in every possible field there is truly exceptional talent.

Leaders at the top of their game will meet genius. Market forces left unhindered will ensure that the best talent rises to the top. When we do meet it, it is thrilling, captivating – and almost always unpredictable.

Genius brings challenge. People – especially young people – endowed with huge ability need careful, thoughtful and strong leadership if they are to realise their potential without negatively affecting themselves and others. Perhaps nowhere is this played out more visibly than in the world of top-flight football.

THE MANAGER

José Mourinho can reasonably lay claim to being one of the best coaches in world football. The jury of his peers would agree: both Pep Guardiola and Diego Maradona have gone on record as naming him the world's best coach, while Arrigo Sacchi of Italy has called him 'phenomenal'.

Famously nicknamed 'The Special One', Mourinho came to English public attention as the architect of Roman Abramovich's Chelsea, moving to Stamford Bridge in 2004 following Primeira Liga and Champions League success with Porto. With Chelsea he won the Barclays Premier League in his first two seasons and the FA Cup in his third, but Champions League success eluded him and he moved in 2008 to Internazionale in Milan. There he won his second Champions League title during his second season, sweeping all before him to achieve the outstanding treble of domestic league, domestic cup and European league. In 2010 he moved again – to Real Madrid, where he won the Copa del Rey in his first season and La Liga in his second. This title success was record-breaking in that Real Madrid reached 100 points, scoring 121 goals in the process. June 2013 saw him return for a second spell in charge at Chelsea.

Mourinho has arguably encountered, encouraged and managed more varied and outrageous football talent than any other coach. He strides across the landscape of modern football in its new, global era, recruiting the best and motivating them to deliver on their excellent potential, and has led the greatest footballing talents in the world.

His Philosophy

Mourinho is convinced that great leadership is founded first on great knowledge. He is flattered by the suggestion that if you can lead at the top of professional football, you can lead anywhere – but does not necessarily believe it. 'I think one of the most important qualities in someone that leads is that the ones that you lead recognise in you a big knowledge of the situation. So you have to know a lot about the area you are working in. I'm not saying that if you know a lot about football you can automatically be a leader in football. I am saying if you don't know a lot about football you cannot lead. That's the main point for me.' Hot on the heels of knowledge though comes a profound understanding of people. 'I have to say we are speaking about men. We are speaking about human beings and human sciences. So is football a sports science? I think it is probably a human science and not a sports science.'

The Challenges

Confronted with the undoubted challenges of managing outrageous talent, Mourinho simply counts his blessings: 'The toughest thing is when you don't have that talent! I have never had a problem with working with that special talent, never, I never had that. I never understood when people say that is a problem, or you can have a special talent but not two or three or four. I want 11 special talents! Maybe I was lucky, maybe I wasn't, but it was never a problem.'

Mourinho has a point. Why would anyone *not* want to have a genius in their organisation? And yet questions can arise: is this person just too much trouble? Is he good value for effort expended? Or will managing him take too much of my focus, to the detriment of the rest of the team? Of course, Mourinho is used to leading a team full of star talent – and that provides a different landscape and subtly different challenges from the case where someone is head and shoulders above their peers. Nonetheless, he has mastered the art – and, like many other football leaders, has achieved great results with world-class talent. For sure, Mourinho has been amazingly successful in this regard – perhaps a sign of his own genius. But what does he actually do that is so successful?

Like all leaders of supreme talent, he must address – consciously or unconsciously – at least five challenges.

Imbalance in the relationship

For a leader working with true genius, a sense of imbalance can easily creep in. As Rangers manager, Walter Smith brought the stunning talent of Paul Gascoigne to Ibrox. He took to heart a comment in a newspaper column made by Scottish comedian Billy Connolly after a high-profile Paul Gascoigne transgression: 'You have to live with the genius, the genius doesn't have to live with you.'

Add to that imbalance the risk of player arrogance. Where does self-belief end and the unpalatable begin? Cristiano Ronaldo scores a breakthrough goal for Portugal at the 2012 European Championships, runs away and stands apart, beckoning his team-mates to come and pay him homage. Play-acting or divisive? A leader needs to deal with any such imbalance in order to manage his team's talent successfully on and off the field.

Capacity to damage others

If genius is not handled with extreme care, resentment and divisions can quickly appear. From Milan to Chelsea and Real Madrid, Carlo Ancelotti is no stranger to the challenge of working with genius: 'The behaviour of these players is very important for the team. You find a talent who is unselfish and motivated for the team. This is the key, and that's very difficult to find – a talent who is unselfish. You have to use the relationship to give him the possibility to understand that the talent is important for the team and not for him – but this is very difficult. Rarely I have found players with talent who are unselfish. It is deep in their personality I think.' Can he name one? 'Kaka.'

Capacity to damage themselves

Genius is so often brittle. The notion of a 'flawed genius' is an all-too-common one. Stories from the artistic genius of Vincent van Gogh to the musical genius of Amy Winehouse show us that the flaw can have the direst consequences. Whether from the pressure to perform, from the intense scrutiny, or from too close an identification of the man with his talent, people of extreme talent appear to have increased capacity to damage themselves.

Living up to expectations

People pay to see genius, and are thrilled when it expresses itself. From a Rooney derby-winning bicycle kick through to the beautiful passing football of Xavi and Iniesta, genius seizes the imagination. One of the great tasks of a leader is how to provide the ideal climate for that genius to flourish. Too much expectation, and the genius can crumble. Too little expectation, and under-performance creeps in.

Maintaining stability

Every leader will recognise the value of stability. When Michael Boyd took over as artistic director of the world-famous theatre group the Royal Shakespeare Company in 2002, he observed that the growth of individual stardom and of a hire-and-fire culture had begun to erode the group's foundations. Recalling his time with a Moscow company where a single artistic director had held a post for 20 years, he noticed how there was a 'tremendous sense of shared language and a depth of human interchange' between the actors. So what is the right message to supreme talent: dispensable or indispensable? Neither seems quite right: keeping genius happy and maintaining stability is not a trivial challenge.

What Imbalance?

The Mourinho approach to the imbalance question is typically robust. One senses there is no question of his feeling less talented or somehow awed by genius. Logically, why would a man of his track record and ability have a problem striking a healthy, balanced relationship with talented footballers? And nor does he see himself as in any way superior. They are professionals together: his role is to lead; theirs to play.

His skill at handling genius became apparent during his first spell at Chelsea, where he struck up a series of friendships that anchored an array of world-class talent. He arrived at Stamford Bridge aged only 41: a comparatively small age difference from his players. 'In terms of mentality, I'm not much older than them – I think I have the ability to put myself at their level. I think it is important to understand. The more you understand them the more you can lead them – there is leadership and leadership, as you know. I never liked the leadership where the boys say, "He's my leader, I have to respect him." I prefer them to say, "I respect him and he's my leader." It is a completely different thing. They can say, "I do that because he tells me to do that and I have to." I prefer them to say, "I believe in him so much, and trust him so much that everything he says I want to do!" I prefer much more this kind of empathy.'

It is a commonly held belief in many cultures that friendship precludes effective leadership. But closeness to the players has always been a defining characteristic for Mourinho. 'Of course, many people say we can't be friends with the players. I say exactly the opposite. If you are *not* friends with the players you do not reach the maximum potential of that group. You have to be friends with them, but they have to understand that between friends the answer is never the answer they are expecting, or the answer they want to hear. They have to understand that, but I think you have to be friends. I don't understand some people that are afraid to be friends with them.'

The friendship approach involves regarding the players as peer colleagues – people who do a job every bit as important as yours. Mourinho gives an example of a symbolic action that betrays very clearly the value a manager really attaches to his players: 'A story from the past. I think there are two ways of travelling with the players in a plane: you travel having a business class where everybody goes in business class, or if there is no space for everybody then the players go in business class and you go in economy class with your staff. If I go in business it's because they go. If there is no space for everybody else, I go behind them. Some time ago a coach arrived in a club and they travelled to pre-season and the first thing they did was to travel executive for the manager and the staff with the players in economy. I was thinking, "Bad start" – and I was not wrong. One of the things you must remember as a leader is your people are more important than you.'

There is a compelling humility about a leader who serves his people – and inspiration when he does it with confidence, unconcerned by any imbalance.

Walter Smith and Paul Gascoigne

Walter Smith believes in doing his homework: 'When you sit down and you say, "I'm going for a player," the pluses and minuses are there and you have to understand the balance before you make a decision. It's up to the manager to reduce the unexpected as much as possible.'

At Rangers, Smith chose Gazza – chose to bring him back after a time in the wilderness. 'He'd been at Lazio for a few years and hadn't played for maybe two and a half or even three years, mainly through injury. So it was a matter of taking a chance with him, knowing that it was going to be a managerial challenge to try and get him back to his best. Because he was a player who you knew if you were able to manage the genius, to handle it, and get the best out of him, then he would be good for your team. And the fans would love him, because genius stirs most people.

'I spoke first and foremost to Sir Bobby Robson and Terry Venables who had had him before and both were quite straight-forward. They said, "If you can get him on your side then you'll have no problem getting him to play. You have to try and keep him on the straight and narrow all the time." This was not the first time I'd had such a challenge in my career, and their advice was right. I believe he felt I was supporting him and sticking up for him when necessary – and he would always play for me.'

Smith was excited by Gascoigne because of his sheer talent: 'A lot of players that are exceptional learn about football as their careers go on. Paul Gascoigne was still the same player at the end of his career as he was at the start. He was instinctive, he had a genius that allowed him to go on to the field and assess the situation and do things that other players couldn't do.'

Both Mourinho and Smith take material steps toward their talented charges. When they do so, imbalance – real or imagined – disappears and is replaced by commitment and understanding.

Uniting, Not Damaging

If the leader gets it right, the team can flourish around a huge individual talent. Mourinho again takes a very simple approach: 'The first objective is for the team to succeed. For this to happen, the team must recognise that the special talent is crucial. Also, the special talent must understand two things: one is that the team is more important than himself, and two is that he needs the team. For him to flourish, the team need to flourish too. I think that is very important – but for me that was very automatic. It was not something that I had to work exhaustively on, absolutely not.'

Mourinho at Inter

When Mourinho arrived at Inter from Chelsea, he inherited a fascinating situation that could have spiralled downwards. 'First of all there is the culture of the country, the culture of the football of that country, and after that is the profile of the people you are working with. When I arrived at Inter I had I think 14 players who were more than 32 years old. I had a team with 75 per cent of the guys in the last years of their careers, and with a history of frustration in European competition. This wasn't just about not winning the Champions League – it was also not even playing quarter-finals or semi-finals – it was a story of last 16 and out. At the same time I had a team that was dominant in Italian football, so a team that had three or four consecutive titles in Italian football, but nothing outside.

'My job was to try and create a team that was able to win the Champions League, but they had to understand that to make a team strong enough to win the Champions League (and that is 13 matches in a season), you have to be very strong in the other 47 matches. So the best way to motivate a team to win the Champions League was to keep winning domestic competitions. If we allow ourselves to be afraid of the Champions League because we are not the best team, and if we focus too much on the Champions League, then we don't win it. And we also don't win the Italian cup, and we also don't win the Italian championship. And instead of the job becoming something extraordinary it becomes worse than they had before. So I had to go with the players in just one direction: improvement. And when you are speaking about players near the end of their careers it is very difficult for them to improve individually. So we have just to focus on the team improvement and let's go and see where we can finish.'

Mourinho focused on uniting the genius at his disposal, creating for them a challenging, but realistic goal. At the end of his second season in charge, Inter won the UEFA Champions League beating Bayern Munich 2–0 in the final. By winning the Italian league and cup, they also became the first ever Italian side to win the coveted treble.

Glenn Hoddle and Ruud Gullit

Glenn Hoddle was undoubtedly a gifted player in his own right. When he arrived at the pre-Abramovich Chelsea as manager in 1993, he was still playing. The Chelsea of that era were not yet the European or even the national force they would become a decade later, and Hoddle set out to make a difference – not least by attracting major talent. 'Ruud Gullit had been World Soccer Player of the Year three years before I brought him across. He had played for AC Milan – and we were Chelsea! And it wasn't the Chelsea of today – it was the Chelsea of no money at all.

'We had a big running track around Stamford Bridge – it wasn't the most attractive of stadiums – so I made sure that Ruud didn't go anywhere near the stadium or the training ground! At the time if he'd seen that, I don't think he would have signed, frankly. But Ruud was a smashing player so I took time to find out what he liked in his life outside football. I wanted to be able to talk to him about things and show that I respected him, the talents that he had and what he'd achieved in football. But he also needed to know that I couldn't make a special case for him off the pitch. My message to him was, "Once you are on the pitch I want you to perform to the highest level you can – but the ethos of the team has to come first." Fortunately Ruud is a really solid guy. He knew his talent: he knew he was one of the best players in the world, but he has this real ability to laugh at himself. So he was really easy to talk to and work with – but I didn't know that when I first worked with him. Then, once we got on the training pitch with everyone else, I treated him just like the others. If there was something to be said that he wasn't doing right I would tell him. I told him what I wanted him to do for the team and he was absolutely first class, he was brilliant.'

Hoddle invested time in getting to know the genius; then used the talent to unite the team. The model would work for him multiple times: 'With other players, you might have a big problem if they are arrogant – but for me the one-to-one approach always worked. I brought players into the team who had exceptional talent, and I knew they weren't going to let me down on the pitch, but you have to make them play within that team frame. The only way to get that balance is to spend time breaking through into that character and finding out more about him as a person. He will then respect you in the end because the conversation will flow and you will end up opening yourself out to him and he to you. I even remember a couple of players who were really into racehorses. I wouldn't know one end of a racehorse from the other, but I started to look up a bit about racing and talk to them a bit about horses and suddenly it just broke barriers down. We had something in common outside football that we could talk about, and I could see them change.'

Neil Warnock and Adel Taarabt

Neil Warnock was 62 and manager of QPR in the English Championship when he says he first encountered genius. He describes it as 'the biggest plus of my career'.

'In my first training session, the staff from the previous management team were there, telling me who was who. They pointed to this Adel Taarabt and told me, "This Moroccan guy – he will get you the sack. The last two managers bombed him out as he never tried a leg, and you will too because otherwise he'll get you the sack as well. He's just a luxury." I watched the practice match and I could see what he had, and we didn't have goals and I knew he would get us goals. There were only about 12 games left in the season, and we needed to get to safety. I remember I pulled him over straight after the game. The conversation went something like this:

Me: Will you get me the sack if I play you? I understand you are a nightmare …

Adel: No, that's not right.

Me: Well, I'm told that you get every manager the sack because you don't train.

Adel: Of course I train!

Me: OK, I am going to play you every game between now and the end of the session and if you play bad I'm going to play you the next game, and if you play even worse I'm going to play you the next game. Do you understand? You are going to be my little jewel in the crown.

Adel: No, I don't understand.

Me: I am going to make you a player.

Adel: Why?

Me: Because I believe in you and you are going to do well.

'I did that and he did repay me. We stayed up and then I signed him permanently from Tottenham.'

Taarabt was a stunning success at QPR that season, and went on to become Football League player of the year. Indeed, in a calculated bid to get the most from his star midfielder at QPR, Warnock decided to make him captain. He recalls, 'The challenge for me then was to get all the other players on board that here we had a match winner, when on certain days of the week he looked like he simply wasn't trying. But I asked them to trust me when I said he would get us promotion to the Premier League, which would benefit everyone. I knew what this lad could do, and they came on board. I told the five lads who could have been captain that they were really worthy captains, but if they went with my decision I might get another 20 per cent out of him, and that 20 per cent would get us promoted.'

With Taarabt as captain, QPR went on to win the Championship. Warnock is rueful, but happy: 'I had to change all my philosophies because he was a luxury at times. I had to change, even at my age, because I never thought I would employ a player who didn't give 100 per cent every game, every week. That's how I thought football was, but I just felt there was something special about him. And in his own way he was giving 100 per cent – just in an English way he wasn't! He was born like that, he wanted to play football and caress the ball from when he was a kid. To take him on board in the first place was the biggest thing, as I knew it was something most of the players wouldn't want.'

And what about this whole question of integrating the genius into the team? 'A player wants to know what his teammates are going to do. Everybody is a cog in the wheel. With Adel, you didn't know from one day to the next! If someone passed to him in our half, he'd just nutmeg an opponent and lose the ball in a dangerous place … So we limited him. I banned everyone from passing to him in our half and fined them if they did! And it worked so well. To see him named player of the year was a huge reward.'

For Warnock, as with Hoddle, Smith and Mourinho, there is something hugely rewarding about spotting talent and embracing it. One of the marks of a great leader is the willingness and confidence to look for, identify, embrace, sponsor and flourish genius – even at personal cost. Football leaders then set about uniting the team around embracing the talent. This requires a clear understanding between manager and player around behaviours, boundaries and commitments; the courage to trust that the player will not let you down at either the level of performance or the level of behaviours; and a strongly held belief from all parties that the team is always greater than the individual, no matter how talented.

Allowing the Genius to Flourish

Great talent needs a stage. If the leader can help create one, then it is likely to flourish. Without a stage, it can become self-destructive.

Arriving at Chelsea for the first time, Mourinho confronted the players with their own talent: 'At the time I don't think they needed another type of leadership – I think they needed confrontational leadership. They needed a leadership to fit their motivation and fit their ambition every day. I cannot be happy by winning two matches, three matches, no – we need more and more and more. I think sometimes you are a leader and always a leader, but sometimes you can be a different kind of leader. I adapt my leadership and there I was a confrontational leader because I felt that was what the team needed at the time.

'I don't remember exactly the words, but I remember saying clearly to Frank Lampard, "You are one of the best players in the world, but nobody knows." In one of the seasons Frank was a finalist in what is now the Ballon d'Or, and I think he didn't win because he was not a European Champion. Between 2004 and 2007 he became for sure one of the best players in the world. So we motivate people also with individual challenges, and for him, for sure, that was a challenge we put there and he understood and he was ready for it. It was a brilliant phase. I learned so much with them, and I think they learned a lot with me too. If Frank's 2012 Champions League had come before, he would have been voted the best. Chelsea were stronger in 2004 and 2008 – but that is the magic of football.'

The blend of individual and team motivation and behaviours is at the heart of what Mourinho does best. 'For any new player arriving, the integration is about getting him to understand we are organised in every aspect and he has to follow us – times, tactics, routines – he has to do it, he has to adapt. We will not change to him, he has to change. So it is about making him feel and understand that he is a special talent, yes – but before him we were a special team … and this special team wants to improve and needs him in order to improve.' Get it right, and the mutual dependence of individual genius and high-performing team becomes a winning formula.

Howard Wilkinson and Eric Cantona

Howard Wilkinson has the distinction of being the last English manager to win the English league – with Leeds United in 1991, the final season of the Football League before the introduction of the Premier League. He had already created a team of distinction when he seized the chance to introduce to English football the mercurial genius of Eric Cantona. The context was not straight-forward: 'When I brought him on loan to Leeds United, he had just been rejected after trialling at Sheffield Wednesday. At that point, I think he'd had something like ten clubs in his native France. His departures from some of these clubs had been, shall we say, "colourful".

'Because of our loan agreement with Marseille, there came a point towards the end of our Championship season when we had to decide whether to buy him for £2.2 million or return him to France. Ironically, the Saturday before that decision was due, he came on in a home game at Elland Road and scored a wonder goal. The crowd were ecstatic. The chairman, who was to pay the fee out of his own pocket, and I discussed this decision at great length. Given Eric's history, it was a huge risk but his behaviour up to that point with us had been exemplary and we decided to complete the deal. But our next season started very poorly and we couldn't get anything away from home. We were due to play an away game at QPR and on the Saturday morning I decided to leave him out of the team and told him so before lunch. By one o'clock he had left the hotel and we had no idea where he's disappeared to. Eventually we found out he was back in France and I then received a transfer request from his lawyer stating that he wished to leave Leeds United and stipulating that he wanted to join Manchester United, Arsenal or Liverpool.

'In the end it was right for both parties that he moved on from Leeds – for a number of reasons. At Manchester United he found a different environment, different culture, different players, different manager and a spiritual home. He became an icon, a god.' Genius needs the right environment in which to flourish, and for Eric that environment was Manchester United. Similarly, Gordon Strachan, who I bought from Alex three years before, had become an icon and a god at Leeds United. Just like Eric, his move from Manchester United and Sir Alex Ferguson to join me at Leeds

United had allowed him to find his spiritual home. That's the nature of football sometimes.'

Across at Old Trafford, Sir Alex remembers Cantona with almost fatherly fondness: 'Eric had a presence about him. He knew he had come to the club of his birth. When I signed him I decided I was going to forget all the stories from his past and allow him to free himself from the inhibitions that were surrounding the boy. What he really wanted was to be loved. He wanted to come to a club that played to his style and I think he got that with us. He was a fantastic player. I remember we played Sheffield United at Bramall Lane in the FA Cup and the home supporters were giving him stick. So he chipped the goalkeeper and then turned to them to say, "That'll teach you."'

If the trick to diffusing the capacity to harm others is to invest in the player and integrate him into the team, it seems that the self-destructive question might have a similar solution. The genius can flourish in a solid team environment. This may take considerable effort from the leader: confronting, nurturing, appreciating, encouraging, challenging. It will also take considerable effort from the player – which not every player is willing to devote – yet another challenge to the leader of genius. The greatest talents of all, of course, work hard and selflessly put their talents at the disposal of the team. But then, as Ancelotti says, there are precious few of those.

Embracing the Expectation

In the world of José Mourinho, there is always expectation. The world expects much of him and his players; he and his players expect much from each other. For him, it is a source of energy – and one of the things he loves most about English football: 'The Barclays Premier League is an incredible competition. I feel very fortunate as a coach and as a manager because I have now worked in four countries – Spain, Italy, England and Portugal. The good thing is to have the chance to compare the different emotions and the experiences of different competitions. We can always discuss the qualities of the football in the different countries, but not about the emotions of the game or the atmosphere as in England. The atmosphere, the intensity and the emotion in England is something you cannot compare with other countries and for somebody that is really in love with the game, as I am, this is the place where you enjoy it the most.'

When Mourinho arrived in England in 2004, everything came together in one huge wave of opportunity: 'Chelsea was a moment in my career where the expectations were in the right moment for myself, and I think they were in the right moment for that group of players and I think we met each other in the right moment in our careers. I was coming from Porto – European Champions and so on – but English culture demands more. It demands you are successful here. Not there, here! This is the country of football. OK, you won the Champions League. You can have it. But come in and do it again now here.

'So I was there in the right moment. And for the boys – people are calling them some of the best in the world after we win; but when I arrive, people in England know Lampard is good, Terry is good, this guy is good, that guy is good, but no impact abroad because before they [had] won nothing. It was like a collision of moments and I needed at that time this kind of (go for it) mentality. The guys desperately needed to make the jump from potential to real, and I think they needed the kind of leader I was. I called it confrontational leadership: confrontation not just inside, but also outside. We make a confrontation between us and the others – this sports confrontation of which one is the best, which one is going to win … We were not afraid to say we are the best, we were not afraid to say we are going to win, or we are special, we are going to prove that we are – so it was perfect. So that season [2004–05] was a season for them to say, "We are the best in this country," and it was the season for me to say, "I'm not just very good in Portugal, I'm also very good here." So it was like an explosion of motivation on both sides.'

Mourinho doesn't just embrace expectation – he deliberately goes out to create it. By extending his confrontational leadership beyond the bounds of the club, he forces the genius of his players to emerge onto the big stage. That is an offer that talent cannot refuse.

Throughout his roller-coaster management rides, Mourinho continues to learn and adapt. 'My big learning at Chelsea the first time was the main idea of motivation of the group [through confrontation]. At Inter it was about the kind of mistake many leaders make, but which here I didn't: older players must not feel that you are there to end their careers. They must feel they have a lot to give till the last moment they are there, and probably the last period of their career will give them what the best years of their career didn't give to them. Why not? The problem comes when people are not able to make the oldest players feel that they are very important. That's why I say you have to understand everything about them: frustrations, ambitions, doubts. You have to understand a lot and work with them.'

Alex McLeish and Franck Sauzée

The story of Alex McLeish and French international sweeper Franck Sauzée brings together the themes of embracing talent and setting expectations. McLeish was manager of Edinburgh club Hibernian, and wanted to create the sort of team the fans loved: 'exciting teams with flying wingers and all that'. Sauzée was a player of exciting pedigree who had won the Champions League with Marseille in 1993. Believing the now Montpellier player had all the talent to light up Easter Road, he courted him in his own back yard – by setting clear expectations. 'Franck was never the quickest player in the world, but he was brilliant, brainy, he could see pictures before you could even see it from the side. He could hit a 60-yard ball and land it on a 50-pence piece – just an amazing individual. When I spoke to him about the possibility of coming he had fallen out of favour with the Montpellier coach and I said, "Look, Franck, I know your career inside out. I know you played for Atlanta, you went to Italy, I played against you with Scotland against France in Paris; you are a quality player. I want to bring gifted players to the club. I want you to not only be a great individual performer, but also to inspire the other ones and maybe get them to raise their game a little bit." I thought at a Scottish Premier League level the Celtic players were maybe going to be a bit too nimble for him – but give him the ball and he'll do something, so we adopted a pattern of three at the back and I played Franck in the centre of them. He was the master of all he surveyed and he ran the show from there. We had a brilliant season – we went to the cup final and lost to Celtic. Our conversation went:

Me: I want to communicate with you every day. There is going to be lots of communication and a great deal of mutual respect.

Franck: That's music to my ears because my other coach he never talks to me and when he does it is only to criticise.

Me: Well, Franck, having spoken to you I would love to work with you.

Franck: And I with you also.

'We still keep in touch. Franck is a legend in Hibs folklore. The fans absolutely adored him and we had a great footballing team with Franck in the starting line-up.'

Where there is real talent, expectation properly handled will act as fuel. Sauzée wanted nothing better than to show his paces for delighted supporters; Mourinho and his players seized the opportunity to show the world they had something special. This dimension of the winning mindset is hugely powerful. It stops short of arrogance; it takes pride in its ability.

Captivating the Talent

At the Royal Shakespeare Company, Michael Boyd commented: 'It's one thing to build such an ensemble from scratch. The trick is keeping it together. Some actors will want to work in film or television. Others will want shorter contracts. There will be those who want to be bigger fish in a small pond, getting bigger roles.'

How then to captivate the talent you've assembled? Boyd reasons: 'People will stay as long as they feel that they are growing with the company, and as long as the work is good, and they feel it gives them a profile and as long as they don't feel that their individuality is being ironed out or homogenised.'

Mourinho focuses on personal motivation and passion, reasoning that a motivated side is a stable side: 'To lead a side you must motivate it, and to motivate you must be yourself motivated. I motivate people with my own motivation. If you are fully motivated, if you show them that, if you make them feel that you have that, they will do well. If you are not a guy with motivation, with passion, how can you make other people feel passion for the game? After that I think you learn with experiences. The moment that you learn that every person is a person, that's the point you become a better leader, especially in a group like ours, in football, with very gifted people.'

In the end, charisma plays a huge part in this motivation. A leader has to engage at a human level if he wants to captivate genius. Mancini has worked with an array of disparate talent – men with contrasting personalities, but united by their skills and appetite for the game. 'When you manage a top team you have 24 or 25 players with different mentalities and they come from different countries and different cultures. It could be a problem to manage these different players. You should treat them all the same way. This can sometimes be difficult, but I know my job and I will have a good staff and together we are able to manage all these players. At Manchester City I had Mario Balotelli, I had Sergio Agüero and I had Carlos Tevez! Players like these are genius and when you are a genius you can do something well – sometimes also something bad. A manager and his staff – the staff is important – work in different ways and sometimes we make mistakes. We don't do everything well – it is impossible that we can be perfect. Some mistakes are helpful because we can learn from them. It is not only players that can make a mistake. When as a manager I make a mistake, then I apologise – and this is very important.'

Mancini certainly did something right to re-energise Carlos Tevez after his return to City from Argentina in the spring of 2012. Putting him alongside his compatriot Sergio Agüero created a spark – genius to genius – that carried their side to the title. 'I think there are some cultures that are strong: Argentina, Uruguay, these players have a strong mentality. In a difficult moment, probably because they come from a difficult life, difficult culture and when they have a good chance to win, or the chance to earn more for their family, I think they have a strong mentality.' As the subsequent season opened, Tevez went on record in the press as saying: 'The problem with Mancini was good for me. I'm enjoying football again, which is what I wanted – to feel this hunger for glory and to be happy like this. I had a pre-season like I hadn't had for a long time. I worked very hard, I feel good on the pitch, light, strong, fast.' The talent was captivated once more.

The Talented Leader

So, is there a formula for handling outrageous talent? Surprisingly, there is – or at least there are some clear pointers from the world of professional football. Not to say that applying them is at all easy – but there appear to be five key principles to consider.

1. Embrace the talent:
    As Mancini says, 'I get great results because I have great players!' Mourinho cannot imagine how anyone would not relish the chance to work with genius. Supreme talent creates possibility. The enterprising leader will welcome it.

2. Know your job and know your man:
    There is no substitute for knowledge. Hoddle takes time to understand his man, so he can motivate him at a deeper level. Mourinho takes time to understand physiology so he can discuss injuries with his players, earning for himself 'credit, respect, admiration'. And your team need to know you are a step ahead. 'How many times I have predicted things with my players and they happened? Many times – and that gives you credit and a better leadership. An example at half-time: "Boys, in this match if we go to the last 15 minutes with a draw they will take risks and we will win it." If that happens … the players say this coach is top!'

3. Offer friendship:
    You cannot be friends with every player. But for Mourinho, making the offer of friendship – welcoming his talented charges as something resembling younger brothers – has delivered success, time and again.

4. Focus on the team:
    Healthy team dynamics are crucial. If the leader can focus on the needs of the team and get his star player(s) to do so too, then the spotlight will move away from the individual and somehow illuminate the whole group.

5. Do it all with humility:
    Once again, humility is a powerful trait in a leader. There is something inspiring about the way in which the 62-year-old Warnock was prepared to be changed by the young genius of Taarabt, about Mancini's willingness to apologise when he gets it wrong and about Mourinho's recognition of his colleagues' worth that would never, ever have him travel a class above his players.

PART FOUR

Personal Leadership

CHAPTER SEVEN

PURSUING A CAREER
UNDER PRESSURE

THE BIG IDEA

Leaders are human beings too, pursuing a career just like the people they manage. By and large the further they get in their career, the greater the personal pressure leaders face. Expectations run high, demands multiply and the buck stops more definitively with them. The temptation in these circumstances to change your game plan is enormous: what if I've been wrong all this time? Alternatively a leader may decide to ignore what's in front of him and refuse to adapt: I will stick to my guns no matter what.

High-profile football leadership is a vivid example of this challenge. The job of manager in the Barclays Premier League is one of the most publicly scrutinised in the world. Amateurs think they could do a better job; experts and critics voice their opinions publicly on a daily basis. And all the time there is the sense that a manager's tenure is limited, and that his future employability depends directly on his team's short-term performance.

In testing times, leadership becomes even more critical to team success. How the leader responds in the pressure of the moment will affect everyone in the organisation, and will most likely decide the success or otherwise of his own career.

THE MANAGER

In 2010, Brendan Rodgers took over as manager of Swansea City. After one season, he had secured for them a promotion to the Premier League that few had predicted. The following season, he guided them not just to safety, but also to an impressive 11th-place finish – and playing some of the most attractive football around. Just a few weeks after the season ended, he accepted the role as successor to Kenny Dalglish at Liverpool. What makes these feats all the more remarkable is Rodgers' relative youth and limited experience as a first-team coach. Before Swansea, he had a total of just 11 months in the leading roles at Watford and Reading. And his professional playing career had come to an abrupt halt through injury at the age of 20. He became manager of Liverpool at just 39.

His Philosophy

Rodgers' philosophy is based on two major principles. The first is around playing beautiful passing football. This includes imparting to local, home-grown talent the belief that, just because they aren't Brazilian or Spanish, it doesn't mean they can't play that way. His second principle is around the club standing for something beyond its own boundaries. In other words the club needs to have a major positive impact on the local community, and give people something to believe in. 'When I work with a team, it is typically about defending our cause, defending our beliefs and how we play. My philosophy is about playing attacking and creative football to win, but always with tactical discipline. Over the years in Britain, our players – especially British players – have been told they aren't equipped to play this style of football. My philosophy is a fusion between British and European styles, tactics and ethos. I've been able to nurture and provide the cause around the principle of defending our belief in the game.'

The Challenge

All leaders experience pressure – and football's leaders are no different. The unusual thing for football leaders is the relentless intensity and public scrutiny. Senior politicians understand this to some degree, as do many other national and international figures. The job has its compensations, of course – recognition and reward, at times on a grand scale. But the pressures remain very real, and almost invariably have career implications – both real and imagined.

Reality

The pressures come at all levels: long term, short term and instant. In the long term, top-flight managers feel pressure to go some-where, to succeed, to build something, to leave a legacy. In the short term, the pressure is on to make good decisions and to produce instant results. Decisions include whether to play or not play a given player, to renew a contract or not, to play a particular formation or system on a particular day, to change things at half-time or to stick to the game plan, to hire a potential colleague or not, to pursue disciplinary action or not, to answer a press question head-on or to keep my counsel. The list is seemingly endless, and the challenges come thick and fast. And all the while, the distrac-tions are there: recent defeats, recent victories, stakeholder demands and needs from players, executives, public, press and others. Instant pressure is what any leading athlete or any student sitting exams would recognise: the pressure to perform at the big moment. The feeling, right or wrong, that it's now or never. It all hangs on this – can I do it?

The inner voice

Set alongside the challenges of reality are the challenges of the imagination. Almost all leaders – and competitors – know it as the 'inner voice'. When British Olympic champion Sally Gunnell overcame illness to break the world record for the 400m hurdles in Stuttgart in 1993, her main emotion was sheer disbelief. She had just added World Championship gold to her Olympic gold – but the personal hurdles along the way had been greater than the simple wooden barriers on the track. Two years before, her biggest opponent had been her inner voice – or as her coach called it, the 'duck on her shoulder'. She was a superb athlete, with amazing potential – and yet she says: 'The voice constantly sowed doubts and negativity.'

Leaders of all hues suffer from a deep underlying sense of inadequacy. The acknowledged number one fear of CEOs is the fear of being found out. Do I really have what it takes? We look into a mirror and we know that deep down there is greatness inside. Then once more frustration sets in: 'If that's true, then why don't I …? Why can't I …?' and the accusing voice takes over again. It is easy to assume that the primary leadership challenge is: 'How do I get the most from my people? If I can create a consistently high-performing team, then we will all be happy and successful (my people, me, stakeholders, shareholders).' But the reality is that the leadership challenge starts inside.

When Brendan Rodgers was first confronted by the tidal wave of daily responsibility at Watford, he admits he was dealing with anxiety: 'I'd been a coach, and been in the background, but now I was in poll position. Yes, I think some fear drives you, I think it still does: fear of failure, fear to not let people down that becomes the lever to drive you on … But I generally felt excited. There was a nervousness, taking those first steps. I was as prepared as anyone could be, but there were still those butterflies.' Did he encounter the negative voice? 'Yes, absolutely. Whatever I'm looking at, the glass is always half full and where there is a negative, there is a positive intention behind it somewhere. So my thought process goes to why is that a negative reaction, then look at the positive element of it. So there's no doubt every sportsperson would go through those feelings of that inner voice, but I'll always try to rebound off the positive voice.'

Walter Smith's inner voice tries to kick in when he makes a mistake. He responds with a rational honesty: 'I think if you're in management, the first thing that you do realise is that you are going to get things wrong. You will make mistakes if you're in a position where you have to make decisions. No one will ever make 100 per cent correct decisions in their management career. They just won't. But you have to get the majority of the bigger decisions correct the majority of times. So my philosophy is to be honest with yourself. All the way through my management career I have tried to assess objectively my own performance as a manager. You have to be brutally honest in that respect.'

Alex McLeish freely admits, 'I've still got the bad parrot that appears every so often, the negative parrot that appears and I get a bit of foreboding at times. However, throughout my career, I've been able to firmly dispel most of these thoughts.' Writer and former tennis pro Tim Gallwey calls it interference. For Gunnell it's a duck; for McLeish it's a parrot. However it shows up, it can lessen a leader's potential and reduce their effectiveness. All leaders have to deal with it, or it will amplify their pressure at every level.

The Story

We do not live in isolation. What we say, what we do, how we spend our time and energy – all these things not only define our own journey, but they impact on everyone around us. Great leaders tell great stories – stories that hang together, are relevant to their people, are engaging and compelling. A great story allows the leader to rise above the pressures – long term, short term and instant. And as the story unfolds, he is not simply navigating his own career path – his is creating meaning for other people.

It may sound suspiciously like a formula. But great leadership stories have three components that define them: a source of inspiration, a trajectory (some sort of life and career progression) and a goal (some sort of destination). They also have two foundational elements: a clear philosophy and the ability to learn and grow. These five components contribute to the leader's story, impacting others and enabling him to pursue a career under pressure.

Where the Story Begins: Relying on your Source of Inspiration

All great stories begin somewhere. When we meet fascinating people, we want to know where they came from – what shaped the person standing in front of us. We want to know if that source could shape us too. Strong leaders will have a well-defined source of inspiration – someone or something that they recognise openly as having shaped them, and to which they look back when they need to make sense of life.

In football, as in other fields of endeavour, these sources of inspiration differ from one leader to the next. But almost every leader can give an example of a great figure from their own profession who continues to be for them a powerful anchor point.

Brendan Rodgers

Rodgers' story began to take shape at Reading when he was a 13-year-old boy – not so much because of the football he played, but because of the influence of a man he admired. 'I played my first game at 13. Then, after travelling to various clubs, I got an offer to go to Reading at 16. The first-team manager at the time, Ian Branfoot, was a terrific influence on me. I felt he had a real duty of care not only for me as a footballer, but also as a human being. So I gravitated towards him because of that feeling: he made me feel important.' Rodgers would take that philosophy with him into his leadership for the rest of his career. But on a higher level, Ian Branfoot simply inspired him to become a manager. 'I look back now at what he did: first-team manager at the football club, and he used to pick me up from the airport and make sure I was home. He would make me feel important every time I was over [from Northern Ireland]. He would just do that little bit more for me and that would make me feel important and special. I sensed the real power and strength of the man. In those early days I could see how hard he worked. There was a real work ethic: he was the manager, but he was also locking up at the end of the day.'

José Mourinho

Mourinho would also go on to play a significant role in Rodgers' story. Meanwhile, one of his own great sources of inspiration goes a fair way to explain his affinity with England. 'I was a lucky man because I have had some crucial moments in my career and one of the crucial moments was when I had the chance to work with Mr Robson.' The young Mourinho famously encountered Sir Bobby Robson at Sporting Clube de Portugal in the early 1990s, where Mourinho worked as his interpreter. They would go on to work together at FC Porto and at Barcelona before Mourinho struck out on his own. 'He was not just a great manager – he was a great person. I think everybody that had the chance to meet him and had a few moments, or in my case a few years, felt privileged. I learned so much from my experiences with him. I always remember with a little smile that after I was upset by a defeat he said, "Don't be sad because in the other dressing room someone is bouncing around with happiness." So I always remember good moments with him, and every moment was a good one.'

André Villas-Boas

Villas-Boas' first interest in embarking on a football career came from a chance encounter with the same man who would become both his and Mourinho's great inspiration. 'I was a fan of Porto. Bobby Robson was the manager, and he came to live in the apartment block where I lived! Out of the blue, without me making questions to him, he took me on board and started taking me to training sessions. My first thought was I have access to something normal people don't have, because he would take me to training and he would give me his training session plans! It was truly interesting. Obviously, when you are a young boy, everybody wants to be a football player, but not everybody has the talent to do it. I didn't have the talent, but I wanted something relating to the game and I found this interest in managing from being with Robson on a daily basis. Then I went on the coaching courses and that opened the door for me to start coaching at Porto.'

Chris Hughton

Hughton cites two contemporary managers as inspirational for him: Glenn Hoddle and Martin Jol. Hughton served under no fewer than ten managers during a 14-year period as assistant at Spurs, but these two stand out for him: 'Glenn was a talker. He was very much involved in everything that we did, and Glenn would generally get excited. We would speak in the changing room or in his office, we would speak about players he was trying to get and the positions he was trying to put them in. There would be a real genuine excitement about players and about the work that he was doing. Martin was the man who got me most involved – where I grew the most. He was a really good coach and a really good man.'

Why it works: the reference point

Each manager has his own reference point: Carlo Ancelotti knows how much he owes to Nils Liedholm, as does Keegan to Shankly and Paisley. When someone is determined to take up this uniquely exacting profession, it is almost always because of someone they respect and admire in the game. Knowing who that is – and what it is they admire – provides a reference point for years to come. The story of Villas-Boas and Sir Bobby Robson is a perfect case in point: 'From the conversations that we had he obviously saw in me a boy full of motivation and interest in being a manager, and whether in football or business, a truly motivated person is able to transcend himself when he is doing something that he loves. Then he can achieve something that is difficult to achieve. So when I think of Bobby Robson, I remember that he saw in me the motivation that I had to become a coach, even at a young age, and he chose me to work with him.' When times get tough, and the unfolding story becomes unclear, Villas-Boas understands at least this one thing: Sir Bobby believed in his potential. Whatever pressures threaten the leader's story, the source of inspiration remains intact.

As the Story Unfolds: Making Sense of your Career Progression

For all of us, the story unfolds one episode at a time. At times we feel in control, at other times not at all. As his career takes shape, the leader needs constantly to be making sense of what is happening, maintaining a perspective that allows him to make good decisions going forward. In leaders' stories there are defining moments: where and how their career began, how opportunities arose, how they performed at the new level, how they took the tough decisions. A leader needs to reflect on these and put them into context if his story is to hang together well.

Getting started

In the event, Rodgers played senior football for only four years. A recurring injury that would have demoralised most people was the spur for him to move into something exciting and new. 'In my final year at Reading I was injured quite a bit, so I took some reflective time. I genuinely felt that I'd wanted to be the best I could, and play at the highest level I could. Now at 20 I realised that I wasn't going to play at the level I wanted because of my knee. I was a typical player, good technically, gifted; I believed I knew the game. I could go and play non-league football, but I didn't have the physical qualities to do what I wanted. I probably came to a conclusion much quicker than other people and I made the decision that if I couldn't play at the highest level then I would set my sights on one day coaching at the highest level.' So Rodgers arrived in the manager's chair through a mixture of circumstance, decisiveness and resilience. Looking back, he would understand the value of these qualities – including his ability to rise above personal disappointment.

Many leaders take strength from the way their careers began. Howard Wilkinson may have stumbled into football coaching, but he realised from the earliest moments that he was built for it: 'It was a Road to Damascus moment. I was in Brighton in 1966 [aged 22, playing for Brighton & Hove Albion]. I was in digs, and I was bored. I went down to the gym pre-season, saw a coaching course advertised and thought I'd give it a go – one night a week and a Sunday morning and it'll be something to do. Within two sessions, I knew that was what I wanted to do. It was as if I'd walked into a shop and found a suit that was made to measure.' It still took some effort, of course. Wilkinson studied for his licences, and, aged 27, made his decision: 'I thought, I can go on playing here or I can do something about what I want to do. I spoke to the Director of Coaching at the FA, Alan Wade, and he suggested I'd learn a lot from a degree in physical education. So I went as player/coach to Boston United with Jim Smith and followed a degree course at the same time. Within a year Jim left, and the chairman at Boston asked me to take over. I was now 28 and in charge of a football team.' Wilkinson was up and running.

Seizing the moment

Sometimes the opportunity to move on and up comes to you when you least expect it. Rodgers' reputation for building something different in the youth team at Reading had attracted the attention of Steve Clark who had been the youth coach at Chelsea. Rodgers recalls: 'I'd had ten great years at Reading as a coach, developing all the way through. I felt like I was on a magic carpet ride – it was fantastic. I loved my career; I loved my life. But then I felt it was time to test my ideas and way of thinking – could all that work at a club that was looking to move into the European elite? José got the job [at Chelsea] in June 2004, and Steve Clark did a pre-season with him, so had got to know and understand what he was looking for in the youth role. And, of course, Steve's teams played against my teams, so he understood the kind of thing

I was doing. The club was restructuring the academy, and the academy director, Neil Bath, had been put in place and was really starting from scratch. So in September they asked me to help form the youth structure – something that José supported at the top end. I was being asked to implement a philosophy that was close to my own way of thinking.' Rodgers hadn't realised he was ready to move on – he was just enjoying doing what he did. But when the call came, he knew it was for him. One of the key skills for leaders pursuing careers is to recognise opportunities when they present themselves. It then requires a choice and often courage to make the move.

Like Rodgers, Hope Powell was very happy in her career. She was 30 years old and still playing when the Football Association called: 'I thought they were going to ask me to work with a new youth team that were setting up – but they offered me the senior England job. It was a real shock. I asked all sorts of questions and debated it – I wasn't quite sure. In the end, someone said to me, "Look if you don't take the job you'll be in the changing room sitting there thinking actually I should have done it." My family and friends also told me I'd be an idiot not to take it! I loved the game, I wanted to get paid for working in the game and suddenly I had my chance.'

Hughton had spent 14 years as a coach at his old club Tottenham Hotspur when he seized the opportunity to take a step closer to management with a move to Newcastle United. He describes it as a deliberate 'move out of my comfort zone'. 'I had decided that management was what I wanted. I got a call from Kevin Keegan. Although I didn't really know him, I'd met him on a number of occasions – normally when Spurs played Manchester City. He asked if I'd be interested in going to Newcastle and assisting him. For me at that time, having had so much time at Tottenham and all of my time in London, that request was too good an opportunity to turn down. It was the road to management – a completely different direction for me, but one I knew I had to take.'

For some managers, the call comes unexpectedly. Others find something stirring inside them, realise it's time and decide to go looking for it. What they all seem to have in common is the courage to seize the opportunity when it comes.

Life on the Big Stage

Many excellent football coaches never manage leading sides. The ones who do have to adapt pretty fast to life on the big stage. The figures make harsh reading: the average tenure for a manager in English professional football is 16 months and 55 per cent of all first-time football managers are never appointed to a second management job.

In 2007, Mourinho left Chelsea. Rodgers describes that time as 'three years of working with arguably the best day-to-day manager in world football'. Rather than seeing Mourinho's departure as a setback, Rodgers viewed it as an opportunity to move up a gear in readiness for the big chance: 'I then had a year's experience of working without him. I felt by working alone I would be fully prepared for what would come next. I had worked with kids of eight and nine through to some of the biggest talents in world football, and I felt I had gained the respect and confidence of players at that level, both from a technical coaching and from a human perspective. So I believed that if I got the opportunity I would be prepared to give that a go and take on the challenge alone.'

In 2008, after nearly 15 years on the coaching journey, Rodgers finally got the opportunity at Watford, a supportive club that was renowned for giving young managers a chance. 'I will always be grateful for the great start that Watford gave me. Although I have to say that the first day walking out at Vicarage Road when the curtains went back and the lights were shining right on me, it felt like I'd had no preparation at all!' Later, he realised that wasn't the case: 'After a short time I realised that all that learning and all that underpinning knowledge was gold, and held me in great stead for my journey as a manager. But I also felt very much that I was now responsible. Now I had not only thousands of active supporters, but also a whole city looking at me. I felt inspired.'

A fascinating feature of leaders under pressure is how they are inspired by it. Analysts in the City and soldiers in the desert pick up on it quickly: the appetite for the big challenge is half the battle. For leaders, welcoming pressure is an integral part of pursuing a career.

The tough decisions

As leaders become successful, so more opportunities arise. The leader who adapts to the big stage and succeeds can expect to face some tough decisions. For Rodgers, after just seven months at his new club, this happened when his old club came calling: 'It happened pretty quickly. I had no desire at all to leave Watford. My plan had been to be at Watford for four or five years. The club had given me a chance, and I wanted to repay them that favour – stay for a significant period of time and learn from the ups and the downs. In the end, my heart overruled my head. I would never have left Watford for any other club, but with Reading it was like going back home. They were the first club I went to at 16, they were a club I felt I knew, they had been in the Premier League, they'd been relegated, they'd just missed out on promotion again and it was a great challenge. But the biggest thing for me was knowing the chairman. I was given a great bit of advice early on in my career, which was if you are a young manager pick the chairman and not so much the club. That's what happened at Watford – the chairman gave the young manager a chance. And going to Reading I knew I would be working with a good chairman. We had a strong relationship. It was definitely a case of the heart taking me back. Once I made the decision I was OK, but it was far from ideal.'

Rodgers tends to make his career decisions at a heart level because of the make-up of his personality. Others will deal with them quite differently. Hope Powell, even with her first big decision, was sceptical: 'To be perfectly honest I thought it was a token gesture. Female, black – I thought it ticked a box and I wasn't prepared to be a tick in the box. There was a player more experienced than me in terms of playing ability, probably not in terms of qualifications, who was the England captain at the time so I challenged [the FA] – why not them, why me? They had to convince me that they'd really looked at my credentials, my reputation on the field (I only had one yellow card in my whole career), that I was well respected in the game as a player … I only wanted the job if they believed I could do it. Once I took the job, I knew I could not fail, because it could have been, "Well, there you go – we've put a woman in place and they aren't up to it." I wasn't going to have that.'

Why it works: self-awareness and self-belief

Leaders who take time to understand their own career journey – how they began, how opportunities have arisen, how they've adapted and how they've made decisions – these leaders develop self-awareness.

After more than 30 years as a football leader, Neil Warnock knows where his strengths lie – and where they don't: 'I think I have been naturally a leader since about 20 years of age. I always quite enjoyed getting my point over! I was never good enough to be a top player, but I knew what I wanted a team to be. I now know that I'm great at leading in the Championship. There's a lot I don't enjoy about the Premier League – the money that's involved, the money that players earn, the discipline, the morals – but I am proud to have led both Sheffield United and QPR into the Premier League. For me, the Championship is more of a workingman's bread and butter – I enjoy the cut and thrust. I'm good at getting clubs promoted. I've done it seven times, and I want to set the record by doing it again.'

This self-awareness is an important step to self-belief. Sports psychologist Professor Graham Jones defines this as an objective understanding of our own abilities to deliver against what is required. This is an excellent tool to have when tasked with rapid and difficult daily decision-making, and the perfect antidote to the pressure of the moment. The heightened tension that comes from inflated expectation can all too easily knock a leader off balance. With self-belief, he can be what his players need him to be – strong, assured and calm.

Managers who are confident in their proven abilities find they have the inner resource to deal with heightened tension. For Rodgers it is about taking ownership: 'I bring it all back to personal responsibility. I have a lot of help from lots of people – lots of support, lots of influences – and I'm grateful for it. But I've arrived where I've arrived by being out there and taking my own responsibility, rather than waiting for the phone to ring or somebody to support me. Knowing what I am capable of has served me well in the tough times – on and off the field. My parents died young, so there have been lots of personal challenges as well as professional. That inner steel, that resolve, that perseverance, has served me well since my time at Reading. I know it's there.' This is the mark of a leader under career pressure. Success is often dependent on inner strength and perseverance, and these in turn are often built up through adversity.

For Carlo Ancelotti, self-belief includes a commitment to what others believe is a weakness: 'Sometimes when I had a problem, at Milan, the owner would say you are too kind, you have to shout and fight against the players. I know I am kind because it is in my character. My philosophy is if you have a horse and you try to teach it to jump, you can stay behind the horse with your whip or you can go to the other side of the jump with a carrot. The result may be the same, but with the whip you stay behind and the horse can kick! And I am not dealing with horses. I am dealing with professional, adult men. We manage men with big responsibilities – family, kids, lots of money. Such a man has to take the responsibility to be professional and motivated.' Others may criticise: Ancelotti knows what works for him and believes in his abilities. He may adapt his approach, but his self-belief means he won't try to change the essence of who he is.

And, of course, both self-awareness and self-belief are excellent weapons against the inner voice, providing the right focus and the inner strength. The Alex McLeish approach is excellent: 'How do I shoot the parrot? I rely on past experiences. I think, "Well, wait a minute. I've got presence in this game; I've been successful. I've solved problems before – I can do it again." You can't get your knickers in a twist. I've seen some coaches and some colleagues say, "What if they win tomorrow and we don't?" and they all sit by the television looking for the results. If I can't control it, I leave it. I block all of that out and try and stay in the focus of what my own team is going to do.' As theologian Reinhold Niebuhr has it: 'God grant me the serenity to accept the things I cannot change, the courage to change the things I can, and the wisdom to know the difference.' Mick McCarthy cites that very quote: 'Those are really wise words for me. I can't change what happened at Wolves. I had my opportunity – I had five and a half years, great years, I look back and think I am satisfied with my time there. I'm proud of what I achieved at Wolves with a million quid and ten new players. So I look back and for 90 per cent of it or more I can pat myself on the back and say, "Well done, mate."'

Where the Story is Headed: Keeping your Purpose in Mind

At some stage of a manager's journey to becoming a true football leader, he realises the significance of knowing his own mind. He begins to ask questions: What do I really want from all this? What will I stand for? What will I become known for? He may have developed self-awareness and self-belief, but the future can still cause anxiety.

As Rodgers grew at Reading, those answers became clearer. 'I had a pretty straightforward objective: to make a difference. I knew if I wanted to coach at the highest level, I would have to be able to have real impact. I had grown up with a wide range of football influences. My father and grandfather were big lovers of Liverpool in the 1970s and 80s, Brazil in the 1970s and 80s, the flair, the crea- tivity – so I grew up with that. Then I was told British players aren't technically or tactically as good as European players – "British players can't do that." So as a young player I spent more time without the ball than with it. The process of knowing myself began with understanding that I couldn't make a difference as a player, but that I could do as a manager. Could I provide a different pathway for young players to get to the top, and maybe one day leave a trail to follow? But to begin with I held a simple objective: could I make a difference to the young kid who is told he isn't technically good enough and he's just got to run and fight? Could I merge the great qualities of the British personality and *also* the technical qualities he certainly has? That was the beginning.' Rodgers was beginning to understand himself. His career goals were forming.

Some 20 years later, Rodgers has emerged as a thoughtful, determined and optimistic leader who inspires through purpose and vision. 'I love the challenge and the excitement most of all. I've spent my life always being comfortable in the leading role. I've played and I've been a loyal assistant in a variety of roles, but I've felt most comfortable when I've been leading a group. My start point when I come across any group of people – but in particular football players – is to find a right, or better still a cause, which the people will fight for. I believe that people will fight for a right, and even die for a cause. So I try to find a cause, which the group can sign up to. After that I seek to provide the vision and the pathway that allows us to defend that cause. When I arrived at Swansea I tied in the city to the feeling, the emotions. My mission was inspiring the city. That was it really. That is the journey that I've wanted everyone to be on.' A taxi driver outside the Liberty Stadium unknowingly proved the point when he told me: 'I love Brendan Rodgers. He gave us all something to believe in. And I love the style of football we play.'

In recent years, Sir Alex Ferguson inspired many through his determination and will to keep on leading and keep on winning. Shortly before his 70th birthday, he commented that he was 'too old to retire'! José Mourinho, for whom Sir Alex is another significant source of inspiration, loved this: 'When I heard Sir Alex say this I was laughing because I was not surprised. He has an incredible humour, but at the same time brightness and common sense. For me he is amazing as he is the same person I met in 2004. I have more white hair and more wrinkles, but he is exactly the same. When I am in my 50s or 60s, I also see myself still in football with the same ambitions and desires. I understand why Sir Alex wanted to continue. It was the same with Mr Robson and I see myself continuing for many years.'

Why it works

For Rodgers it's about making a difference. For Sir Alex it was about keeping on winning. For Mourinho it's about staying at the top of the game for 20 more years. Rodgers, Ferguson and Mourinho all have purpose and drive. Just as a mark on the horizon offers a compass bearing, so a clear purpose keeps a leader's career on track.

Foundation One: Staying True to your Philosophy

These managers clearly illustrate the first three essential components of the leader's story: the inspiration, which often kicks it off and acts as a reference point; the career progression and handling of defining moments, which creates foundations for self-awareness and self-belief; and the career goal, which creates purpose and drive. The next component that underpins a leader's story, and one that football managers speak of with enormous passion, is philosophy. How I think. How I think about my work, my people. How I think about football.

Ancelotti explains its importance very simply: 'When your 11 players run on to the field, it is your philosophy that they are about to act out.' José Mourinho concurs: 'I think it is very important for every manager to have their own philosophy for everything

– the way you want your team to play, the way you want to lead your team, the way you want to work every day – everything must be very specific. To have a mentor is one thing; to try and copy is another. With a mentor you can improve and have a base for evolution, but when you try and copy, the copy is never the same as the original. So I think you have to learn from people with more experience who have had success, but always keep your own personal identity.'

Being Reading's first-team manager did not work out for Rodgers. In essence, it was a turnaround task that went wrong. Reflecting on the painful experience of his short (seven-month) tenure, Rodgers lays the blame squarely on his own shoulders: 'I got the timing wrong. I tried to create a lull in the club, and build over three years. I never really grasped the club's expectations, and I set them some unrealistic targets.' This may well be right – and sound leaders tend to accept responsibility rather than deflect it. But the root cause is worth examining. Under the pressure of career expectation – sensing the judgements being made of him as a coach and manager – Rodgers made a dangerous error: he moved away from his philosophy. 'We just weren't getting the success. It was too sporadic. We'd play really well, see lots of elements of the philosophy, then we'd lose again. The defining moment for me came at Loftus Road against QPR. I went for a team that was steadier, more solid. I remember standing watching the game, and the players were terrific there – they were real good, honest players. But it wasn't a team of mine I was watching. We lost that game 4-1. I had gone away from my beliefs. I hadn't inspired the team. We had a mismatch between what the players were trying to do and what I was trying to do. I had lost my integrity as a manager.'

This was a career-defining moment for Rodgers. A leader's philosophy is so significant that, if he departs from it, then he departs from his true self. Not long after – just a few months into the job he had so wanted – Rodgers left Reading. Crucially, he remained in learning: 'I came away after that and did some reflecting and soul searching. I needed to go back to my beliefs, whether or not we pulled it off. If I was going to go down I was going to go the way I wanted to. For the first time in my life I had veered off the track I was on, and I couldn't accept that. From that day I was in a better place.'

This demonstrates the power of reflection. Rodgers returned to his deep instincts and his true vision – the self he really knows. It was too late to save his post at Reading – but he had his integrity back. And that would be his springboard to success. Six months later he was offered the manager's job at Swansea City, the ambitious Welsh club looking to reach the Premier League for the first time. He had learned some real lessons: 'By the time I began at Swansea, I had renewed belief in my philosophy. In fact, that belief was probably greater than before: but I had to be more clinical in my decision-making and get to the end point much quicker than I had at Reading.'

Why it works

Leaders who stay true to their philosophy – true to themselves – are inspirational. They're almost unshakeable – which can be inspirational in itself.

Swansea came as a great opportunity for Rodgers, but it certainly carried a feel of 'now or never'. 'It was a hand-in-glove fit. The club had started out on a comprehensive cycle [of renewal] five or six years before, and the board wanted a certain way of working and playing. So I came in and now I had to show my character. I had thought my career as a manager was over before it had started and

I hadn't known whether I was going to get a chance. But now I knew the rules of the game. The experience at Reading had taught me that. I now knew I was in the business of winning.'

Strongly held philosophies work. Swansea and a complete commitment to his dream appear to have been the making of Rodgers. Building on foundations laid, among others, by Roberto Martinez, he crafted a side that distinguished itself playing fluent, passing football. In his first season, Swansea won promotion to the Premier League via the play-off final at Wembley where they beat Reading 4-2. The pressure was relentless. The bookmakers immediately installed Swansea as favourites for relegation, and the talk was of a season of ten points. Instead, sticking to Rodgers' attractive brand of flowing football, they finished a notable 11th – highest of the season's three newcomers, a mere seven points behind Liverpool, and claiming such notable scalps as eventual champions Manchester City along the way.

The offers were bound to come, and within weeks of the season ending, Rodgers had made the big move to Liverpool. On his first day, he began publicly to rally the club and the city behind his philosophy and vision: 'I promise I'll fight for my life and for the people in this city. This is long term, and that appeals to me. I am very proud. I feel I have been blessed with the opportunity to manage the club. I am really looking forward to working with some of the greats of this football club. For me it will take a bit of time to introduce how I want to play and the philosophy I want to bring.'

Foundation Two: Remaining in Learning

The final component of the leader's story is a mindset for continued growth and learning. Great leaders never stop learning. From the beginning of their story there is an appetite for their work that drives them on; and throughout their career, they remain committed to growth.

Building a solid foundation of skills

At some stage in their career journey, all successful football managers build a skill base that will eventually ensure they are equipped to handle the demands of a career at the top. These technical capabilities and the ability to communicate, teach and coach will form the basis for what they do each day and will give them credibility among professional players, regardless of age. As Sam Allardyce says, 'You need to know how to plan and make the sessions the right way because footballers are very quick to pick up on what you do wrong!' Beyond the daily work, this deep understanding of the game will be a bedrock at moments of high pressure. Like Mourinho showing his players that he has reliable knowledge in every relevant area, Allardyce comments, 'I know this stuff. No one knows it better than me.'

As a young man, Rodgers invested in building a solid foundation. For ten years he coached young players at Reading in a sequence of appointments that took him from one age group to the next. 'It was a constant progression, growing in each role and moving up every two or three years. Every season was a step forward. The club was growing, the players were growing, the staff were growing and obviously then I was growing with them as well. There was no single defining moment – it was a lot of hard work from many different people that allowed us to grow and grow our way of playing and working.'

Dario Gradi provides a perfect illustration of how to remain in learning even after decades of experience. 'You have to keep learning. I always say that to the coaches and players. Even when I'm coaching the under-12s, I tell them "you haven't come here to have fun – you've come here to learn. So listen, learn and work at it." I'm still learning. I'm not just having fun. I do enjoy it, of course, but I tell them "I'm here to teach you and it's not much fun if you don't learn. My fun comes from you learning. I know I'm a good teacher because I've taught a lot of people to become good players. But I'm no good if you don't learn so you've got to play your part in it."'

This message of hard work and determination is the common thread to high-achieving managers as they lay the bedrock of their skills – however and wherever they happen to build it. Allardyce says, 'You *can* get a job without coaching badges, based on your experience and what you've done as a player throughout your career. Coaching badges are a good way forward, but I always felt I could coach – I could decide on my experiences in football what I had to do. I was 28, and I realised that what I most needed to get was a skill in management. I found out that the PFA ran management courses from a business school in St Helens, adapted for football. The lectures were generic, teaching us to manage in any industry – which I liked. They had a sort of crash course – we had little or no time then as we were still playing so we only got that small summer period. I had to adapt it to football a bit myself – think about what happens for a manager when he gets his job – and that was the interesting bit.'

For the ones who are deliberately building something over time, there is a danger of frustration and wanting to seize the reins too early – not a mistake that Rodgers made: 'I was fine because I was so young. I had time to grow. I was a sponge for knowledge, and I had an inherent belief in young players. My ethos was always to find them, to care for them, and to develop them. The only frustrations I ever had in that time were wanting to have the best facilities, wanting to have the best players. But the challenge was hugely formative. I was asking the players to play differently, and all the time there was questioning from senior officials at the club: why would we be playing that way when the first team play like this? I stuck with it. It wasn't conflict; it was education. I learned to be happy with the sense of thinking differently. Exercises were different, team management was different, how I was preparing the team to play was different.' When others might have felt hindered, Rodgers saw it as learning.

For David Moyes, learning and self-development is – and always has been – a driving passion: 'I think you have to have a real desire to go and find it. You can read books and you can learn and you can pick up things, but I had a real passion. I wanted to get out on the road and I wanted to find new things. I qualified as a coach very young, but my reason for becoming a coach was really to become a better player. Then the more I went on the coaching courses, the more I started to think I really enjoy being around people who talk about football. I couldn't wait to be standing at the side listening in – talking to the Scottish coaches about football.'

Moyes studied for and achieved his UEFA pro licence not once, but twice – in England as well as Scotland. 'Once you are qualified, it doesn't matter which country you become a qualified coach in. But I wanted to show that I could do it in both countries and I wanted to see if there was a difference in the two badges – and there was! Again, I was trying to educate myself. I was a player and I played all season, and when you got four to six weeks in the summer you had to take a big chunk out of that to do your coaching. But it was sort of a holiday for me because I really enjoyed being around and listening to football people.'

A real and lasting commitment

As Moyes' summer programme testifies, truly to adopt a learning mindset requires a real commitment. In 1998, at the very outset of his career as a professional coach, he desperately wanted to go to the World Cup in France to observe training and preparations first hand. 'There was a period of time [around the 1998 World Cup] when I wasn't a wealthy footballer by certain standards. To be fair, I had support from the English PFA who helped pay for my tickets to the games because they understood that I was trying to be involved with some coaching in the national side and they helped with funding. But I just didn't have that level of cash to be in a different hotel each night. So I hired a car and I drove myself, two or three times sleeping in the car. That year I had gone to a lot of the countries to ask if I could go and watch training, but found that it's not easy to get into the international training camps – they can be a bit guarded and security conscious. Strangely enough the only people who said I could come and watch were Craig Brown and his team at the Scotland camp. No disrespect but, in truth, the last people I wanted to see were Scotland – I knew these guys pretty well already! But I ended up going and watching Scotland training and preparing for the World Cup and it was very valuable.'

Moyes would also argue that the commitment must not waver over time. It's important to remain in learning, whatever the circumstances. As recently as summer 2012, determined to see at first hand the European Championships unfolding in the Ukraine, he ended up staying in a youth hostel when he was too late to find a hotel. 'Just because you get your job, you can't put your feet under the table and say "I've made it now and this is it." Self-learning and self-development is essential for me. I watch a lot of football just because I know there are a lot of things I can pick up. If I was out of work I'd go to South America and have a look at what they are doing – at why so many players now in Europe and the Champions League are from Uruguay, Brazil, Argentina ... I'd love to get out there for a couple of months and see if there's anything that maybe I'm missing and that I could introduce to what we do.'

He concedes it's a challenge to find enough time for this when you are leading a professional outfit full time, as he does at Manchester United. 'There are other things happening closer to home too. When I see how Spain have improved, and how Germany are bringing on all their younger players on a conveyor belt – there is so much I would like to do given more time. I don't think I'll ever find the complete answer to all of it, but to go and have a look is always a good beginning.'

Why it works

Mick McCarthy is a great example of how learning works. He does not suggest that he is a Moyes-style learner – but he finds value in it all the time: 'When I look at all the things I've done in my career, and people ask me what I've learnt, I often say I have no idea. But when a situation arises then I'll know what I've learnt because I'll deal with it through my experience. Most of us would like to have a solution that we could write down and say, "This is how I do it." I can't do that. But when it comes to leading people and making decisions, I realise how much I've learned.'

And like other components of the leader's story, the learning element works for both the leader and the people around him. People are simply inspired by leaders with a learning mindset. Moyes experienced exactly this effect from his earliest days: 'People saw me out and about, and they were saying, "There is someone who is out to learn, out there trying to improve himself." They were willing to help.'

The leader who can stay in learning even in the toughest times find it a sure route back to balance. André Villas-Boas left Chelsea in January 2012 after only nine months in charge: 'When I stopped first there was an emptiness – so I go back to my family at the beginning. Then I wanted to fill the emptiness that I was feeling with the game and learning and self-development. I went back to the things that make me the person and manager I am. I made sure that I saw as many games as possible to prepare for an eventual comeback. I watched players that I didn't have the time to see when I was working. I met together with my technical staff, the ones that went with me, to ask how we failed and why we failed to make sure we take these lessons into the future.'

The Authentic Leader

All leaders will come under pressure as they pursue their career – this is normal. Great leaders respond by ensuring that the story they are telling is joined up, compelling and full of integrity. In short, they are authentic – they lead out of who they are.

For all leaders wanting to tell an inspiring story with their life and career, these basic principles emerge.

1. Identify and rely on the source of your inspiration:
    The source for many is a person – often someone you know or knew intimately, and who has modelled for you a way of being to which you aspire. Knowing who this is and why they have inspired you is a starting point for your story, and can be an anchor for the leader under pressure.

2. Turn experience into wisdom:
    All leaders' careers will involve both decision-making and upsets. Successful leaders analyse their decisions without regret and look on upsets as contributors to growth. Making sense of their story as it unfolds – including a critical but not

destructive appraisal of their own responses – builds self-awareness and then self-belief. And these two qualities make them stronger, wiser and better leaders. Villas–Boas holds dear a quote from a Lisbon University professor called Manuel Sergio: 'He told me one thing – "the person that you are triumphs over the coach that you want to be." So in the end you are a coach, but first of all you are a person. You are who you are. You can't pretend to apply things that you don't feel.'

3. Keep your purpose in mind:
    The leaders who win know their purpose. They may adapt their style, they may change their approach, but they know what they want to achieve, what they believe and what they stand for, and they stick to it.

4. Stay true to your philosophy:
    Brendan Rodgers is an authentic leader because he has a philosophy that he stands by, he knows who he is and he doesn't have to pretend to be anyone else. His philosophies of flowing football and deriving meaning for a club and its city together enable him to deliver fully on his promises. When he went away from them, he realised his mistake and from that moment on he was able to be himself with no fear.

5. Be a serial learner:
    Great leaders have a learning mindset. The desire to learn and the ability to find learning even in the tough times sets them apart from their peers. It affirms humility over arrogance, growth instead of staleness. As Rodgers says, 'Stay at the leading edge of the game. I may grow older, but the players are still young. For their sake, I must never stand still.' Learning is the fuel to the leader's story.

CHAPTER EIGHT

SEEING THE BIGGER PICTURE

THE BIG IDEA

Leaders need to be excited by their subject and committed to their cause. Without it, they will not inspire. But the line between commitment and obsession can be a thin one, and in high-pressure environments, it can be almost impossible to see where that line needs to be. Imagine a business leader in a crisis, working all hours at his desk. At one level, it is good for him to be immersed. But how effective is he? And how long can he maintain the pace?

Managers in professional football are subject to the same traps. A series of defeats or poor performances – even a short series – creates pressure. The default reaction to this for many is to seize the problem with both hands and to wrestle with it, day and night, until it is resolved.

The motivating force for leaders under pressure can often be fear; and fear can distort reality. So they can end up spiralling into reactive and poor decision-making, losing their perspective, their health and potentially their job. Great football managers are able to work with fears, emerge from under the pressure and regain a perspective from which they can lead their team to improved performance and get to sustained success.

THE MANAGER

Harry Redknapp is one of the great characters of the English game. A successful midfield player with West Ham United in the mid–late 1960s and early 70s, he played alongside some of the true greats of the game: Geoff Hurst, Martin Peters, Bobby Moore. His professional league management career began in 1983 at Bournemouth, where he led the team for nine years, building a reputation as a great judge of footballers and as an unfussy, straight-forward leader. His break into the big time came at former club West Ham in 1994 where he produced a sustained period of high performance. He is acclaimed as the man who revived the fortunes of Portsmouth Football Club, leading them in 2002 to promotion to the Barclays Premier League for the first time. After a short time down the English south coast at Southampton, he returned to lead Portsmouth to their highest finish (ninth) in half a century, and later to FA Cup victory in 2008. In recent times he led an entertaining and talented Tottenham side to their first ever UEFA Champions League season. The ensuing Champions League campaign saw Spurs beat AC Milan over two gripping encounters to reach the last eight of the tournament. In November 2012 he was appointed as manager of Queens Park Rangers.

His Philosophy

Redknapp is a big-hearted leader who invests all of himself in whatever he does. He is passionate about football and yet he is extremely passionate about his family too, about his country and about improving the lives of people less fortunate than himself. He holds dear values he would describe as old-fashioned: responsi-bility, duty, teamwork. He is committed to attacking football, and builds entertaining sides. He is an uncomplicated man who despairs of trends in modern football, which he sees as eroding the traditional values of the simple and beautiful game.

The Challenge to Balance

High expectation, instability, stakeholders, genius, triumph, despair – managers face them all. They all create pain in the moment – the short-term challenge. But the long-term challenge to the leader in football is how to achieve and maintain a balance that will allow him to approach both the good and the bad times with equal ease, and to make the best possible decisions at every turn.

Almost all the challenges managers face are a threat to balance. Turns of events on the field, distractions off it – they can all knock a leader off his chosen path. So significant are these that Redknapp says he's almost forgotten what balance is: 'I mean, you go in in the mornings and you never know what is going to hit you. You can be with 50-odd footballers, kids, everything. "Harry, we've got a problem with this kid. He's got involved with a girlfriend whose previous boyfriend is a dangerous guy on the estate where he lives, and we've got to move the family off the estate because they are in danger." You never know what is going to hit you. Every day somebody's not well, or the mum or wife isn't well, somebody's children, there's always something going on – and these things are obviously important too. You are responsible for everybody, your coaching staff could have a problem – it's really non-stop. Now with mobile phones you are never away from it, you are on call 24 hours a day really.' One moment from Redknapp's past tells the story: 'When I was at West Ham, one of the players got arrested. He'd been in a fight up in Essex somewhere. So the phone goes at 3 o'clock in the morning and I've got family of my own – it's a horrendous time to get a phone call because you fear the worst –

who's ringing at this time of the morning? And someone says they are from the police and you think, "My God, what's happened." It's non-stop. You are always into it. I really find it very difficult to switch off.'

Deeper even than the most serious distraction though is the enemy we don't see: fear. Fear clouds the judgement of leaders, turns us away from our deeply held values and beliefs, turns challenges into stress, knocks us off course. When fear and not reason becomes the driver of what leaders do, then everyone around them suffers.

When fear becomes the driver

Arsène Wenger names a fear that many face – the fear of what people will think. 'We have gone from a vertical society to a horizontal society where everybody has an opinion about every decision you make, everybody has an opinion on the internet straight away. Basically the respect for people who make decisions is gone because every decision is questioned. So one of the most important qualities of a good leader now is massive resistance to stress. Under stress you become smaller and smaller until you cannot give a message out any more and that, of course, is something that is vital. Many people underestimate this challenge.' Fear, then, hampers a leader's ability to lead.

Sir Alex passionately agrees: 'I see a lot of situations where a manager is under pressure and he's not getting good results. Even though most of the players want him to do well and try their best, somehow they can't do it. They fail simply because the fear of the manager about the results at the time drip-feeds into the players' minds. I see it all the time. It's the *Manchurian Candidate*, the drip, drip, drip in the head and eventually … they give in. As much as they would like to do their best for the manager, you can see them draining away. Some can pick themselves up, some can get out of it, some can recover, but I do see it happen – how that fear has a draining effect on the players when the manager is under pressure.'

For many leaders, the deep underlying fear is one of failure. Rejection, inadequacy, not leaving a legacy – all of these are common; and all are entwined with the sense a leader has that he might not succeed. As Redknapp simply puts it, 'We all want to be successful in what we do – none of us want to be failures.' For many in football, that translates very simply into a fear of defeat on the pitch. Chris Hughton admits, 'My fear is about losing games. In spite of all my experience as a coach and a manager, it has not got any easier. The fear is still there.' Redknapp shares that fear, and it is reflected in his reaction to a defeat: 'I get so committed to it. The journey home afterwards – it's just ridiculous really – I could take a friend up to a game and I could not speak to him all the way home for three hours. I just want to shut myself off.' And what fuels the fear for Redknapp is his great passion for the game. It is hugely important to him and so, of course, he will feel defeat very deeply. 'It's difficult; it's life-consuming almost. I mean if football's not going well, for me, I can get so low about it all. I've had a few bad experiences at Christmas when results haven't gone well, and then Christmas is a nightmare. Then I'm no use to anybody. I have the grandkids round – it's sad, it's pathetic really – but that's how it gets me.'

Fear, however, has an upside. When moderated, it can drive passion, performance and right behaviours. Hughton recognises that in himself: 'If anything, it makes me focus on preparation going into games. I would like to think that I am better prepared going into games than I was a year ago and two years ago.'

A great perspective attributed to Mohandas Gandhi is that we live inside a circle bounded by our fears. In other words, fears limit us – our ability and desire to explore, to learn and to perform. Imagine for a moment the inner circle being our comfort zone. There are many benefits to living inside the comfort zone – it feels relaxed, easy-paced, with no fears. However, over time this can be dull, uninteresting, and unchallenging. If we step beyond our comfort zone, we find ourselves in the learning zone. Here the downside is clear – it is uncomfortable, stretching, and can be quite salutary for us as we realise how much we do not know. Yet, it is interesting, challenging and potentially exhilarating – and is the place we need to be in if we are to grow at all.

There is one more zone beyond this: the terror zone. Here, challenges become stresses, we become afraid and we learn very little. Life in this zone is not healthy and not productive. So leaders need to be able to judge how to stay in their learning zone without creeping into their terror zone. They need to ask themselves: 'How can I grow my learning zone and shrink my terror zone so that fear comes less readily in moments of challenge?'

Arrest the Fear

When fear shows up, it needs to be dealt with quickly or it can become debilitating. Leaders experiencing fear of whatever type need first to stop the boat rocking.

The first thing to do is to identify the fear for what it is, and put it into context. It is said that the celebrated England rugby fly half, Jonny Wilkinson, would wake up on big match days and feel the pressure of the day in his stomach so that he could not eat breakfast. Then he would recognise it, welcome it, go on to the practice field and kick dozens of goals before returning for a big breakfast. Seeing it for what it is constitutes the first step; implementing some kind of routine response is the second.

After losing a game, a natural fear for Chris Hughton would be losing the next: 'If we've lost on Saturday, then that night I won't be in the best of moods. I accept that, and so do people around me. Sunday is typically a hangover day. I put the defeat into perspective: if we lost a match against Manchester United 1-0 and played really well, then my level of disappointment won't be as great as if we've lost at home to a team that's bottom of the division and we're in trouble. That tells me what processes of recovery I need to put in place. Then from Monday morning we are getting ready for the next match.'

What's the worst that can happen?

The recent period of economic austerity in Europe has prompted a revival of the old English wartime refrain: 'Keep calm and carry on.' This has a very practical ring to it, and is a genuinely useful principle of leadership. Mick McCarthy embodies this idea, not least because of his sense of perspective. 'I'll be honest with you; the fact that I'm never ever going to be skint helps. I'm not going to be out of work because I have belief in myself and think I did well.' This self-belief is also a practical antidote to fear.

For Walter Smith, this calmness is accompanied by a natural instinct to take ownership of his own circumstances: 'I don't think any manager that's worth his salt will sit down and kid himself that he played no part in a defeat. You have to sit down and make an honest assessment of what's gone wrong and at the time admit, maybe just to yourself, that you made those decisions and they were wrong ones at the time. Perhaps you shouldn't have made the decisions as quickly as you did. But if you're going to manage properly, you have to know that there will be times when you will make the wrong decision and you have to have the strength of character to carry on and continue to pursue the goals that you originally set out.' Smith is putting the defeat into the perspective of a larger goal; and provided that goal is not under threat, then the fear needn't take hold.

What's the best that can happen?

Positivity is also valuable. Stronger leaders are optimists. Not pie-in-the-sky dreamers, but forensically positive. Redknapp is deeply aware of the need for him to stay positive during the tough times: 'I can't go in and let the players see that I'm down or that I think things are going wrong. As down as I can be at home or when I'm driving the car to the training ground, once I walk in there if I'm going to be down then we've got no chance. It soon transmits to the players how you are feeling so you just can't do that.

'You've got to come out every day and you've got to be up and you've got to be bright and you've got to get them all going again because otherwise the players will pick up on that – they don't miss a trick. So I find I have to be strong, I have to be positive. Every week is different, one game has gone on to the next game. OK, we got beat last week – we're ready to go again next week and make sure we get the result. When you do win it's such a fantastic feeling! I drive home in the car and I can just be driving along and I punch the air and people must think I'm mad! I can do that about 20 times on the way home.'

Sir Alex Ferguson believes himself to be lucky. Speaking in the days before the showdown matches at the end of the 2011–12 season he observed: 'I don't panic, I lost panic a long time ago. But I certainly concern myself about Sunday's game coming up. I concerned myself about last Sunday's game because we are in an important time of the year now. You have to have an optimism that something is going to happen for us on Sunday. The dangerous rat is the one that's sat in the corner; I've got to hope that [the right result] can happen.' This is rational optimism. On this occasion, it went the other way – but it's this never-say-die attitude that infects the United players week in, week out – evident in their frequent injury-time winners, most notably with the miracle at the Nou Camp in 1999 against Bayern Munich that saw United crowned champions of Europe.

McCarthy rejects the description of his being unflappable, but agrees he's 'fairly stable'. 'I stood 3-0 down against Blackburn, last game of the season in 2011 and everybody was going mental. [Wolves needed to reduce the deficit to two goals in order to avoid relegation to the Championship.] I said we'll get a goal; we'll score. I've got to believe it. If I stop believing I don't think anybody else will believe. As long as the referee hasn't blown his whistle, we have got a chance. I said something will happen, either we'll get a goal or Spurs will score – we are staying up. They were looking at me as if to say he's off his head! We scored with three minutes to go. I thought there was about 15 minutes to go. Does that make me unflappable? Does it show I have belief? Bloody-mindedness? I don't know, but I always think we can win, always, no matter who we are playing against.' McCarthy's dogged optimism is his way of banishing the fear of failure.

Wherever it comes from, fear rocks the boat. Leaders must be unafraid to name their fear, put it into context; they must show self-belief and acknowledge that the outcome could be very positive. This approach calms the waters and opens a new perspective.

Take a Step Back

Before they can establish or regain long-term balance, leaders in any changing environment first need to understand what's going on.

215

They need a picture of the battle. In Richard Attenborough's 1977 epic war film about the battle at Arnhem, *A Bridge Too Far*, there is a pivotal scene where four senior allied officers are standing on the balcony of their impromptu headquarters, looking out over the battle. Watching that scene, there is a palpable sense of relief after the fog of the battle: at least the leaders have a picture of what's happening! Leadership expert Ron Heifetz from the Kennedy School of Government has written extensively on a concept that he calls 'Adaptive Leadership', in which he describes a set of principles that leaders in a fluid environment can use to navigate the territory. A fluid environment is one that requires constant reassessment and reworking – and professional football is such an environment. One principle Heifetz proposes is the Balcony and the Dance.

Daily work can often feel like a dance – constantly on the go, surrounded by people, occupying one small part of a larger stage. Taking a step back is like looking down on that dance from the balcony – you suddenly have the perspective and the time to see the wider picture without the pressure to be constantly involved. A good leader needs to see things from within the dance *at the same time* as from the balcony. The 'dancing' is essential for a leader if he is to keep connection with his people and a sense of reality. It is an act of leadership to take time to experience first-hand the work you are asking your people to do. And the 'balcony' is the perspective he needs if he is to recognise patterns and make short- and long-term decisions. The trick is to do both at once.

Howard Wilkinson believes the balcony enables a leader to stay in the game full time, working from his passion without it becoming an unhealthy obsession. 'You've got to keep your eye on the ball and over the horizon, all the time. Some [aspiring] leaders haven't got it, they haven't got the intellectual ability to deal with these complexities – they are one-dimensional. Then you get the others who try to do it part time. There's nothing wrong with picking your kids up from school, taking time for the family and so on. But in this game, you have to have a deep passion and commitment.' And what was Wilkinson's own balance when he was at the top of his game? 'I don't think it was unhealthy. My wife might say different, but then in this country it's very difficult to get off the treadmill averaging two games a week. I have to say, my staff helped me to maintain my perspective.'

And the principle runs a level deeper. The great leaders know how to get on to their *own* balconies. In other words, they know how to look at themselves, observe how they are reacting or behaving, and make the necessary changes – in the long term, but also in the moment. It's the hardest thing to do. The players who can do it can avoid red cards. The managers who can do it command a whole new level of respect and authority.

Walter Smith was in a tough place when he lost his job at Rangers in 1998, despite his sustained success. He now recognises he did not take enough of a step back and use the time out effectively. 'When I got the sack at Rangers, it was the first time in my life I had been unemployed and it was a strange feeling. I'm a boy from a working-class area of Glasgow so a work ethic was always instilled in me and there was an element of guilt that I wasn't working. So I spent the close season in a kind of void, wondering how I was going to get out – where would I get offered a job? I accepted the job at Everton, but in many ways, reflecting on it, it was a decision that I made in a little bit of haste. Everton on their own are a fantastic club, they're a proper football club, they've got a fantastic support base – but the timing was wrong.'

Everton was a tough job for Smith, who nonetheless acquitted himself well. But he learned from experience, and when he left the club three years later, he got his perspective back. 'I remembered how

I had jumped too quickly the previous time, and said to myself, "Well OK, I'll make sure that when I do come back, if I do get the opportunity to come back, I'm more careful this time." Taking a step back served Smith well. He took his time, spent a period with Sir Alex at Old Trafford where together they won the FA Cup in 2004, and then took over at Scotland – a move he would never regret.

Take the Broader View

Once perspective returns, then so can balance. But just as fear is a very personal thing, so is the recipe for achieving balance. All the great football leaders seem to have a mechanism for restoring balance – but these mechanisms can be quite varied.

'Football! It's the most important of all the small things in life.' – Carlo Ancelotti

In some ways, that says it all. The Italian manager comes back time and again to this wonderful balancing perspective. Redknapp takes a similar view: 'I look at my life and I think, "I'm so lucky. I should stop feeling sorry for myself because tomorrow I will go up to Victoria School and see all these little kiddies in wheelchairs …" I see so many people that get dealt such a bad hand. I mean, what are we feeling sorry for ourselves about? We've lost a game of football! I need to stop feeling sorry for myself. When Bill Shankly passionately said that football was more important than life or death he could not have been more wrong.'

Remember your goals

While longer-term goals can help leaders handle pressure, they can also help restore balance. Hope Powell's bigger goal has been to make a real impact on and for the women's game: 'When you look at where women's football is placed, when you compare men and women's football, we are the second-class citizens. One of my responsibilities is to promote the game and raise its profile in the long term. At some level, everybody involved in women's football has that responsibility. The game will always be here, we hope, so it isn't about me or any one player. It's a bigger picture and that's really important to me.'

This objective helps her maintain perspective. Is she obsessed with football? 'Not even close. I'm not obsessed with the game. I'm obsessed when I'm in it and I'm working and I've got a job to do. But the minute I get in my house it's forgotten.' Nor do her goals need to be that specific to have a balancing effect. 'I know that we want to be the leading nation in women's football. What that looks like, how long it takes … I just know that so long as we are making progress daily, so long as we can compete against the best and win sometimes, and develop the players coming through, I feel like we are getting one step closer.'

Where this long-term goal helps specifically is in banishing any fear of getting things wrong. 'I believe I am quite a good decision-maker – perhaps for that reason. I don't have a problem making decisions. My mentor said to me, "At the time you make the decision just remember that it's the right decision. It's OK then to change your mind and make a different decision." So I'm quite happy to say, "Right, we are going to do this," hoping that it will be OK – and if it isn't, I'm happy to change it and say, "Well, actually that didn't work – we are going to do this instead." For example, I might be on the field in practice and I'm coaching and I have this session drawn out. I'm putting on a session, and it doesn't actually work. So then I'll tell the players right, off we go, off the pitch – I'm not happy with that and I'll have a minute and

I'll re-jig it and I'll do it again. Some leaders are afraid to admit that something actually doesn't work and change it.'

Attitude of gratitude

One of the most important contributors to balance is thankfulness. This practice is incredibly regenerative. Redknapp puts it like this: 'I have a good life; I am very lucky when I look at where we have come from and where we are now. We have been married 44 years, we've had a great marriage, we've got seven grandkids. I mean, life is fantastic really – we have been very lucky. I've been very lucky to have done the job that I've done and be involved in something I love. It's just been amazing really.'

Glenn Hoddle found that gratitude was the key to maintaining a healthy perspective as England manager. 'When I was in the England job, my word there was a lot of pressure. It felt as if the whole country was on my shoulders. For four or five weeks I probably had more pressure than the prime minister – because even he was putting pressure on me to win! You can imagine what it was like. We took the players and their wives to the West End to go to a show to build team spirit in the weeks before we went to France, and the word got out. For about a mile before the theatre the whole of the streets were full! And it hit me just sitting in the bus with my wife: wow, these people – it was as if we'd won the World Cup already. The weight that I felt was enormous – and we were just going to the theatre! I learned then that if I could approach pressure with real gratitude, the pressure would actually shift before my eyes. It's an amazing thing, and I wish I'd known it when I was 20. But if you can take a real pressurised situation and be grateful for this pressure – suddenly you diffuse it, it disappears. I felt like I wanted to go and start the game right then, not go to the theatre – and that's how I wanted the players to feel. And the key is, I have to do it from within myself genuinely. It's quite easy if things are going well to be thankful, but when there are real burdens and pressure and you are unsure, that's the key moment. And I find if you can attack it from a different angle with that same emotion, you dismantle the pressure. If you don't the pressure builds up, and can quickly take you to your terror zone.'

Sir Alex is thankful when he looks back to his childhood: 'I always look at my background and how I was brought up and I was lucky with my upbringing in Glasgow. I don't think it's hard because you never think it's hard, but thinking back to my days there sustains me. There was nothing there. It was the end of the war. It was a different world. There were families with 17 kids and stuff and you just wonder how they survived. And there was rationing, of course. I can still remember that: you are brought up in an environment and an upbringing like that you can refer to all the time, that's your reference point.'

It's not surprising that the act of setting football into a broader context restores perspective for its leaders. What is notable is how the great leaders do this systematically, and how effective it is.

Take Time for Renewal

Finally, there is the hugely important task of finding a place of renewal. Renewal is the critical need for a leader to pause, refresh and grow – to lay in for long-term, sustained performance. Again, where that place is varies considerably from person to person.

Writing time

Walter Smith is now committed to it: 'It's important for anybody in management to set aside a bit of time if you have a problem, whatever that problem is. It's sometimes easier if it's a footballing one. I can sit down on my own, watch, make up my own mind, look back on a game, look back on something. I always set aside a period in a week and I would always scribble down different notes during the week and then set aside a period where I sat down and went through them and made sure that I wasn't missing anything – just to make my own personal assessment of what was going on. Sometimes for me it would be the office, but sometimes when you're involved all the time, people keep knocking at the door, disrupting the train of thought. A lot of the time it would be at home in the evening. I'd just take an hour to sit down and say right, that's it, try and clear everything away – and plot a course of action.'

Brendan Rodgers also enjoys what he calls 'thinking in ink'. 'I write a lot, and I'm always thinking and I have little blocks of time to write. Reflection is important to me; it allows me to move on quicker. It's really the lever that helps me. I wouldn't over-analyse a big event, but I would think first, make little references to moments, use them as referrals and plant them into my story.'

Routines

Whatever form they take, having regular relaxation and renewal routines is an excellent route to balance. Neil Warnock had a sacred match-day wind-down routine during his time at Sheffield United: 'When we got a good result at Bramall Lane the old guy, Derek, used to fill the bath and bring me a cup of tea as a way of warming down. I would lie in that bath thinking about when I was a kid running around with my dad, and how happy I was when we won and thinking about all of those thousands of people that I made happy. You can't put a price on that. I'd go home and put my pyjamas on and be in bed by 7 o'clock, and everyone would be asking if we were going out! But my wife knows me – she knows how tired I get after a game, mentally and emotionally tired, absolutely drained by 7 p.m. – so the first job when I got in would be to go upstairs and get into my pyjamas.'

Family and friends

Putting family first may sound obvious, but it can be very hard to do. Warnock has learned this lesson the hard way: 'I used to travel up the motorway, I used to do 18-hour days, I couldn't let anybody else watch a player. It wasn't a shock when my first marriage broke down. Now my marriage and the kids are everything – I have a completely different perspective. I have to employ good people and I have to trust them and I have to have my breathers and I have to have my rest. I'm not a manager that comes in at 7 a.m. and leaves at 7 p.m. like some managers do. I like reading the papers at home and making a few calls … I very rarely come in before 10 a.m. I have days when I'm in till 10 p.m., but they are few and far between. I have been picking my son up from school the last few years at 4 p.m. One chairman said before he hired me, "I've heard your wife lives in Cornwall. I'd like to put in your contract that you have to be at the training ground at least five days a week." I said, "We've got no reason to talk any more then because you've got the wrong manager."'

Time out

When the season is in full swing, Redknapp says he finds this one almost impossible – but admires his colleagues who can do it. 'I remember meeting Ron Atkinson when he was Sheffield Wednesday manager. West Ham were playing on the Sunday and Ron came to do the TV coverage. The day before they had been leading at Old Trafford in injury time, and Manchester United got two goals right at the end. It was a game when Fergie jumped on the pitch [to celebrate]. Big Ron came into my office on the Sunday before the game, and I said, "I bet you had a good night last night, Ron," thinking he must have been feeling horrendous. He said, "Yes, we got the karaoke on and got a Chinese takeaway. A few of the lads came round, we had a great night!" And I was thinking, "I wish I could do that." I couldn't do that – I'd be in such a state. I wish I could do what Ron did, switch off, go home and get on with it, but I've never been able to do that.'

Mick McCarthy refreshes by 'being normal': 'I catch the tube, I go up into London, I jump in a cab, I chat to everybody. I tend to think I'm a normal bloke with an extraordinary job and a career behind me. Not many have got that. I go to the pub and have a pint and if someone comes and talks to me I just generally try and be me, just try and be normal. I play golf, I cycle, I try and keep myself fit. I've got a great family – I've been married for 32 years to Fiona – and we've got three great kids. We're a great family unit too, which helps. I've got great friends; I've got a real fabulous back-up. Fiona will say it's the support system that we have, it's lovely.'

Time in

However, there is some measure of renewal even within the game. Howard Wilkinson remembers a day when Redknapp travelled home from a Spurs match, watched the highlights on *Match of the Day*, flew out the next morning to Palma, watched Real Mallorca, flew home in the evening and got back in time for *Match of the Day 2*! Redknapp admits that has renewal value for him: 'I love watching football – I have always been a great sports fan all round. My father was a fanatical sports fan – loved his football, good football, non-league football – he lived for football and boxing and all sports – loved his cricket, and I've been the same really. I loved the Olympics; I watched the cricket last week … I really relax. But football is my main passion. It's great for me.' Many speak about needing time away from work. For Redknapp, the passion is so intense that he finds rest even within it. Some may consider this dangerous, but for some leaders such as Redknapp it is clearly helpful.

The Thankful Leader

Leaders battle with stress and fear, and football's leaders are no exception. Success is no antidote – it is too short-lived. What is needed is perspective – the ability to step back and see the bigger picture as well as the detail. The lessons from football's leaders are clear.

1. Arrest the fear:
    Leaders don't often admit to having fears, but pretty much everyone has them. When fear surfaces, strong leaders can see it for what it is and take action to arrest it. Helpful techniques are to ask what's the worst that can happen and what's the best.

2. Take a step back:
    The balcony offers a route to a healthy perspective – especially if a leader can get on to his own balcony. Rodgers got on to his balcony and understood that he had sacrificed his philosophy against QPR. Villas-Boas got on to his after he left Chelsea, and took a route back through learning. Mancini gets on to his balcony and apologises when he's wrong.

3. Take the broader view:
    A sense of perspective will tell you that when you're in it it's a tragedy, but when you're looking at it it's a comedy. For a

leader, understanding that your work and role may only be the most important of all the small things in life is a sure route to restoring balance. So is the practice of remembering your wider goals and so is an attitude of gratitude.

4. Take time for renewal:
   Whether through writing, routines, family and friends, time out or even time in, renewal must be a high priority for a leader. However, it is easier said than done. What works for one leader doesn't come close for another. Ron Atkinson can relax with the team after a narrow defeat, Redknapp can't; Mick McCarthy takes time out, Redknapp takes time in.

In summary, the leader who can get on the balcony, look at his circumstances and be grateful for them will reduce his own anxiety, regain perspective and function effectively once again as a leader. He will make better decisions and get better results. The fearless leader probably does not exist, but the thankful leader does.

PART FIVE

The Great Challenges

CHAPTER NINE

CREATING SUSTAINED SUCCESS

THE BIG IDEA

Success – especially in football – is fleeting. True sustained success is rare in almost every occupation. The world has its great institutions, from the British monarchy to the United Nations, and its centres of excellence, from NASA to the Kirov Ballet. Many have received sustained public investment to help them, and despite this, most have endured periods of foundational challenge. Their ability to weather the roughest of storms in part defines them and their success.

The great challenge to a leader in business is to create sustained success, to create an organisation that ultimately defines the market in which it operates, something that investors treasure and competitors aspire to. In football, the daily challenge to the leader may feel different, but the nature of it is essentially the same: he needs to manage the daily pressures while also conceiving of and implementing something lasting. Those who can do this are the toast of their profession.

THE MANAGER

Sir Alex Ferguson is one of the giants of the global game. In a football leadership career that has spanned some 40 years, he has broken records and achieved heights that bear comparison with the greatest in any field of sporting endeavour. He announced his arrival on the football management stage with an astonishing spell at Aberdeen between 1978 and 1986, taking a club with a 25-year trophy drought to sustained success and a famous defeat of Real Madrid to win the 1983 European Cup-Winners' Cup.

In 1986, he joined Manchester United. Very quickly seeing the need for radical rebuilding, Ferguson embarked on the parallel tracks of short-term, high-impact methods and long-term foundational transformation. He quickly achieved stability, but when in his fourth season there was no obvious evidence of sustained improvement, a public assumption grew that he would not last in the post. Victory in the FA Cup in 1990 changed all that, and three seasons later United were champions of the newly constituted Premiership. Perhaps even more significantly, the now-legendary United youth side of 1992 had emerged: Ferguson had created a pool of talent and strength that would be the source of much of the club's sustained success for years to come.

He guided United to a further 12 titles in the first two decades of the Barclays Premier League, finishing no lower than third on any occasion. In this era they have become perhaps the most powerful global brand in football. They have been champions of Europe on two occasions and FA Cup winners four times, winning the extraordinary 'Treble' of European Champions League, Premier League and FA Cup in 1998–99. In that same year, Ferguson was awarded the KBE by Her Majesty the Queen for services to football. He retired from football management at the end of the 2012–13 season.

His Philosophy

Sir Alex has a simple philosophy of leadership in football: that no one is bigger than the club. This hard-fought principle, often quoted in football circles, is at least in part responsible for the consistency of

Manchester United. Where other clubs might break some rules or at least bend them to accommodate a star player, United does not. Stars are created at Old Trafford, or they are imported – almost invariably they shine brighter as a result of their stay at United. But ultimately they come and go; and after quarter of a century of achievement and growth, the club's fortunes show no real sign of waning. At some level, Ferguson has embodied the club. He is one of a select group of leaders to become so synonymous with a global organisation that it has become unclear which one has shaped the other.

His achievements at Manchester United stand alone in the history of English football. No manager has remained longer at a single club; and no manager has achieved such consistent excellence. This extraordinary success has come through a dynastic set-up in the playing staff.

The Challenge

Building something to last has always been difficult; doing it now in a world where crises abound, where short-term gain is king and where individualism is rampant would seem almost impossible. Very few football clubs can be said to have achieved sustained success across generations of footballers; fewer still can be said to be dynastic – ensuring a succession that enables continuous achievement beyond the career span of specific individuals. To do so requires commitment and strength of character from key players, consistently good financial and resource management and a leader's clear vision of long-term success.

Two of the very few clubs in recent times to have achieved sustained success at the highest level in England are Liverpool and Manchester United. For 30 years Liverpool could reasonably claim to have established a leadership dynasty; while Manchester United, under one very powerful and talented leader, have at least established a dynasty of star players – recreating a winning line-up generation after generation. Only in exceptional circumstances will even the longest-serving outfield player deliver 20 years at the highest level: Ryan Giggs at United and Paolo Maldini at AC Milan are salient examples. Ferguson was at Manchester United for over a quarter of a century, overseeing wave after wave of talent.

Paul Ince is himself a professional manager, and a player who achieved great success under Ferguson. He ascribes the dynastic effect at Manchester United to Ferguson's great force of character: 'People forget how many teams that he has actually built. He has gone through transitional periods, but has produced four or five great teams since 1986. I don't think that there's another manager in world football that could do that.'

It's not that Sir Alex Ferguson has all the answers, nor that the wisdom of the unforgettable Liverpool managers can be bottled and sold on. But what they have done is exceptional, and bears a second look.

Solution Part One: Build for the Long Term

Unsurprisingly, where one of the primary challenges is short-termism, leaders who achieve sustained success build with one eye on a longer-term horizon. Peter Schmeichel observed that Sir Alex always planned for the four- to five-year time frame. The Liverpool football club of the 1960s, 70s and 80s was famous for its long-term thinking – expressed most obviously in the continuity of its leadership. Kevin Keegan was one of the most celebrated of Liverpool's array of attacking players that graced the 1970s: 'Typically, if the manager goes now, then all the staff go with him. When I went there we had Shanks, and then we had Bob Paisley,

really as a physio and assistant manager (he wasn't even fully qualified as a physio!), then we had Joe Fagan, then we had Ronnie
Moran and then Roy Evans as reserve team coach – so five of
them. And you always had one or two heroes around – Ron Yeats,
Ian St John and Tommy Smith were still at Anfield when I went
there. They weren't playing much – in fact they had pretty much
finished – but before they left completely and went to other clubs
they stayed for a good while ... So you had this sort of boot room,
then you had these older players who had younger players learning
from them to carry on that legacy. It was very powerful.'

The work of Sir Alex at United and of Bill Shankly and his
successors at Liverpool would suggest five principles to enable
long-term building:

1. Make strong and rapid decisions:
   Ferguson attributes his long-term success in no small part to his
   ability to make decisions. He began his football management
   career with East Stirlingshire at the age of 32. Like many
   managers, he did not have a career mapped out in front of him.
   Nor did he have any clearly articulated long-term goals: 'I don't
   think that when I started at 32 you could say I had any leadership qualities in the sense of where I was travelling in life. I
   think what I brought to it as a 32-year-old was I was always a
   good decision-maker. I was always prepared to make a decision
   – right or wrong – so I had that in my favour.'

   The decisions the young Ferguson was making were quite
   different from the ones he made in recent years as manager at one
   of the world's leading clubs. Decisions now are about how to grow
   players' careers, how to motivate, how to shape and mould a team,
   how to create balance across a squad, how to balance the needs of
   Premier League and Champions League – amongst others.

Decisions then were around how to garner a team at all! 'When I started out as East Stirling manager I was part time. I managed to gather 13 players by mixing free transfers with young players. My first match was a friendly against Kettering and then the following week we played against Tranmere Rovers, with Steve Coppell playing centre forward for them … Quite an introduction! Looking back, it was easy to work with 13 players, it had nothing like the complexity that I faced at Manchester United in recent times.'

The ability to take tough decisions under pressure is one mark of a great leader. Walter Smith worked as assistant manager to Sir Alex first at Scotland and later at Manchester United. He observes, 'Alex is prepared to make difficult decisions and that demonstrates his strength of character.'

Ferguson goes further: 'I've *enjoyed* taking decisions. It probably all goes against my thoughts of 25 years ago when I believed I could do everything. That's the unfortunate thing about being young; you think you can do everything. So the lessons have got to be learned on the way and today, past 70, I'm still looking to make changes.

'My job was to manage United and to produce results. In that way I'm no different to any other manager. I'll not be regarded in the same way if I'm not successful. Everything to me is black and white: if it's on the football field and I see something that I feel is a retrograde step for the club, I have to act and make decisions. In management you have to build to make decisions. Sometimes you're not right, but that doesn't concern me too much because the important thing is being able to do it.'

If he is famous for his ability to focus on the next horizon, then it is the strength of his short-term decision-making that creates the space for him to do that.

2. Build a great store of knowledge, and share it:

    Sir Alex has always believed in the value of a great store of knowledge. Roy Hodgson firmly believes this is what lies behind Ferguson's greatness as a football leader: 'What makes him successful first of all is his knowledge of football, and it comes through putting in such a lot of hard work. He has an encyclopaedic knowledge of players. He knows so much on so many different aspects of football – both today and delving way back into the past. He would be an ideal partner on any football quiz!'

    Gérard Houllier also believes Ferguson's knowledge is his bedrock: 'People talk about him as a reference. Even Laurent Blanc, who was the national team coach of France, refers to him. I remember attending a few coaching sessions with him in Scotland and everything he says is immediately written down by those on the course. What he says is always common sense, which is a combination of knowledge and experience. And he likes to share. He is known as a person who is outstandingly successful, but also someone who is accessible regardless of his level of standing within the game. His expertise, his work attitude, loyalty and enthusiasm make him practically the best in the world.'

    Leading without knowledge is difficult. Deep knowledge of the core of the business earns respect and enables accurate decision-making. Deep knowledge *shared* suggests a different level of leadership – where someone is investing in the long-term health of an organisation and even of the wider environment in which it operates.

    Deep subject knowledge is both impressive and essential in a good leader. There is no substitute – people are too canny. A leader can get away for a while on native intuition, but as the saying goes: 'You can't fool all of the people all of the time.'

3. Focus on people, but avoid sentimentality:

   While Houllier agrees on the knowledge point, he also draws attention to Ferguson's legendary people focus: 'He has great expertise – he knows football inside out. He also has a great expertise in man management and knows how to deal with people, which is very important. Over the years he's seen a lot of difference with players and the mentality and change of attitude, but he has adapted himself to that. He's a very loyal person: loyal to his players and loyal to his friends. His mixture of enthusiasm and enjoyment is apparent. I would imagine that enthusiasm is infectious to his players.'

   Ferguson always has a goal in mind – whether better working conditions when he was a trade union official in Govan or winning the Premier League again in his final season as manager of Manchester United. In his tenacious pursuit of his goal, he will decide whom he can rely on and he will confront destructive behaviour: 'It's a horrible thing to say, but you can't be sentimental in this job.' And it has nothing to do with a player's public profile. In his dealings with people, Sir Alex will do what it takes. But he is nothing if not a shrewd judge of people – and he gets it right time and again, choosing great players and leading them to great achievement. 'I love the players that I've had and I've been very, very fortunate to have had great players who've come through my career with me.'

   A young Alex McLeish felt that touch at Aberdeen: 'I was always quite a vociferous character when I played the game, even in school. Even playing with my mates at home I was loud and rough. I carried it on through juvenile football and into professional football, and at Aberdeen I encountered other guys of the same ilk – Willie Miller, Stuart Kennedy,

Gordon Strachan, Mark McGhee. There were some really strong characters and then we ended up with a certain manager, and this incredible man met us head-on, took charge of that group of boys and moulded us into a European trophy-winning team.'

Elsewhere, the Liverpool boot-room focus on people was expressed through respect and professionalism. One of Keegan's most vivid memories is of how players were treated when eventually their time came to leave the club: 'When players left they were never shoved out the door. When it was time to go, the manager would always sit down with them and say exactly the right thing. It might have been something like, "You can stay here – everyone likes you in the group and you're a good footballer – but you need to play football and you'll get more football elsewhere." He found out from the manager instead of finding out from a second or third person, or from a phone call. The manager was – and still is – very important to a player: he needs to sit down in a room with his man and paint a picture of where he sees it. Because the way he sees it is probably the way it is going to go. The level of communication in the group at Liverpool was far higher than today. Now we have all the means of communication, but it's far less personal. Players get emails and texts to say, "Go and talk to somebody if you want to leave …" People aren't talking face-to-face.'

In the context of task, team and individual, this is about dealing with individuals in the framework of the task. Sir Alex, like Bill Shankly and Bob Paisley in years past, focuses on his people; but always in his mind is the task. The over-riding question is: 'Which players are going to win us the matches that will earn us the titles?'

4.   What got you here won't get you there:
Speaking to the BBC shortly before the end of the trophyless 2011–12 season, former United goalkeeping legend Peter Schmeichel summed up the widespread admiration of the manager: 'Sir Alex Ferguson's achievement this year is one of his greatest. No words can praise him enough. For someone of his age to keep moving with the times and understanding what makes these players tick is incredible. He always looks ahead.' Schmeichel has put his finger on another critical attribute of the dynastic leader – the wisdom to move on and try something new. When Tiger Woods had won his first major at the age of 21, he did not rest on his laurels. Instead he worked with his coach to deconstruct his swing and rebuild it again, this time better and stronger. He had the humility to realise that what he had – world-class though it was – would not get him to sustained world leadership in golf.

When the 45-year-old Ferguson arrived at Manchester United in November 1986, he inherited a club that had not known real success since the George Best years and the European Cup of 1968. Living in the shadow of the other great north-western dynasty that was Liverpool FC, they had started the season poorly and were second to bottom of the First Division. By working on – among other things – the basics of fitness and discipline, he took them to 11th at the season's close. But, as Brendan Rodgers would discover more than 20 years later at Reading, instant results are not easy to come by – not when you're trying to build for the future. And in December 1989, United ended the decade just outside the relegation zone. Sir Alex would later call this 'the darkest period I have ever suffered in the game'. Public and press were calling for his dismissal.

Then in the New Year, the dawn broke. Popular belief has it that an unexpected 1-0 win in the third round of the FA Cup away to high-flying Nottingham Forest was the turning point. Certainly that match ignited a run that saw United go all the way to Wembley and win the trophy. But Ferguson would cite the explicit support of the board for his longer-term plans as the main driver for his success. One of the early difficulties he faced was that the team 'was too old. The problem with human beings is that when they get older and they are playing at a club like this, how many challenges can they accept without being successful? It's very difficult. So players that have been here a long time and are in their 30s, you have to question whether they can go another battle. By that I mean winning the league. The whole campaign is a battle. It's not decided in the first game or the last game – it's decided in 38 matches, or at that time 42 matches. Although we were second to Liverpool in my first full season I knew we couldn't win the league with that team, so while all that was happening, we were rebuilding the youth in the club. We were doing OK. One or two came through: Lee Sharp and Lee Martin became first-team players. Some were on the fringes: Mark Robins was successful in terms of his goal-scoring ratio and had an ability to score in important games. So there were signs we were on the right track.' It was Mark Robins, in fact, who scored the winner in that decisive cup match against Forest.

Once Ferguson had done enough to win his first trophy, the seeds of sustained success began to blossom. 'The definite breakthrough was the youth team of 1992. They were phenomenal, absolutely phenomenal. Seven full internationals came out of that team. Extraordinary, and we continue to see the effects today.' For the record: the seven were David

Beckham, Nicky Butt, Gary Neville, Ryan Giggs, Robbie Savage, Keith Gillespie and Simon Davies. The team won the FA Youth Cup that year, and were runners-up the following season – a year in which they were joined by Paul Scholes and Phil Neville.

What Sir Alex did was a significant act of leadership: like Tiger Woods, he acknowledged the flaws in a winning system, and used them as a springboard for something newer and better – something that would last.

5. Invest in the next generation:
Sir Alex has infused the club with his own character – but it is a two-way street. The two have moulded each other. He speaks with admiration of the United of half a century ago who built for the future: 'This club has traditionally been good at working with young players. They won five youth cups in a row in the 1950s, and they created the Busby Babes. That would have been a phenomenal team but for the disaster of 1958. Who's to say how long it would have lasted, that particular team? But they were young; they were only boys, 21 years of age. They were fantastic footballers.'

He attributes his appointment as United manager to his work at Aberdeen, and attributes his success at Aberdeen to the investment he made in the upcoming generation of players: 'At Aberdeen I did exactly what I would later do at United – I built a football club. We had a great youth system at Aberdeen: we brought young players through continually and that was part of the success at the club.'

When he landed at a club rich in history, but starved of real success, he observed straight away the need to recapture the traditional commitment to youth in order to develop sustained success for the future: 'When I arrived there wasn't really a good youth system. So at first I was involved completely in the youth effort. We started a system. I set up a meeting with all the scouts throughout the country and told them exactly what I intended to do and what I expected from them. Scouts are as important as your coaches – it's only through a good scout you get the right quality of people into your football club. In the early days all [assistant manager] Archie Knox and I did was trial, trial and trial, so that the coaches would have the material to work with. We were bringing in boys from everywhere. The scouts set about their jobs very well and by doing that got the message across to the board what my long-term approach was to building a football club: focus on young people. By hard work we got to a level around about 1990 where we were starting to make a change to the dynamics of the club.'

Sir Alex acknowledges this wasn't easy: 'No criticism of [predecessor] Ron Atkinson, because management is a job – was then and still is today. It is a results-based industry, so for a lot of managers they have to concentrate on the first team. I've never been that way. The club's got to be out there for sure – we've got 11 men on the pitch and five on the bench and we've got to be out there performing today. But at the same time you are thinking long term about bringing the talent through. So I've never worried about the result of the first team, I've always worried about the foundations of the club. I've always felt it's not building a football team; it's building a football club. There needs to be a foundation there built on young players. We have over time got to the level where now we are turning out some very, very good young players who are all playing today – and not all at our club. Many of the ones we didn't take are playing for Scotland and England, and we felt they weren't as good as the ones we had — a fantastic position to be in.'

For certain, his plan caught fire. 'Bobby Charlton in particular was a great support. When we found young Ryan [Giggs] at 14 years of age I said to Bobby, "You need to come down and see this kid — he's unbelievable." So Bobby came down to the far pitch on Littleton Road down the far side and I'm standing there and I'm watching a game. Bobby's walking across and by the time he gets to me, Ryan's been on the ball about 20 times. He walks from the pavilion end over to the pitch and says, "That must be him there!" He knew right away because Ryan was like a terrier chasing a bit of silver paper in the wind, his head was up and he was off the ground, floating about the place. Fabulous. Bobby and [then chairman] Martin Edwards supported us in everything we tried to achieve with youth.'

The academy system at Manchester United is at the heart of the club's long-term success and represents the dynasty that Ferguson built. This work appeals deeply to his people skills. But he did not do it all himself and had to rely on his academy team to implement his vision: 'Building up young players to the necessary level of self-belief and skill is a job for our academy when they arrive. They are rebuilding their character. If they can rebuild a player's character to the level that he can handle me, then he's got a chance. That's a fact, because when they got to me they would have to be men.' Here again, the focus is on people, but without a trace of sentimentality: 'We've no time for a weak person in the first team. When they see weakness [at the academy], they keep working at it. Because a player would not only be dealing with me, he is dealing with 76,000 people expecting them to win each week – and that's a different issue altogether. So the rebuilding of a character that's strong in terms of handling a crowd and the senior players in the dressing room: big stars, expectations, media, all these things – it's not done in the wind. It's a building process, and the academy people are good at that.'

There is a real pride in Sir Alex's eyes as he considers how this academy team has reproduced something in the finest traditions of the club: 'They have recreated history at Manchester United by developing these fantastic young players. It has given everyone the satisfaction that they are doing their jobs properly: the scouting, the coaching, the decision-making about who was the best one to bring into the club, all these things. So this has created a foundation for Manchester United as it is today. This is absolutely what has built lasting success.' For Sir Alex then, building a football club is synonymous with investing in the next generation and in creating sustained success.

And the final part of the loop? While Sir Alex entrusted this sacred work to his academy team, he was far from losing touch. Peter Schmeichel recalls a visit to United's training ground in the later years of Ferguson's managerial time at the club: 'I walked around Carrington with him and we watched the kids train. He said, "That fella over there will make his debut in 15 or 16 months." That's how he plans. But he never says that to the player. He just talks about the next game.'

Ferguson is not the only manager to place such emphasis on youth. Brendan Rodgers was convinced of the power of youth work from his earliest days at Reading, and makes the connection between the next generation and the club's culture and values. 'Some young players grew and went right through to the first team. Development is a decade really. It starts with the youngster who can't tie his laces at the very beginning, making him feel important, secure in the environment, allowing him to play with freedom.' So the work on mindsets begins young. Culture, philosophy, values, morals are all words Rodgers uses to describe his focus during his decade as a youth coach. 'I worked on inter-personal skills in relation to the young players: shaking hands, little simple things, please and thank you, not simply expecting things, reiterating hard work, making them work. It was important to operate on their level, getting myself feeling how they feel, building rapport, building trust. Once they could trust me, I could incorporate core values: collectiveness, unity, pride. It was a commitment to nurturing.' This is significant, core work for a leader in any sector. Business leaders – like football leaders – need to invest real energy and resource in ensuring the flow through of talent to where it can best be used.

And nor does it stop there. For those who will move up to the elite squad, there is considerable preparatory effort: 'I want them to smoothly come across, and then be able to go back and forth. At Swansea, young players used to jump from youth straight to the first team, which was too big a jump for them. So instead we put in place a bridge, to prepare them for that jump. The biggest thing with the young players is managing their expectations: walking alongside them, understanding them, creating possibilities.'

Dario Gradi talks of the 'extreme pressures' on young players moving up. He recalls the moment when the young Rob Jones moved on to the high-intensity environment of Anfield. 'When I signed him as a schoolboy, I went round to his house with his forms and promised we'd look after him. When we accepted the offer from Liverpool, I rang his mum and said we'd accepted and she asked if that would be good for him. She reminded me that we'd said we would only do what was right for him. I told her he'd be playing against Manchester United on Sunday and marking

Ryan Giggs and I thought that was quite good for him! So when he went, I said, "You'll be alright on Sunday. You'll do alright against Ryan Giggs. He might beat you but, when he does, you'll know what you did wrong. You know how to play full back. There's nothing you don't know about playing full back. So don't worry, you'll cope. If you are worried when you get the ball, just kick the f***ing thing up the pitch as far as you can. Don't worry about it, don't overplay." Anyway, he played well. The following week I had reason to speak to [then Liverpool manager] Graeme Souness and I told him what I'd said. He said, "I told him the same thing. I told him to kick the ball out of the ground if he wanted! But he didn't, he played well." Six months later he was playing for England. Terrific.'

Rodgers also agrees there is a considerable role for the senior players here: 'The young players are only as good as the senior players and the senior players at Swansea were magnificent, taking that responsibility themselves. They work with them on the field – they support them and encourage them, they give them advice. The key thing is they aren't distant with them – that they don't see themselves as Premier League superstars, but instead they see themselves as people united in what they are doing as part of the club. And to have individual, assigned mentors is also a great idea. We had that process at Chelsea: John Terry, Didier Drogba and others were great for the young players. There was a lot of integration there.' Another connection between the youth and club culture: if senior players take a leadership role in this way, club values get passed on and become even stronger in the first team itself.

Gradi's three decades at Crewe Alexandra – including a 24-year unbroken spell as manager – make him one of the most enduring figures in the industry. He is acknowledged as one of the most dedicated and successful developers of young people in the game. He has great technical focus – a commitment to footballing skills that has launched a significant number of highly successful careers. David Platt, Rob Jones, Danny Murphy, Robbie Savage, Neil Lennon and Dean Ashton among others bear testimony to his abilities. 'There are certain core skills a successful footballer needs – and he has to learn them young. I say to our under 12s when I'm working with them, "We might be doing this every week but it's a skill that you won't be able to develop when you are 18 or 19. We can't get you to receive the ball from the back players in tight situations if you've not done it as a kid. You are going to make too many mistakes, which means you've got to be able to screen it. You need to use two feet and you've got to be able to do that in the game, and you've got to get into the drag so you can dodge people. They're simple skills and quite easy to teach, but if you haven't mastered them by the time you're 15 or 16 then you aren't going to." I remember working with Alan Hudson and he had a weak foot when he was 17 or 18 at Chelsea, and we worked ever such a lot on his weak foot. But he never used it in the game. It was too late.'

At a big-club level, Sir Alex believes the cornerstones of good youth work are a consistent environment, and an all-round view of care – including the tough subjects: 'The people we had running our academy – some of them were with the club for 20 years. They are part of the fabric of the club. So what you've got is consistency and experience of how to handle young people, and of what Manchester United really means. It's not always an easy job. We get a lot of kids from broken homes now – the father and mother have split up, and you have to deal with both sides of it. The most important thing is the care we can give them. Of course, we do the educational thing, but there's also development of character – getting them to understand it's not an easy job. We tell them, "It's a commitment. You've got to do it 100 per cent – you can't do it part-time at this club." We have to make them well aware of the dangers of drugs, we help them understand financial matters and all about what's appropriate. There's been a real change here. We got Ryan Giggs to sign his first professional contract for four years on a quarter of what these guys are getting. You sometimes see them drive off in their flash car, and we immediately do something about it: the insurance is ridiculous money, and the message it sends out is all wrong. Drink can be a problem too. And then girlfriends come into their lives, of course, from 16 to 19. Then there are agents – do they have a good one or a bad one? We support them across this whole range of challenges.'

From the tireless work of Sir Alex comes this clear message: building the next generation is the essential work of a leader if he is to achieve truly sustained success.

Solution Part Two: Build Something Bigger Than Yourself

One of the toughest balances for a dynastic leader to strike is around how much personality to invest in the organisation. Too little, and he loses the power to shape something; too much and it becomes dependent on him – with all the limitations and the dangers that carries. This part of the solution has three elements.

1. Infuse the organisation with your character:
    Exactly how dependent Manchester United has become on the personality of Sir Alex will only be seen now that he has retired from the front line. But no one could argue with the extraordinary success that has sprung up from the marriage of the institution and the person.

Ferguson does not think of himself as a leader in the traditional sense – more as a person who shapes others: 'I would
never describe myself as a leader. I think time has given me an
opportunity to influence people's beliefs, to give them faith in
themselves. Confidence and your personality get through to
them. I always feel my teams mirror me, my personality, and
that's what I always head for, that one personality.'

Paul Ince explains how, over time, Manchester United has
become almost a direct expression of the manager's character:
'When you sign for Manchester United, you want to play for
Manchester United because for me it was the biggest club in
the world. After about a year of being there I wanted to play for
Alex Ferguson. In my eyes, he is Mr Manchester United. I
wanted to learn from him and pick his brains and play for him.
You know what he expects from you and the fact that he wants
you to come and play for his team gives you such a lift in your
career. That someone like Sir Alex has recognised you as a
player that can actually come and do a job for Manchester
United and be a part of a side that won the title after 26 years
was great.'

George Graham, a highly talented, title-winning contemporary of Sir Alex in management, agrees with Ince: 'His
biggest strength without question is his desire, and age has
nothing to do with desire – you can have it as a youngster,
you can have it at middle age and you can have it in your
older years. Alex has always had that desire and he's still got it.
He's actually built his Manchester United success from scratch
and he's instilled his own personality and character. It's very,
very hard to define that.' In other words, there's no way of
bottling and selling what Sir Alex does. But the message is
that any leader seeking to build long-term success needs to

ensure his character – that is, his behaviours, values and beliefs – permeate his organisation.

Bill Shankly was another leader with plenty of charisma. Keegan will never forget his first day of training under him: 'It was the end of the first day. I was just someone they had plucked from obscurity. Shankly walked over to me and said, "You will play for England," and just walked off. In that moment, I knew I would.' In all his dealings, Shankly communicated a deep affection for the club and especially for its supporters: 'He would remind us, "You are privileged to play for these people. Everything you do here, you do it for them."' He also communicated a very personal interest in the players: 'He was unbelievable. He had something special with everyone. With me, I think it was that we were both miners' sons. But he was like that with everybody – he didn't have favourites. He was always going over to people and talking to them and giving them messages. Some would get it, others wouldn't. He would go over to someone if he wasn't very fit and say, "Chocolate is no good for you, son …" Of course he was actually saying they could be fitter, they could be a bit slimmer, they could maybe train harder. Little personal cryptic messages.'

This is *not* about the leader declaring himself the best thing since sliced bread. Rather, it is about him using the strength of his character for the good of all in the organisation.

2. Establish enduring vision and values:
Paul Ince pays tribute to the sheer presence of Sir Alex – a presence created by his adherence to compelling values: 'It's the respect and standards that he has for his club and his players: how they should behave, how they should work in training and respect each other. There is awe about the man, when he walks

in, when he speaks everybody shuts up and that is a great trait to have.' Of course, Ferguson's reputation as a match-winner alone goes before him, and helps to establish something special. But to have real impact on generations of newcomers requires some process – formal or informal – of induction. A player arriving at the club needs to see and feel that he is joining something special, something bigger than himself. The importance of this hit Sir Alex a few years ago: 'It was a moment when we came to commemorate the anniversary of the Munich air disaster, and I realised that some of the young foreign players weren't aware of it. We showed them a video of the team back then, and Bobby Charlton came to speak about it. The response was amazing – and I mean the emotional response. And that was a very poignant moment for the football club in terms of players from other countries like Brazil, immediately realising how big a tragedy it was and how big the club has become since then. So we do more of that now when players arrive at the club, to get them well clued in around how we've grown to the famous club we are now.'

Now that Ferguson has retired, Arsène Wenger is the longest-serving Premier League manager. Like Sir Alex, he has infused his club with his character and has established clear values that have significantly enhanced performance. He also sets a high premium on vision. 'I would say a person who is a good leader is a person who has ideas and has a vision of the world. To have a vision of the world, you have to have a philosophy of the world and values that are important for you. So I must say the first work a leader has to do is analyse what he wants, what is important to him, and the second step is to make that real. Our job I find very interesting because it's more than being an intellectual. An intellectual guy is a guy who lives for his ideas; a football manager is a guy who needs to have ideas as well, but then he has to show that these ideas work and to transform it into a practical aspect. That's why I find this job interesting: at the end of the day you can check how good your ideas are. I believe as well a leader can be a fantastic person who can influence other people's lives in a positive way. Therefore he has a great responsibility.' Have the right impact on those lives and you begin to create something enduring.

The values that Bill Shankly lived out at Liverpool would endure well beyond his own tenure. Keegan has a prime example: 'Possibly his most powerful value of all was honesty. If you did something wrong you were told: if you had a bad game you knew it, if you'd done well you knew it. So there was a passing on of genuine information and feedback all the time. If someone was pleased with you, you knew it. But no one said too much. At Liverpool, we never criticised anybody to other people – it's just not what we did. Then it was all about Saturday, about winning, about playing for Liverpool: how lucky you were to play for Liverpool, we don't do that at Liverpool, this is what we do at Liverpool. There was this real buy-in to how lucky you were, how privileged you were to be given the shirt to wear and run out wearing it in front of the crowd. That's how it felt and still to this day I feel it.'

The values point is not a new one in itself. What is significant in the context of sustaining success is when the values are established in conjunction with the leader's character, and when they are established in such a way that they become a central part of the organisation and they outlive him. Powerful sustaining values are embodied by a leader – and then taken up with the same intensity by his successor.

3.   Ensure your succession:

In his book *Good to Great*, author Jim Collins suggests that one of five traits of a truly great leader is to ensure his own succession. In 1974, Bill Shankly retired from the role of Liverpool manager. He was loved by just about everyone in English football, revered by the Anfield faithful and profoundly respected by his players. The question everyone was asking was who could possibly succeed him? Rumour had it that Brian Clough, then manager at Leeds United and future great at Nottingham Forest, would be the successor. But the club had plans to keep the succession internal. In the manner of a royal family, the role fell to the heir apparent — Shankly's assistant, Bob Paisley. Keegan recalls that time: 'The great thing about the transition was the ship just sailed on. When Bob took the job, my first thoughts were, "He's not a communicator, he's just a real, solid, down-to-earth guy."'

Likeable, knowledgeable — but did he have what it takes to lead a team of champions? 'From the start with Bob we were all committed not to let him fall. It was a case of: "He's too good a guy, he means too much to us." And then he went on to become so much more successful even than Shanks because that team just grew and grew. I only had a year with him, and they went on to great things. What he won was incredible.' The Shankly-Paisley succession was a superb example of a leadership transition. And the key to its success did not lie exclusively with the outgoing man. 'If Bob had had an ego he'd have wanted to change things. But he just thought, "OK, I'm number one now: I've got my main players, I've got the same staff behind me, Bill's gone, but we worked together 20 years" — and off he went! Nothing changed in that year I was there, and as far as I know nothing changed afterwards either. We kept the same training routines, the same fitness pre-season, the same people looking at teams. That's all very clever because most people go into a business and think, "I've got to make my mark on this, I've got to change this" – and sometimes you don't, especially if it's successful. Ego's the biggest thing.'

Perhaps it is the absence of ego that makes a great leader into a great dynastic leader. Wenger is a firm believer in ego-free succession: 'I find that above all the club belongs to the fans, and not just to one person, and it has to be a model that survives you when you go, that survives the biggest players when they go and economically it is just a viable model. That for me is the biggest part to think that this club will just become bigger and bigger and when I leave I feel a hugely proud moment that this club can go further and continue and get even bigger and become even stronger.'

At Manchester United, of course, for several years it was the great unanswered question. Who would be able to succeed the great man when he eventually stepped away? David Moyes is the man tasked with the challenge, but Howard Wilkinson believes that Sir Alex has bequeathed to the club a form of continuous growth that goes beyond Ferguson as an individual: 'I think Manchester United can ask no more from Alex than what he has already given. What he's left there is fantastic. It's the board's responsibility to manage that change. They might ask him to help them, but it's their responsibility to put in place a strategy for the change. In my humble opinion it would not have been a case of "we need to find another Ferguson." It's surely more around how do we keep steady the ship which has cruised along so well, now that we have a new captain?'

Wherever the responsibility lies, it is a clear challenge: sustained success only translates into dynastic success with proper succession.

The Dynastic Leader

We have seen two parts to the work of a leader who seeks to establish a dynasty.

1. Build for the long term:
    This involves bold decision-making, developing and sharing deep knowledge, building loyalty, strategic reinvention where needed and investment in talent. Sir Alex's decision-making clears the space for him to think and plan for the long term; his great knowledge and his willingness to share it wins him lasting respect, the effects of which ripple far beyond his own club. His focus on people in the context of the task, reminiscent of Bill Shankly, ensures he builds loyalty, his acknowledgement of the need to reinvent ensures new horizons of growth and his investment in the next generation has carried him and the club across a quarter of a century.

2. Build something bigger than yourself:
    Both Ferguson and Shankly have bequeathed their very characters to their clubs, both have fashioned enduring values and Bill Shankly ensured his succession. And this was the last great professional challenge of Sir Alex Ferguson's managerial career.

    Amid all the achievement and desire for success lies once again the great leadership challenge of humility. Shankly showed it in his willingness to appoint a successor when the time was right – and a truly dynastic leader must have humility at his core. And establishing structures to ensure sustained success in an organisation that embodies his values long after his departure is his greatest task of all.

CHAPTER TEN

CRISIS RESPONSE AND TURNAROUND

THE BIG IDEA

The ideas of crisis and turnaround are closely linked. Turnaround is needed where dramatic improvement is required, for example when results have been allowed to drift and the organisation is no longer operating at the expected level. Crisis is, by definition, more dramatic and extreme. But, at its core, a business in crisis requires turnaround – some kind of profound shift – if it is to revive its fortunes.

One of the key elements of both concepts is choice. A crisis is effectively a point of choice – a place where a leader asks 'How shall I respond?' Most of us think of it as a dramatic and negative situation – and so it may be – but the word essentially means a 'decisive moment' or a 'turning point'. However, the Mandarin characters for crisis (wei ji) actually mean 'danger' (or 'risk') *and* 'opportunity'. Crisis is all about provoking action, and the thoughtful leader asks 'Where is the opportunity in this?'

A second key element of both concepts is action. Crisis provokes action, and only truly radical action will drive the reversal in fortune and form that leads to successful turnaround. Leaders in a crisis may feel the pressure, but they at least have momentum driving them forward. Turnaround from a standing start – such as years of accepted under-performance – still requires radical action, and thus brings a challenge all of its own.

In football, almost all managers are appointed into some kind of crisis or need for turnaround. Up to 98 per cent of professional managers in the four English leagues will be sacked at some point – an expression of frustration by the shareholders or at least of a strong desire for urgent change. The new manager often arrives on a wave of hope and expectation. What he typically inherits is low confidence and stretched resources. His primary goal is to deal with the crisis and set the team back on the path to long-term success.

THE MANAGER

With 21 major honours in 11 years over two spells as manager of Glasgow Rangers, Walter Smith is one of the most successful professional leaders in the modern game. He arrived at Rangers as assistant manager to player-manager Graeme Souness in 1986 and, when Souness left for Liverpool in 1991, Smith became Rangers manager in his own right. Between 1991 and 1997, he led Rangers to seven consecutive Scottish Premier League titles, securing the domestic treble in 1993. After leaving Rangers in 1997, Smith guided Everton through a notoriously difficult four-year period, beset by financial stringency, before taking the post of manager of the Scotland national side. In his three years as Scotland manager he again presided over a significant upturn, leading them 70 places up the FIFA world rankings. Then in January 2007 he returned to Rangers as manager for a second period to preside over the turnaround of a club whose on-field results had slumped. Initially the club were able to provide Smith with a level of resources to upgrade the team but then, in early 2009, Rangers were hit by a financial crisis which would see Smith unable to sign any players for a two-year period. Remarkably, despite such uncertainty, Smith continued to dominate Scottish football during this period, winning three more consecutive league titles, two league cups and a Scottish cup.

His Philosophy

Smith's core philosophy is to instil a winning mentality in the group that he is working with: 'Whatever your context and challenge as a football manager, the one thing we all have to do to be successful is to win. So we have to get that winning mentality in our teams.' At Rangers, Smith had many successes, winning titles and having trophies to show for his efforts. But the winning mentality he insists is not contingent on winning trophies: 'Many managers like David Moyes and Tony Pulis are winners because of the winning mentality they have instilled in their teams to ensure consistent progress. When I was at Everton, we had a good few problems to overcome including significant financial aspects. But even during that troubled three and a half years, the club was able to stay in the Premiership and to maintain decent levels of performance. There were no trophies, but for me that was like a win. We achieved a winning mentality.'

The Challenge: Building the Aircraft While it's Airborne

It is ludicrous to imagine building an aircraft in the air. Two things would be going on simultaneously: the minute-to-minute operational challenge of keeping the aircraft flying, with all the challenges of navigation, communication, technology, engineering, safety and passenger comfort; and the foundational work of design, sourcing and manufacture of components, heavy engineering, assembly, testing and the rest. These are clearly incompatible. And yet when a new manager is asked to take on a failing or underperforming team in crisis, this is effectively what he is being asked to do. Week to week there is training, coaching, analysis, selection, inspiration – not to mention a whole raft of stakeholders from owner through fans to the press, and, of course, the matches themselves with all the preparation, execution and fallout they bring. Then at the same time there is foundational work that will transform the club altogether: setting and communicating a new vision, getting buy-in from players and stakeholders, reshaping the squad, buying and selling, dealing with anxiety, resentment, questioning and monitoring progress against the overall goal.

Success in crisis response or in any form of turnaround requires a leader to strike a balance between the immediate needs of the team (keeping the aircraft airborne) and the long-term needs for future success (building a plane that will keep on flying for years to come).

The Response: Creating Turnaround

Glasgow Rangers is a fiercely proud club with an undeniably great history. In the summer of 1986, Graeme Souness took over as manager and brought with him an experienced assistant manager Walter Smith. Souness arrived at a club in a poor state of repair that had not won a major trophy for seven years, and trailed their bitter rivals Celtic by some distance. Like many leaders in these situations, Souness faced a broad array of challenges, which Smith recalls well: 'When we got there, like a lot of football teams – and like a lot of businesses – there had been no real investment in the team. The standard of player we found at that time was probably lower than it had been for many, many years. Since the Ibrox stadium disaster in 1971, most of the money had been ploughed into making sure they had one of the best and one of the safest stadiums in Britain. So the team struggled a little bit. The management team's challenge was to get in fast, make the changes and try and get the team to be successful. So phase one was about having an impact by bringing in some new players, throwing out old mindsets, doing the management basics well – and hoping the results would come, which they did.' In this first phase Smith, as assistant manager, observed Souness applying the first two rules of turnaround: get early results, and start to shift mindsets. It was an experience that would serve him well as a manager in his own right.

Getting early results

Sam Allardyce arrived at Bolton in 1999. He recalls that in the early stages, many players simply didn't want to be there: 'They felt their career was going to be benefited by going elsewhere and making a few more bob. Everybody knew that Bolton was in a financial dilemma, so they all wanted to be the one that got away.' This undercurrent can be very dangerous, but is not uncommon when a team is in crisis, and typically it was not out in the open. Most dissatisfaction only came to the surface once a player got his agent to begin the process.

In this climate, Allardyce did two significant things. The first was to keep an assistant, Phil Brown, who knew the players well from the previous leadership and could provide instant benchmarks to assess whether or not a player was really trying. The second was to secure some good early results on the field: 'Good results will make life very difficult for those that want to get away. If you keep getting results, players actually start to like it again – they begin to think, "it's not so bad here" – and quickly the team gets on an upward spiral. In that way the cycle of negativity gets broken.'

Martin O'Neill is the master of the early impact. Taking over at Sunderland in December 2011, he took the team from 17th to 10th in the Barclays Premier League, winning four out of his first six games and inflicting only the second defeat of the season on eventual champions Manchester City. This was a considerable impact on a side that had taken just five points from 18 before he arrived. What's his secret? 'I try and prepare as well as I can a couple of days before arriving, to learn as much as I can – which won't be phenomenal! Then something happens in the mindset of the players. We all know that everything is down to the performance and the result at the weekend. So we focus entirely on that – to get a result from somewhere, because that more than anything else will give the players the confidence to carry on. You can talk to them forever and a day about the changes you might make at a football club, and that's all fine – but it's all in the future. Players need the instant result and the best way to do it is get it on the field.

'Our first game against Blackburn Rovers, we played really well in the match, had just a little bit of luck and scored twice late on to get three very valuable points. That gave the lads confidence heading into the Christmas period. One way or the other we just seemed to deal with injury setback after setback. By the time we played Manchester City on New Year's Day we had midfield players playing in full-back positions, we had centre forwards having to drop back and play in midfield … But all in all we had gained a bit of spirit at that time and the players saw it through and actually won the game in the very last minute. It is remarkable because a couple of days later we travelled to Wigan and won at Wigan. Now whether we would have won at Wigan had we not won against Manchester City is always debatable, but as the great Jonny Giles once said to me, "Ifs, buts and maybes – if you keep them out of the equation you may be able to think a bit more clearly."'

O'Neill brings with him into a turnaround situation an energy that is both practical and positive. He welcomes the chance to address low confidence, and seems to bring about early results almost by sheer force of character. Once they got going, his Sunderland side hit a run of form, their confidence growing by the week, proving the value of early results.

Shifting mindsets

Like any turnaround leaders, football managers find that shifting behaviours in their people is critical. Arriving at Rangers, Graeme Souness and Walter Smith found some things that needed to change. When players have become convinced they are second best (or worse), they can begin to behave negatively or disruptively both off and on the field. Complaining, blaming, getting angry, arguing, dropping heads, making unforced errors. All of these behaviours are detrimental to any team – but especially to a high-profile football team looking for rapid improvement. Gérard Houllier's fourth foundational value is 'be a winner'. Smith, Mancini and others speak of 'a winning mentality' and 'shifting mindsets'. But what does this actually mean?

Returning to the idea of the iceberg, we can only achieve lasting change to our behaviours if we do shift our mindset. A manager can tell a player to stop complaining, and he may well do so – for a while. But unless he shifts the feeling of injustice that has led to his behaviour, he will simply return to the complaining.

The behaviours Souness and his assistant manager Smith encountered were being driven by a losing mindset – and they had to address it head-on in order to achieve lasting change. 'We had a group of players who hadn't won a championship for nine seasons. At Rangers, that's probably been the longest spell for 60, 70, 80 years. Nine years before, at the same time as Celtic began their championship-winning run, Rangers themselves had a good team. But Celtic had a terrific team and they went on to win nine straight titles under a fabulous leader, Jock Stein. Rangers were reaching European finals, winning cups, and having good runs in Europe, but Celtic's dominance and a lack of investment at Ibrox created this losing mindset. When success is elusive, players start to consider that that's normal and that they can't rise above it. It was important to instil in them the belief that those days are over and there's going to be a total change.'

Easier said than done, of course. But Smith recounts that Souness had an interesting strategy: 'When we arrived at Rangers, everybody got the impression of massive changes. In reality, the changes were pretty modest: only three or four players brought in – Chris Woods, Terry Butcher, Graeme himself. We worked with a squad composed mainly of the players we had inherited. We got an immediate reaction from them though, and won the championship and league cup in the first season.' The management team appreciated the impression of the clean sweep, but did not get carried away by it. They were at all times grounded in reality.

The legacy challenge

Towards the end of the 2011–12 season, Manchester United's supporters were smelling blood and singing 'City's cracking up.' In the title race United's winning mindset was coming to the fore, just as City's old losing mindset seemed to reappear. Jim White, writing in the *Daily Telegraph*, spoke of the 'continuity of success' in the Old Trafford dressing room, where the 'long-serving, medal-accumulating players pass on winning habits to new recruits'.

There was no crisis at Manchester City. Here was a club with new, ambitious owners, massive recent investment and seemingly limitless opportunity. Yet to seize that opportunity required a real shift. For Mancini, the losing mindset was a deep underlying challenge that demanded turnaround action. The team he inherited from Mark Hughes in December 2010 was not in serious danger – indeed a top-four finish looked possible. But they were not yet consistent, some of their expensive signings were not matching expectations and the great promise of the Abu Dhabi investment was not yet coming good. Mancini faced the legacy mindset of 'typical City' – the club that snatched defeat from the jaws of victory, that created anxiety when the match should have been won and that always dwelt in the shadow of United.

So how did Mancini tackle this need for turnaround at City? 'First you need time, because if you don't have time then it's difficult. You can't work on the players' heads in one month, three months or six months. You also need luck because if after one year you can win, then it's easy because the players follow you. You also need to work hard. We worked hard, very hard, and they were not ready to work hard like we worked them in the last two years. But in the end if you win, the players are ready to do this. After that we work also with their mentality because the players understand that it is not important only to play; it is important to win. They understood if we arrive in second position it is not enough, and we should play always to win. We do this also during the training session. If you can understand this, you can change your mentality.'

Don't declare victory too early

Had Manchester City declared victory too early after the investment? It is unclear how much of the initial posturing a year before Mancini's arrival was media-generated, but the signature signing of Robinho was to prove unsuccessful and initial momentum was lost. At Rangers, the huge first-year success of Souness was almost wasted, when the club failed to invest – and

Smith believes they did declare victory too early. 'In our second season when we were looking to build even further and be stronger, we didn't manage to spend the money that was necessary to continue the improvement. Graeme Souness had been a fantastic player for us in the first season, but he was finishing playing. Terry Butcher who was our captain and on-field leader broke his leg. We won the League Cup earlier on in the season, but didn't have the size of squad to cover for injury and suspension, so we suffered towards the end.' The club learned its lesson though: 'At the end of that season, we managed to do what we should have done a year earlier – invest greatly in the team, bring in another level of player and propel the club to sustained success.' Best-practice turnaround happens in both the immediate and the longer term.

The power of symbolic actions

One of the most powerful tools for shifting mindsets is symbolic action from leaders. With the new owners at Rangers came new management, and with the new management came new players. Smith is sure that the freshness of the new blood made all the difference: 'This vitality was a huge thing. All the players and staff who continued into the new era could sense it. The owners had no need to physically go down into the dressing room … Just the act of bringing a new manager, especially as high-profile a manager as Graeme Souness, made everybody in that dressing room realise that the new owners were serious. They were not expecting the team to stay where it was.

'Everyone knew that they had to rise to the challenge that was being thrown to them if they wanted to remain at the club. Success hadn't been there for a great number of years, but now it was expected once again. They were going to have to step up to the plate. The actions of the owners were as important as anything Graeme said or did in the dressing room.' Smith has a point. 'Handling a crisis is not a one-man show. Each major stakeholder has to play their part: vision and investment from the board, ownership and commitment from the players.' In addition, clear, decisive action was taken at Rangers that left no doubt in the minds of the players about what was acceptable and what was not. At City, Mancini appeared to do the same: from the training-ground regime to selling key players, he was also unambiguous.

Tony Pulis arriving at Stoke City took very forceful and early symbolic action that was also intensely practical: 'Initially we were in a very difficult situation because we were a mid- to low-table Championship club and surviving on gates of 11,000. We found it very, very difficult initially to attract players. We weren't the biggest payers in the world, but luckily for me the loan system had just kicked into place where you could actually take seven players on loan. We weren't able to do much business when the transfer window was open, so as soon as we were able to loan players we loaned fringe players from Premier League clubs. Players like Patrik Berger and Salif Diao arrived, which not only gave the club a massive lift, but also enabled us to attract better players from Championship clubs. So we had a plan which we stuck to, we managed the resources available well and it worked for us.'

Symbolic actions reverberate throughout an organisation, and show that the turnaround leader means business: he will not easily be diverted from his task.

Transformational leadership is a contact sport

The words change and transformation are often used inter-changeably. In fact, they carry quite different implications. Change is often fleeting. A manager can change the shape of his team at half-time, and then change it back again when they take a two-goal lead. This change is not permanent. Transformation – like the caterpillar becoming a butterfly – is truly radical. And there is no going back. What was required at Rangers in 1986 was a full-blown transformation. And what was demonstrated is that leadership of this type is a contact sport. It's all about how you engage with people. Walter Smith recalls: 'It was important to demonstrate that what had been acceptable previously was acceptable no longer – and for that, actions are initially as strong as words. I think once you are in the midst of the turnover, things naturally lift and naturally get carried away and there's a freshness there that makes management a little bit easier than it is over a longer period.'

One of the first things Souness had to do was make assessments – work out who would fit where and who wouldn't fit at all. 'These are the first decisions you make as a manager and even if you don't know for sure, you often have to make an early assessment. When you go in there are some players who disappoint you, some players who surprise you – so that early assessment is important.

'If you're one of the players who's been retained, you're feeling good about yourself – but you're also feeling some weight of expectation. You begin to believe you have a role to play in getting to the next level and making this club great again. That's the message that must be communicated to everyone. But words are easy. In football especially you have a 90-minute period, sometimes two 90-minute periods in every week where you actually see your work – it's actually there and it stares you right in the face. So when we were asking players to change their mindset, then we were able to see whether they're really shifting. Allowing for a little bit of time for a team to come together, we can see whether that mindset is changing within the players who were previously there. On the majority of occasions, once you make your decision on a player and you're quite happy with the way he's playing, they are the ones who have normally reacted in the proper manner and the ones that you're happy to keep.'

The early contact is not always easy, and takes gutsy leadership. David Platt says of Mancini's arrival at City that he was 'never afraid from the beginning to ruffle feathers and to confront people when they disagreed with him'. Just as Mancini would do with Manchester City ten years later, Rangers had to keep their eyes on the prize: 'The most important thing was achieving a lift in the whole club – a lift in everyone who played, everyone who supported and everyone who wanted to come into the new thing we were building. And as Rangers began to achieve success, that created an expectation of more success and a next level of perfor-mance for players to rise to. Then they had to show they could handle that on a longer-term basis.'

When, during Smith's second spell as Rangers manager, the severe financial situation necessitated that every player be made available for transfer, it took courage and openness for the manager to break the news to the squad. This approach was rewarded in a way he did not expect. 'What I never thought would happen was the strengthening of bonds both within the squad and with the management. Because we put everyone up for sale, effectively every player was in a similar situation. We then went through a few transfer windows where we transferred some players and cut our squad size down, and did everything that we were asked to do in a financial sense. We ended up with a squad of players that remained more or less the same for two full seasons, and they created a terrific bond that as much as anything helped us through the situation. It may have happened by accident, but it was a factor in the team remaining successful despite the financial problems off the field.'

Talk with people

While Smith's arrival back at Rangers in 2007 originally looked like a turnaround situation of an underperforming team, within two years it evolved into a full-blown case of crisis management that he could not have anticipated.

Interestingly, though a man of action to his core, Smith also knows the power of words. His first priority in the maelstrom was his team. 'As soon as we were told that we had a problem in a financial sense and that every one of our players was going to be put up for sale, I felt it was important to be straight with the players right away. So I held a meeting and explained the financial situation to them and told them we had no other path to go down other than to make everybody available for transfer. I then had fairly regular meetings with them just to explain to them where we were financially without going into minute detail. I explained to them why they weren't getting offered contracts when they were coming to an end and being allowed to run out. And looking back, to be quite honest, it was the right thing to do.

'There was always the chance to talk, which is the advantage of having a small workforce of maybe 24 guys, roughly speaking. They are there every day. You're in contact with them every day. I don't like to have too many formal meetings with the group – I like to keep these for when they really matter and when I've got something to really say. To keep continued success going, you have to keep taking stock with the team on a fairly regular basis. If they're at the top of the league, they'll always imagine that they're being successful. But at times I had to show them that their performance levels had fallen. They might still be winning, because a lot of the time you can be good enough to still win while playing at a slightly lower level. But I had to generate the spark to keep them at that high level. So I would use my instinct to know when a team talk would have real impact. Too many and you lose your impact; too few and they think you don't care.'

So his advice to a leader in crisis or turnaround would highlight regular, frequent, honest communication. 'I would sit everyone down – and explain the situation on as honest a basis as I possibly could to make them realise exactly where they are at the present moment, and where I hoped to be in the short and long term. And I would keep that level of honest sit-down, clear-the-air communication going quite regularly in the short term. Once you settle down and start to get on with the turnaround, you still have to have these sessions so that everyone knows exactly where you are – but at longer intervals. Football is slightly different in a sense, in that the world knows where you are anyway: your wins, your defeats, your position in the league – it's there for everybody to see – there's no hiding place. But in any crisis situation there has to be a real honesty and some real straightforward talking done in the initial part of it – to lead people out of it.' Leaders in business will recognise this. Straightforward conversations about results – real and projected – are essential, and not only with front-line staff, but also with management, board and shareholders.

'In the crisis, chief executive Martin Bain and I were left with the task of the day-to-day running of the club, and I think when you have the problems in the manner that we had, then the relationship you have with your chief executive is probably as important as any at the club. Martin was fantastic in helping me handle the overall situation. It was a hard time for him as well trying to handle the club, keeping everything going and making sure that we had enough support to make us competitive on the field, while still trying to juggle with the banks and financials in the background.'

No engagement with significant stakeholders is wasted. In October 2009, Smith commented in one of his post-match press conferences on the extent of the financial constraints at Rangers, and explained how all of his players were up for sale. 'It's important to explain the overall picture to everyone concerned. When they see circumstances arising and decisions being made, both supporters and media can be quick to jump and blame people for making those decisions. If leaders in football have got a problem financially, then they should tell people that they have got a problem financially. Supporters contribute an awful lot of money to the club's wellbeing, and if that money is not getting spent in the manner they would like, then they have a right to know that as well.'

Likewise, Martin O'Neill is a great believer in talking to people in any form of turnaround. When he arrived at Aston Villa, the club could not be said to be in serious crisis – but, as with every managerial appointment, the owner was looking for an early impact – a turnaround on a smaller scale. 'Whenever you have time – let's say you sign for a football club pre-season, and you've got a number of weeks to work with them – then it's worth having that individual meeting with players. At Aston Villa, I had a fortnight before the season kicked off and sometimes in life that fortnight seems like six months, which was great. It gave me a chance, for instance, to convince Gareth Barry, who wanted to leave to go to Portsmouth, to stay in order that things might improve. He hadn't been involved in the England team for some time. So I sat down and had a conversation with him – and then he proceeded to play his best football. Now not for one minute do I think that the talk had everything to do with that, but it did steady his mind. And he played so well for us that next season that not only did he get into the England squad, in time he got into the England team and cemented his place there. Of course, for him personally, he went on to Manchester City and won medals, so it has gone well.'

Low points will happen

Looking back on extraordinary success in both the turnaround and the crisis situations, it would be easy for Smith to forget the low points. But he is clear they happen: 'At Rangers, the low point was in the second year. We didn't do enough to improve on the first year's work. That brought us down a little bit, but then we managed to improve and get a few other players in and the whole place received a massive lift again. That was effectively the moment when Rangers went on and dominated Scottish football for that nine-year period.' The lesson here is that a slump after the initial post-crisis success does not spell disaster. Once again, the challenge for the leader is to remain grounded in reality.

'In many ways, Everton was a far bigger test than Rangers, where all the background circumstances were there for me to front a level of success. At Everton they weren't, so we were flying by the seat of our pants a lot of the time. It was a crisis: a period of intense turmoil, with a hundred small decisions to be made every day. The questions come from every angle – they come from the team, from the bank manager, from the chairman – hundreds of things at once. The most important thing though is to show your people – your staff and your players – that you're leading and you're not being affected by anything that's happening off the pitch. That's an important aspect of it. To show the confidence that you're going to get through it and you're going to take them with you. That for me was the main leadership challenge in crisis.' The leader in crisis needs to be calm and assured – and Smith demonstrated those qualities again during his crisis-hit second spell at Rangers.

The Commander

Of Professor Keith Grint's three styles of addressing a problem (command, lead, manage), the ideal one for crisis is command. He writes, 'A *Critical Problem,* e.g. a "crisis", encapsulates very little time for decision-making and action, and it is often associated with authoritarianism. Here there is virtually no uncertainty about what needs to be done – at least in the behaviour of the commander, whose role is to take the required decisive action – that is to provide the *answer* to the problem, not to engage processes (management) or ask questions (leadership).'

In today's leadership environments, many new leaders face something akin to crisis on arrival. In football leadership, someone has almost always been sacked – provoking a mini-crisis in itself. Smith faced a graver than usual crisis in 2009, and (albeit in very different contexts) both he and Mancini on arriving at City faced the need for turnaround. Without generating hysteria or causing unnecessary pain, in each instance both men took command of the situation. Essentially, that command style required three things:

1. They had answers:
   Both men knew what they wanted to do and did it, confidently driving through their own approach to achieving turnaround.

2. They acted decisively:
   Both men made rapid changes to the playing staff, shifted training methodologies and confronted unhelpful mindsets.

3. They held their nerve:
   Mancini as City's old losing mindset seemed to reappear, Smith after Souness left in 1991 and again in 2009 when his

squad was put up for sale – and undoubtedly countless other times in circumstances that will remain behind the club's closed doors.

Most turnarounds need delivering over two horizons. The first is the very short term: steadying the ship, so to speak. This is especially important in a true crisis, and is where the O'Neill-style quick results are needed to steady the nerves. How long a leader has depends on the environment – but it's typically months, and sometimes weeks – never years. The second is the medium to long term – setting the ship on the right course. This is where the Souness, Smith or Mancini-style building to trophies is required. Here, the leader may well have years – provided the trajectory is right. But no leaders in turnaround are given long if results elude them. Souness, Smith, Mancini and O'Neill all began their tenures with wins. This is not essential, but it is highly desirable. In football as in business, it does not take too many reversals before questions get asked. The successful commander drives through the short term and adapts for the long term. No wonder it only falls to a few to do it well.

CHAPTER ELEVEN

TRIUMPH AND DESPAIR

THE BIG IDEA

Professional football at the highest level is a game punctuated by enormous highs and lows. For the football leader – just as for the business leader at the top of a company with shareholders – the line between success and failure is thin and not always well defined.

Both joy and pain are ever present; and one gives way to the other with astonishing frequency in high-pressure environments. How leaders handle success and how they handle failure goes a long way to defining them in the eyes of their own people and of a watching public.

THE MANAGER

Mick McCarthy has played and managed with distinction at the highest level of football. At international level, he led his country in separate World Cup final tournaments as both a playing captain and as a manager. At club level, he played top-flight football with Manchester City in England, Celtic in Scotland, and Lyon in France – most notably winning Scottish Premier League and Scottish Cup honours while at Celtic. While playing at Millwall in the second flight in 1992, he moved overnight from player into his first management role. He has moved role only four times in 20 years: first to Ireland, then to Sunderland and on to Wolves, remaining in each post for between four and six years. His Sunderland team won the Championship in 2004–05, and his Wolves team equalled the feat in 2008–09, leading the table for 42 out of 46 weeks. He would go on to be Wolves' most successful manager in 30 years, leading them in three consecutive Premier League campaigns. McCarthy made his fourth managerial move, to Ipswich Town, in November 2012.

His Philosophy

McCarthy appears to the watching public as a tough, Yorkshire-born former centre-half who eats people for breakfast. In reality, he is a very thoughtful leader of people who leads out of decency, integrity and passion. He refuses to blame, or to complain. He takes ownership for his failures and his successes. He believes in setting and modelling high standards of behaviour, and he believes in the inherent decency of people. His appetite for ownership and responsibility lies at the heart of his ability to deal equably with whatever triumphs and disasters he encounters.

The Challenge

The 19th-century author Rudyard Kipling suggested we should seek to 'Meet with triumph and disaster and treat the two imposters just the same.' How many of us get carried away with the ups and the downs of our lives and careers? When something goes well, we think we're invincible. When we fail, we can begin to experience an abyss from which we fear we will never escape. This black-and-white view of a world that has countless subtle shades of grey is one example of what psychologists call 'crooked thinking'.

Consider for a moment the dangers of this brand of thought. One victory becomes in our minds a guarantee of great achievements and riches to come. For a football manager in the Premier League, this is incredibly dangerous. The pressures on him to succeed are intense and come from a raft of people with considerable personal interest. Players look to him to lead them to glory, owners need to see some payback on their often massive investments and the fans, week in week out, arrive at the ground expecting and demanding results. Equally, even a short run of poor or unexpected results can prompt a leader to ask deep and unsettling questions.

Leaders in this situation can all too easily lose their sense of objectivity, and find themselves drawn down one of two dangerous avenues.

The trap of triumph

There is nothing wrong with celebrating success. Ignoring success – or skating over it too fleetingly – can lead to resentment in leaders and their people. McCarthy is a great believer in enjoying the moment: 'My latest success is always the best one. Getting to the World Cup finals with Ireland in Iran was just surreal. I am the manager that's taken the Irish team to the 2002 World Cup finals. Someone hit me and wake me up! So that was great, but then when I got Sunderland promotion that was better, getting up with Wolves and staying up that was better, staying up a second year was better and whatever I do next will be better than all of them.'

Who would argue with the right of a cup-winning side to parade the trophy on a bus? Neil Warnock contrasts moments of triumph at Scarborough, Notts County and Plymouth with the QPR promotion campaign of 2010–11. 'At Scarborough when we got promoted, there were amazing scenes with an open-top bus ride through town. With Notts County, two promotions and two Wembley play-off finals, two open-top bus rides – coming back up the motorway to Nottingham with all the flags flying – unforgettable. Plymouth had never ever been to Wembley – we got there and got promoted. To see all the people who still talk about the open-top bus ride coming down the motorway from Wembley – grandads and young kids with their flags out of their doors, windows – superb. At QPR, we'd been through the mill with all the point-deduction business. We won the league, got promotion and we never had an open-top bus ride, we never had a celebration dinner, we didn't have anything at all. It was a moment lost. Fans remember these moments all their lives.'

Warnock is right. Achievement deserves celebration – especially when hard work has played a part. It also allows leaders to show their gratitude publicly – managers to honour players, owners to honour staff at all levels and the club to honour the fans. But success is fleeting. Ask just about any high-level, high-quality professional football manager. And because it is fleeting, the leader who pays it too much attention opens himself up to dangers on two horizons. In the short term, the trap is to grasp at positives that are not really there, or not really relevant ('we had more possession than they did'), or to seize on a single win or a short run as a sign of turning a corner. When subsequent events prove the manager wrong, he loses credibility. The long-term trap is even more dangerous. The scent of success is heady, and as an admiring world begins to celebrate a manager's achievements, it's very easy for him to start believing his own publicity and then to miss the warning signs of the mire ahead. The same admiring world will be only too eager to cut him down at the earliest signs of frailty – real or imaginary.

The slough of despond

The second of those dangerous avenues leads to becoming obsessed with failure. Four straight defeats for your football team do not make you an incompetent manager, but the spiral from upset to despair is slippery and very common. McCarthy has never really suffered from this – although he admits he nearly went there as a player at Manchester City: 'I had a torrid time of it. The manager Billy McNeill left me in the team – he trusted me, which I appreciated. I remember it vividly. I had a month or six weeks where I struggled. I stayed in, I went out; I drank more, I drank less; I trained harder, I trained less; I tried everything to rectify it.' Characteristically, McCarthy took ownership of the situation and told himself to 'just get on with it. I got myself back playing.'

Warnock's blackest moment came in 2007 when Sheffield United were relegated from the Premiership just one year after their promotion. After a series of three defeats in the spring, they achieved two great results under pressure against their closest rivals for survival: a 3-0 home win against West Ham and a 1-1 away draw at Charlton Athletic. Then they played Wigan Athletic at home in the final match, needing only to avoid defeat to ensure Premiership status. On the same day, West Ham played at Manchester United – and needed at least a draw to survive. Dramatically, West Ham won at Old Trafford – and Wigan won at Bramall Lane. The 2-1 defeat meant that Sheffield United were relegated by a single goal. 'We had 38 points, which was unbelievable – that would be mid-table some years, but we got relegated by one goal. It was like an arrow – really painful: the worst moment of my career. I stood with the rain pouring down on me with a few minutes to go, knowing I'd got my boyhood club relegated.' But straight away came the determination: 'It felt unjust, but then again I was determined to show [chairman] Kevin McCabe how good I was. I thought: right, I'm going to go somewhere else now and do it. I couldn't quite do it at Palace, but that drove me on again …'

Football is a game of high stakes and narrow margins. One goal would have changed it. Is it wrong to feel that somehow the fates have conspired against you? Perhaps not, but it is almost impossible to avoid. The critical issue as a leader is not whether these thoughts come into your mind. It's what you do with them that counts.

Staying Centred around Setbacks and Upsets

Leading football managers have to have strategies to deal with the knocks. Some have their preferred approach that clicks in whenever the punches come. For others, it is entirely situational.

Take ownership and responsibility

One of the great temptations when things go wrong is to blame everyone else. Psychologists call it externalising. It's the referee's fault, it's the board's fault, it's because of the injury list. The act of blaming has two effects. First, it tends to alienate others and sacrifice the support and sympathy they might otherwise offer. Second, it immobilises the victim – the person making the excuses. As long as a leader is trying to convince himself and everyone else of his innocence, he is not focusing on taking steps to solve the problem.

World-class football leaders internalise responsibility. In February 2012, McCarthy took Wolves down to London to play QPR. McCarthy was in his sixth season at Wolves, and his second successive Premier League campaign. Achieving stability in the most competitive top flight in the world is not easy when resources are limited, and McCarthy achieved it in significant measure by the standards of the club. However, the season was tough and Wolves were in the bottom three. A week earlier, after a 3-0 defeat against Liverpool, club owner Steve Morgan had personally given the team a dressing-down – a move that McCarthy now admits undermined his leadership. On the day at Loftus Road, an inspired substitution by McCarthy saw Kevin Doyle score the winner within a minute of running on the field. Wolves were out of the bottom three, and the BBC called it a 'huge win'. But eight days later, it all went wrong. Wolves conceded five goals at home to local rivals West Bromwich Albion. McCarthy apologised for the performance, and within 24 hours was sacked.

McCarthy's reflection on this incident is unquestionably that of a centred leader: 'It's sad, of course, but I look at myself and I had a role in it. I don't blame all the players and the chief executive and everybody else. I've signed the players; I've worked with them. There are mitigating circumstances in and around that, but of course I've had a role to play in it. The trend was simple: we were going in the opposite direction to the one we wanted. But that was who we were as a team. I had eight players in the team that got us promoted from the Championship who I'd signed from Luton, Leicester, Bohemians, Hearts … Frankly, we were a bottom-eight team, always going to be scrapping against relegation. I thought I was going to keep them up because I'd done it for two years previously. It was sad, but I didn't walk away with any bitterness. I generally don't because I know I had a role to play. So I've left on the best terms – and that is true of every time I've left a club.'

McCarthy's broad shoulders are inspirational. Too many leaders are ready to blame everyone except themselves. This affects both their own view of the world, and everyone else's view of them. At tough moments, great leaders take ownership, and the world applauds. It's not easy though. In 1999, McCarthy's Ireland needed to beat Macedonia to qualify directly for the European Championships of the following year. They conceded an equaliser in the 93rd minute of the match. 'I didn't sleep a wink that night. I was in bits. Not a wink. I watched the telly all night and I knew the press were waiting for me. I got up and put my best suit on and I went downstairs. I looked a million dollars – chest out, chin up, and I looked them all in the eye and said, "I believe we have a press conference this morning, lads – do you want to see me?" They were all like "yes please!" So I arranged it, did it, knocked them out, talked about it. I was dying, but they didn't know that. I looked them all in the eye; they were blown away by it. They asked me afterwards, "How did you do that?" I said I just did – they didn't know I was dying. I smiled at them all and did it all. Shook all their hands and I think that rubbed off on everybody else that day.'

Control the controllables and quickly move on

One of the key features of managers who take responsibility is their focus on what they can control. The line McCarthy took with the press after the Macedonia match is typical: 'As usual we now are in the play-offs, playing against Turkey. I can't do anything about last night – that's done, so we've got Turkey to play. Yes, we should have won – it was a bad goal to concede, but is me crying about it going to change it? If I talk about it for the next 20 minutes, are we going to be in the European Championships? So I'll go and watch Turkey now and get on with that. I will deal with the things I can.'

In a very similar way, Carlo Ancelotti learns lessons then moves on to where he does have influence – which is usually the next match: 'We have a problem today. We lost a very important game last night. But today is not a time to regret, to think about what happened yesterday, the last game … Instead, we have to focus for the next game. That is the only way you can do.'

There is an old proverb that goes: 'The past is a thief – it steals the present and the future from us.' Leaders who dwell too long on their – or others' – mistakes find that they lose their mastery of the present.

After a defeat, no matter how big, McCarthy refuses to dwell in the place of pain: 'Once I've seen the players on Monday and we've trained, I'm back at it. So Monday might be a dull day, and I think it is for any of us that have been beaten, but it doesn't carry on for the rest of the week. I'd have the staff in early and we would sit on the static bikes and watch on the big screen. So we are watching and at the same time we get an hour's exercise on the bike and chat about the game – four of us generally, five with the analyst. So I might arrive on a Monday morning, badly beaten and thinking we were crap. But when I've watched it, I've got it clear in my head and I've taken the positives. We've got a lot right, and we've analysed that. Then we move on. We've lost that game. No point crying over that one, let's get on to the next one. The only way we can prepare for the next one is getting over that one.' Leaders must get the subtle blend of learning from their mistakes without becoming defeatist or despondent.

Go back to your belief wall

Warnock's response is not to dwell on thoughts of victimhood and injustice. He picks himself up quickly, and self-belief cuts in. What goes through his mind is something like: 'I'll show them. I'm not done yet.' And even when his next club after the Sheffield episode, Crystal Palace, went into administration, the self-belief was strong enough for him to continue, and he moved on to QPR.

Self-belief is a critical part of an elite athlete's make-up – and it's essential for a leader also. Olympic gold-medal swimmer Adrian Moorhouse, writing with performance psychologist Professor Graham Jones, defines it as: 'An unshakable belief in your ability to achieve competition goals'. They suggest it is all about understanding the unique qualities and abilities that make you better than your opponents. Many elite sportspeople use the concept of a 'belief wall' – a mental construct built of the bricks of undeniable achievement. Thus a runner might look left and right to his opponents in the starting blocks, and say to himself 'I have beaten every one of you over this distance before.' That is a brick from his wall. The stronger and more solid your wall, the more powerful your self-belief and the more it takes to knock you off balance.

Choose optimism

One of the most powerful characteristics of a football leader is optimism. This is not a Pollyanna-style refusal to accept reality. It is a rational, almost forensic approach to charting the best possible route. Warnock's approach is an almost dogged version of this. He admits he is a man for whom hurts remain. He is not the best at letting go. But he does lift up his eyes and set his jaw: 'I do look back at QPR and think, "Two years of my life to get where I wanted to be, taken away." It is unfair, but my philosophy has been when one door does close it's a new opportunity and a new part of your life. Exciting things are often just round the corner – and it's not very often that they crop up when I'm low. I know what I'm good at – I enjoy management and I love making people happy. So I look the world in the eye, and never give up.'

Ancelotti shares this approach: 'I am optimistic in life. It is very important – especially in football. I prefer to wake up in the morning and think about the good things and the sunshine – to wake up with a smile. I think sometimes people create problems, but for nothing.' Optimistic leaders do not ignore reality – but they are careful not to exaggerate existing problems or to invent new ones.

Look for the win

Perhaps the most powerful of all the strategies is to apply the aikido principle. In most martial arts and other combat sports, the main idea is to block what your opponent does and then punch back. In negotiation, this is equivalent to saying: 'No – you're wrong. *This* is how it's going to be.' However, in aikido the philosophy suggests you take the punch your opponent is offering and use the energy to your own advantage – and to others' benefit also. In negotiation, this is like saying: 'Now that's interesting! I wonder where it might lead us?' Applied to the arrows of life, this is the difference between painful resistance and open-minded enquiry.

Except for the extraordinary Anfield dynasty of Shankly, Paisley, Fagan and Dalglish, British football history is not littered with examples of successful transitions from assistant to manager. After Souness left Rangers, the chairman turned to Walter Smith whose task was made even tougher by new UEFA rulings. But Smith saw the situation as an opportunity: 'Looking back on it, UEFA's introduction of a "three foreigner" rule actually helped me. The majority of our "foreigners" were English, but they still ranked as foreigners – so we had to change the staff quite a bit. Graeme and I had been planning to do that in the summer anyway, and everybody at the club from owner down knew it was going to happen. We were going to be allowed a couple of seasons domesti-cally to make the change, but we knew the time was now – no doubt influenced by our European prospects. After winning a couple of titles in a row and heading for a third one, you really wouldn't want to make that many changes – but I knew we had to do it. In the end, it went very well. We had one or two disappointments at the start – normal when you're changing and trying to form a new team – it takes a little bit of time for them to settle in. We had two or three months of up-and-down results and then we settled and went on a fantastic run.' Smith's positive mindset had resulted in a neat aikido move – taking the problem and turning it to his advantage. He now had a team that he could call his own.

Put the setback into context

The past may well be a thief, but this can be true of the future too. An optimistic view of the future can be powerful, but a leader who faces the future with fear will find it hard to overcome the challenges in front of him. The key is to avoid catastrophising – the sort of thinking that says: 'This is the worst thing that could possibly have happened to anyone, now it will all go downhill and there's nothing I can do about it.' José Mourinho has a good way to re-frame defeats: 'I always say a defeat must not be a start of a period; it must be just the end of a great period. So when the defeat comes you cannot think this is the first of some, but just the end of a period of victories and good moments.' This theme recurs time and again among good football leaders.

McCarthy took over at Sunderland in the final quarter of a campaign to avoid relegation from the Premier League. 'My start at Sunderland was terrible. I lost the first nine games because we had to play to win every game – draws wouldn't be enough for us to avoid relegation. I'm not sure that filled everybody with confidence in a manager who'd never been in the Barclays Premier League. We actually played well in many of the games, but we weren't good enough. Worse was to come – I lost the first two games in the Championship, 2-0 to Notts Forest and 1-0 to Millwall. So by now I'd lost the first 11 games on the bounce, and we were playing Preston away who had a great home record. If we'd have had a loss we'd have got the record for the most consecutive defeats, and we went and played great and beat them 2-0. We finished third that year, lost out in the play-offs.' The Preston victory enabled McCarthy to recover his naturally positive mindset.

Wenger's Arsenal travelled to Manchester United in August 2011 and were beaten by the startling scoreline of 8-2. Even Wenger was shocked. 'We were titanically bad, but we managed to get the boat over the iceberg. We come back to values and ideas, because nobody can predict a football game. I'll give you a recent example. If you go to 100 people and ask them before the semi-finals what will be the 2012 final of the Champions League, most of them would have said Barcelona against Real. But it was Bayern Munich against Chelsea. That shows you the unpredictability of a game and you have to accept that as a manager as well. And therefore at some stage you cannot base your career on the way you see the game and on individual results. You have to base it on ideas and values that are important. When I go through a difficult period, I think how can I improve the results – but my checklist is more, "Am I in line with what I think is important in my job?" That's why I think it's important to not just think about winning the games, but also think about what is important to me in this job, in the way I see the game. Because when you go through crisis periods, that is what will help you survive.'

David Moyes' career low point came during Everton's European campaign of 2005–06: 'We had lost to Villarreal in the Champions

League that year and dropped into the UEFA Cup. We went to play Dynamo Bucharest in Romania. I think we were 1-0 down at half-time and we weren't doing a lot wrong – then we lost 5-0. For me that was probably as bad as I've felt because we were out of the European competitions that we had worked so hard to get into. I didn't question myself, but I did need someone to help me get going again. I don't know that there is anyone that every now and again doesn't need someone to give them a pick-me-up and get them going again.'

Moyes did well not to feel sorry for himself. In his recollection, he doesn't dwell on what could have been: he doesn't bemoan his fate, he doesn't beat himself up, he doesn't catastrophise. Instead, he puts it into context: 'I don't think there was anything specific that I could identify to work on. With the quality of the players we had, we should have been good enough to get through. Maybe the disappointment of losing the Champions League game, which would have got us into the group stages, had a big effect on the players that night. Either way, we just got caught out. It wasn't for lack of preparation. People who are leaders of companies will always know there will be days when – for whatever reason – it all goes wrong. It's how you recover and how you get back on track that counts.'

Return to the source

Finally, it is valuable for a leader to have some place of refuge – either physical or mental. Moyes simply says, 'I have an inbuilt thing in me that I know where I have to go when it's not going well.' For him, it's about personal foundations, something akin to a belief wall: 'It's very difficult to turn to other leaders in the sport because it's a competitive world. My staff were helpful, but in the end it was inside me that I found the drive to go back out on the training field and carry on. That night certainly was a test for me.'

Staying Centred in Success and Adulation

Dealing with setbacks is no fun; dealing with success can be just as difficult. The world watches how a leader responds, and generally does not appreciate anything that looks like arrogance. The common theme among the great football leaders is to enjoy the moment, then return to the task at hand. Glenn Hoddle contrasts his experiences of success as player and as manager: 'When I was a player I would bask in it a fair while. As a manager I would have the night. The next day I would get the recognition and the congratulations, then two or three days later that's in the history book and you are actually planning for your next season, or your next goal.'

McCarthy's approach could best be summarised as pride where justified, but always softened by humility: 'Probably my greatest moment in football was as a player. Quarter-final of the World Cup in Rome, captaining the team. I don't think I'm eloquent enough to describe how it felt. I would say it's fantastic, amazing, brilliant, but it's better than that: the pride, the emotion, the hairs tingling on the back of your neck. Being on the pitch in Rome – Mick McCarthy, in the quarter-final of the World Cup in 1990 – no way! What was I doing there in the first place? Everybody told me I wasn't good enough and I couldn't play, well b******* to that! I had the captain's armband on, leading them out, and it was just amazing, and it was wonderful. Even when we lost and I walked off that pitch in tears, I was full of pride. Franco Baresi came after me to swap shirts. I admired him so much – even more so when he ran up to swap shirts with me!'

Alex McLeish recalls with deep satisfaction his Scotland side's 1-0 away win over France in a World Cup qualifying match: 'We were pretty sure that they would go 4-4-2 with Claude Makelele and Patrick Vieira in the central midfield. We opted for a 4-1-4-1 formation – James McFadden up front with support from Darren Fletcher and Barry Ferguson – to cover our bets. It worked really well. France had a lot of possession, but rarely threatened our goal, and James scored the famous goal and it was brilliant. Great memories. But we didn't paint the town tartan that night – we came back home. Work to do.' In the final analysis, Scotland failed to qualify for the World Cup finals, despite the victory.

At club level, McLeish's high points have been even more poignant. 'The highlight in England to date would have to be the Carling Cup final [with Birmingham in 2010] – winning that, and coming ninth in the league the season before. A few guys said, "You should have lost the last few games because you made a rod for your own back – the directors will expect you to finish higher than that next season." It's not in my nature to lose a couple of games! It's in my nature to win every single game. So we got the Carling Cup, and then for many reasons we end up relegated. I went from an extreme high to an extreme low, and believe me in football the highs and the lows are absolutely massive.'

For David Moyes, the greatest team performance of his career so far came when Everton qualified for the Champions League in 2005: 'The night that we played Manchester United, we needed to win to get into the Champions League – and we did. Everton's got a tough football club image and I think that night it matched that. The night – the level of the game – matched what Everton stands for, and we had to play probably the best team in the country and we were able to get a result against them. It was a night where the football club itself showed what it stands for and what it's made of.'

It's as if Moyes and his team didn't do anything extra special that night. What they did was bring together all they had, stood up for what they believed in and played with passion. And Moyes did not get carried away. Wisely so: despite this memorable achievement, their painful Champions League exit came only six months later.

For Hope Powell, it was the night in France when England's women qualified for the 2007 World Cup: 'We had to at least draw the game, we hadn't qualified in 12 years. We went to France with a crowd of 19,000, we came away with the result and we qualified for the World Cup. That was great.' But she takes equal delight in the 2011 World Cup campaign: 'We wanted to top the group, we had a strategy, the players implemented it, we weren't expected to beat Japan [the eventual champions] and we won the game. There were some really good performances – players owning [our philosophy] and delivering.'

All of these managers admit to great elation at the point of triumph. And all of them are quick to put it into perspective, to remind themselves of what needs doing next and get back to business as usual. This is a key behaviour for the successful leader – both in football and in business.

Not Passing on the Pain

More than half the battle in dealing with setbacks is within the leader. But once he has understood his own reactions and has chosen his response, his next challenge is how he will impact his team. This is an area where leadership is at its most visible. In the heat of battle, a ship's company look to their captain. When a team loses – especially when it is a heavy or unforeseen defeat – the players look to their manager for clear leadership. At that moment, the manager is probably dealing with deep emotions – anything from regret, inadequacy, failure through resignation and despair to anger and resentment. The watching public – and especially angry and upset fans – can sometimes feel that the manager takes things lightly and moves on too fast. In reality, this is rarely the case. When McLeish describes his ultimately unsuccessful battle to avoid relegation from the Premier League with Birmingham City, the pain is palpable: 'Relegation hit me really hard – as hard as anything has ever hit me before. It was a real horror.'

The leader's question then is around how much to share. Integrity says share everything. The vulnerable leader has a particular power and, in any event, keeping back information from the team can feel in some way dishonest. But courage can sometimes demand that the leader deal privately with pain that would only adversely affect the players.

After the 8-2 defeat at Old Trafford, Wenger centred himself as he always does, by taking the long-term view. Then he connected with the players: 'At that moment you come back to the team and say that is important for us, that is our culture, that is us, so let's come back to what we are good at and what we want and that sometimes helps get the team back on track. Unfortunately, at this moment, you have to begin in the emotional place. When you go out of a game like that you know that now you face a storm. The storm is in the media, the fans, the disappointment that you will have to stand up to. That's the moment that you have to show leadership qualities and show that you are strong and show that you don't panic. So basically I don't say anything profound to the team like that on the day because they are hurt, and I am as well. Anything you say in that moment could be even more detrimental. I try to get them to pick up, individually I speak to them, and give them two days off and come back on Monday and we start fresh again.' The weekend then allows everyone to be a little more calm and long-term focused: 'The drama is strong enough at the weekend that you don't have to add any more to it, you do not need to say they were absolutely disastrous, they know it. And I believe as well that the big results don't have that much significance in the long term. They have an emotional significance, but no great footballing significance. Against Manchester United we conceded four goals in the last 20 minutes, we were down to ten men and we had played three days before at Udinese. Of course, people don't want excuses, but I can put it into context myself, and I know that this team is not as bad as the result was.'

McLeish believes in holding on to the pain himself: 'When we were relegated I was absolutely devastated. I was trying to find the positives in it and the only positive I could find was such was the quality of that league that season that I don't think any of us deserved to be relegated. I think the only ones that were far below everyone else were West Ham; they were completely out by about six points or something. That's when you start to beat yourself up and that's when you start looking back. But I definitely try and keep all the pressure away from the players. Some players hide it, but there is definitely emotion, there's a few in tears and I think you just have to say, "Look guys, thank you for your efforts through the whole season."'

Walter Smith always endeavours to approach the highs and lows of football management with equal measure. 'There are periods of turmoil in management when there's a lot going on. I just try and manage as best I can. I think it's an instinctive thing that you have in you to lead. You have to hold your nerve in front of the team, protect the team from stuff that shouldn't be coming their way and provide stability amidst the turmoil. I think that's a natural part of the job – one of the natural aspects that you shouldn't really take a great deal of praise for putting in place. You have to do this as a leader.'

In times of upset, McCarthy deliberately steadies himself before dealing with his players: 'I try and maintain or regain my centre. I think if you are up and down they have no chance. I treat people consistently; I'm consistent in my behaviour. So even when we went to Preston looking to end our run of 11 defeats, I'm still preparing the same way I prepare for every match. Saying we have to win this only adds pressure to the players and that's not fair. They can see if you panic. If they see you treating a game differently, they detect your anxiety and that does them no favours.' David Moyes would agree: '[After a setback] I have to go back to work on my own behaviours and my mood. I think you need to correct yourself first, so that in turn you are able to correct the group of people you are working with and help to fix them.'

Glenn Hoddle agrees with the protective role of the leader, but is also committed to taking lessons from the pain: 'I would want my players to be upset and sad that they have lost, I wouldn't want them to be too jovial if they have just lost the final! Then together, under pressure, we can find out so much more about ourselves and each other [teammates and staff] than when we are winning and life is easy.' Leaders in business as well as football will recognise this: the greater learnings come out of the tougher times.

Passing on the Joy

Most leaders would not hesitate to share joy and pride at moments of triumph. As manager of the Republic of Ireland team in the 2002 World Cup campaign, McCarthy took a couple of small steps to ensure his players shared his pride in the team and the campaign. 'I had always felt the match shirts needed to be more than just a shirt. I have all these shirts at home but I haven't a clue which one's which. So we had the occasion printed on our team shirts – the opponents' name and the date. That way the shirt meant just a little more to the players.' Then there was the national anthem. 'So many people over the years had accused members of the Irish team of being "not real Irishmen" and had pointed to how players didn't sing the anthem when it was played. One man wrote to me with the anthem in Gaelic phonetics! I loved it. We all learned it and sang our hearts out. I wanted them all to celebrate what they were doing and what they were standing for as players.'

One important consideration though is when to celebrate and when to refocus. Glenn Hoddle takes great delight in the shared joy of a team: 'It's really important that the players and the manager celebrate success together. There's a great feeling of camaraderie that comes from working together as a unit for a period of time when it's gone really well. The players will take their lead from the manager. They'll enjoy the feeling, then when it comes round to the next season or the next match, they're looking to the manager to lead the refocus. But for the manager, you are planning again almost as soon as you've enjoyed the success.'

Keeping a successful side's feet on the ground while encouraging proper celebration is an art. Wenger again takes a long-term view: 'Again it comes back to values. When you have a team like we have with 18 different nationalities you have first to create a culture, a sense of who we are as a unit, what makes us different from other people, how we can create something that is common to all of us. So you have to recreate a new way to behave – an Arsenal culture. To define it, I go through what is important to my group. It's explicit. We sit down and we go through how we want to behave. That counts also for our response to success.' Wenger understands that his long-term values as a leader will dictate his team's behaviours in the face of both temporary triumph and temporary despair.

The Masterful Leader

An old Chinese story tells of a farmer whose only horse runs away. 'How terrible!' say his neighbours. 'Maybe!' says the farmer. The next day his horse returns, bringing along three wild horses. 'How wonderful!' say his neighbours. 'Maybe!' says the farmer. The following day his son tries to tame one of the wild horses, but he falls off and breaks his leg. 'How terrible!' say his neighbours. 'Maybe!' says the farmer. The next day some soldiers come along to force young men of the village to join them in war. Because the lad has a broken leg, he is left behind. 'How fortunate!' say the neighbours. 'Maybe!' says the farmer. The soldiers, still one man short, take the young man's cousin instead. 'How dreadful!' say the farmer's neighbours. 'Maybe!' says the farmer. That night a landslide covers the house in which the cousin would have been sleeping if he had not been taken by the soldiers. 'How fortunate!' say the friends. 'Maybe!' says the farmer.

Joy and pain in football – like in business – both tend to be short-lived, and can turn on a single result. The compelling image is of the masterful leader who remains centred in all circumstances, radiating to his people a steadiness that they can rely on. Few would claim to be that all the time; but in the whirlwind of senior professional football, the centred leaders have a noticeable advantage.

1. Instead of despairing, great leaders take ownership and responsibility:
    There are few sights more disheartening for a team or organisation than a leader who blames everyone and everything but

himself. Ownership is the key. The owner cannot be a victim. He also moves on quickly from defeat while taking the learnings, is strong in his fact-based self-belief, is deliberately and forensically optimistic, puts setbacks into context and treats crises as opportunities for growth. He also has a source – a place of refuge to which he can return.

2. Instead of exaggerating success, great leaders take satisfaction and put it into context:
    In that way, Moyes could take both Champions League quali-fication and exit in his stride.

3. When it comes to sharing the pain, great leaders make choices: Different circumstances require different approaches from a leader. Sometimes it is good to show vulnerability, at other times it is essential to protect your people from the vagaries of the environment in which they work. The key is to do what you do intentionally and with careful consideration of the impact you will have.

4. When it comes to sharing the joy, great leaders celebrate well and yet remain measured:
    Not to celebrate genuine success appears heartless and is counter-productive. But great leaders somehow manage also to anchor their people in something more long lasting.

If there is one lesson to take from all this, it is the tendency of great leaders to take ownership of their situations, however difficult. In the words of Mick McCarthy: 'Of course there was mitigation – there's always mitigation. But I signed the players and I picked the team.' Such an approach displays integrity and inspires respect. It is a mark of the masterful leader.

AFTERWORD

This book offers an insight into the work, thoughts, feelings and practices of some of the most recognisable leaders in the world game. It does not tell the whole story, of course – there is much more.

But it does tell one very important story: a story often repeated, and yet often forgotten. It is a story of human beings. Despite their differences in culture, frames of reference, personal insight and professional perspective, all the managers I have met agree on one thing. Leadership is all about people. Whatever his goals, whatever his grand vision – no leader will achieve anything truly worthwhile without the ability to inspire his people.

The great football leaders need to know their technical skills – they are all coaches first. But it is their willingness and ability to really connect with their players on an individual and personal level that marks them out from the crowd. The leader who invests the time and energy needed to get below the surface with his people will be breaking records when his peers have fallen away. This is the leader who will leave a true legacy.

May this book make a real contribution to the growth and understanding of leaders and their people both in football and beyond.

A NOTE ON THE AUTHOR

Mike Carson worked for McKinsey & Company for five years and is now a partner and co-owner of the consulting business Aberkyn, specialising in business and human transformation. He's a leadership expert and a Manchester City fan, and lives in Winchester with his wife and four children.

A NOTE ON THE TYPE

The text of this book is set in Bembo, which was first used in 1495 by the Venetian printer Aldus Manutius for Cardinal Bembo's *De Aetna*. The original types were cut for Manutius by Francesco Griffo. Bembo was one of the types used by Claude Garamond (1480-1561) as a model for his Romain de L'Université, and so it was a forerunner of what became the standard European type for the following two centuries. Its modern form follows the original types and was designed for Monotype in 1929.